1.00

GOOD HOUSEKEEPING'S

# Advanced Cooking is Fun

by Margaret Coombes and Suzanne Wakelin of
Good Housekeeping Institute



EBURY PRESS

SBN 85223 009 5


Chestergate House, Vauxhall Bridge Road, London SW1

Second impression 1975

Cover design by John Elsegood
Photographs by Barry Allsuch
Drawings by Dinah Dryhurst

Recipe testing and conversions
by Elizabeth Evans of Good Housekeeping Institute

FILMSET AND
PRINTED BY BAS PRINTERS LIMITED
WALLOP, HAMPSHIRE

# CONTENTS


| | | page |
|---|---|---|
| | FOREWORD by Margaret Dalloway | 4 |
| | INTRODUCTION | 5 |
| | CONVERSIONS | 6 |
| Chapter 1 | The Science of Cookery | 7 |
| 2 | The Science of Food Care | 25 |
| 3 | The Science of Meal Planning | 45 |
| 4 | The Art of Meal Planning | 54 |
| 5 | Sensible Shopping | 86 |
| 6 | Food Storage | 99 |
| 7 | The Food on the Table | 109 |

RECIPE SECTION

| | | |
|---|---|---|
| Chapter 8 | Starters | 118 |
| 9 | Fish | 126 |
| 10 | Eggs and Cheese | 136 |
| 11 | Meat | 148 |
| 12 | Poultry and Game | 178 |
| 13 | Vegetables and Salads | 186 |
| 14 | The Sweet Course | 194 |
| 15 | Baked Goods | 212 |
| 16 | Petits Fours; Cocktail Savouries; Candies; Preserves | 234 |

REFERENCE SECTION

| | |
|---|---|
| BASIC RECIPES | 242 |
| FOODS IN SEASON | 248 |
| INDEX | 251 |

# FOREWORD

Home Economics teachers and their students who have enjoyed and appreciated *Cooking is Fun* will welcome this companion book, *Advanced Cooking is Fun*.

It is a real pleasure to be able to write a foreword to a book which explains the scientific principles behind our more advanced work in such a palatable and readable manner, at the same time suggesting useful and interesting experiments with food which can be carried out to support the theories. Fifth- and sixth-formers will enjoy the opportunities offered to carry out tests and investigations, to make their personal observations and recordings and to form their own conclusions about the foods and the cooking methods they are using.

The book is realistic and up-to-date in its approach to shopping, the storage of food, advanced cookery terms, meal planning and the more sophisticated forms of entertaining. The treatment of these topics has sufficient depth to be of value to both 'O' and 'A' level candidates.

The mouth-watering recipes and suggestions for entertaining will not only attract the examination candidates, but will also tempt their colleagues to join the Home Economics Group so as to enjoy the pleasures of preparing, serving and eating delicious and attractive food. This book could indeed form an excellent basis for a fifth- or sixth-form Gourmets' Club.

The fact that *Advanced Cooking is Fun* uses metric measures will make it most welcome at a time when schools and young people are in the lead in 'thinking metric'.

Speaking personally, I can say this is a book I shall be delighted to own and use, and one which I thoroughly recommend, not only to schools but to all cooks and hostesses, whatever their age.

MARGARET DALLOWAY
*Inspector of Schools, Organiser of Home Economics, Bristol L.E.A.*

# INTRODUCTION

If you've been using our earlier book, you will already know that cooking *is* fun. That still applies with more advanced cooking. In fact, the more you learn, the more fun you can have experimenting, adapting and devising your own recipes. Cooking is truly a creative art, in which attention to detail, flair, inventiveness and adaptability all play a part.

In this book we aim at encouraging students to ask questions instead of taking everything for granted. Equipped with a basic knowledge of cookery and with the extra background information given here, you may well find yourself wondering about such far-reaching questions as why we eat, why things go wrong in the kitchen and indeed why we cook at all.

Why do we eat? Because the body needs food and water to maintain it, to repair damage to its tissues, to provide energy and to protect it from disease.

Why do things go wrong? There is usually an underlying basic reason for poor cookery results. The chapter on 'The Science of Cookery' will help you to understand why a mayonnaise curdles, why a cake sinks, and so on.

Why cook? To make foods more appetising and digestible. But it is necessary to know how the constituents in foods change during the cooking in order to obtain first-class results. Once you grasp the science of food and cookery you can follow a recipe more easily, you can if you wish adapt it, and you can take short-cuts by making full use of modern convenience foods, mechanical aids and new techniques.

As this country is still in the transition period of changing from Imperial to metric measures, we decided to describe the size of such things as, for example, a can of baked beans as 4 oz. (approx. 110 g), because we do not yet know what metric sizes the manufacturers will choose. Other ingredients are given in metric terms, and in working out the recipes we based the quantities on a 25-g unit. In the case of baking tin sizes and so on, we have put the Imperial measurement first, because this is how the articles will still be described in the shops. With measurements we ourselves can control, like rolling out pastry to a given size, this book gives the metric figures only.

Scattered through the book you will find a series of helpful drawings showing different techniques that are used in advanced cookery.

# CONVERSIONS

The recipes in this book were tested and written up using metric weights and measures, and were not converted by rule of thumb from imperial versions. They will give a slightly smaller recipe quantity. The new British Standard metric measuring spoons (2.5 ml, 5 ml, 10 ml and 15 ml) have been used in place of the old variable teaspoons and tablespoons. For more exact conversions and general reference, the following tables will be helpful:

**Mass (Weight)**

*g = gram; kg = kilogram*

| | | | |
|---|---|---|---|
| 1 oz. | = 28.35 g | 2 lb. | = 907 g |
| 4 oz. (¼ lb.) | = 113 g | 3 lb. | = 1.36 kg |
| 8 oz. (½ lb.) | = 227 g | 4 lb. | = 1.81 kg |
| 16 oz. (1 lb.) | = 454 g | 5 lb. | = 2.27 kg |
| 1½ lb. | = 681 g | 10 lb. | = 4.54 kg |

**Capacity**

*ml = millilitre; l = litre*

| | | | |
|---|---|---|---|
| ¼ pint | = 142 ml | 1¾ pints | = 994 ml |
| ½ pint | = 284 ml | 2 pints | = 1.14 l |
| ¾ pint | = 426 ml | 2½ pints | = 1.42 l |
| 1 pint | = 568 ml | 3 pints | = 1.70 l |
| 1¼ pints | = 710 ml | 3½ pints | = 1.99 l |
| 1½ pints | = 852 ml | | |

**Length**

*cm = centimetre*

| | | | |
|---|---|---|---|
| 1 inch | = 2.54 cm | 1 foot | = 30.48 cm |

**Temperatures**

| *Fahrenheit* | *Celsius* | *Fahrenheit* | *Celsius* |
|---|---|---|---|
| 32°F (water freezes) | = 0°C | 325°F | = 163°C |
| 205°F (simmering) | = 96°C | 350°F | = 177°C |
| 212°F (water boils) | = 100°C | 375°F | = 190°C |
| 225°F | = 107°C | 400°F | = 204°C |
| 250°F | = 121°C | 425°F | = 218°C |
| 275°F | = 135°C | 450°F | = 232°C |
| 300°F | = 149°C | | |

To convert °F to °C, subtract 32, multiply by 5 and divide by 9.
To convert °C to °F, multiply by 9, divide by 5 and add 32.
*Note:* Centigrade is another name for the Celsius scale.

**Energy**

The basic unit used in calculating energy in nutrition is the Calorie (Kilocalorie), but it is probable that when the S.I. (Système International or International System) metric units are adopted in the U.K., the unit of energy known as the *joule* will be adopted. The equivalent value is as follows:

1 Calorie (Kilocalorie) = 4.19 Kilojoules

## CHAPTER I

# THE SCIENCE OF COOKERY

The main purpose of cooking is to make food more palatable and more easily digested. The processes of cookery make use of four main scientific principles:

1. The expansion of gases by mechanical, physical or chemical means.
2. The softening of cellulose and the bursting of starch grains by the application of moisture and heat.
3. The coagulation of proteins.
4. The action of those micro-organisms which can be useful, e.g., yeast. (The micro-organisms which cause natural decomposition of food are dealt with in the chapter on 'The Science of Food Care'.)

In this chapter, the expansion of gases and the action of yeast are covered in the section called 'Why Does it Rise?'. The softening of cellulose and the bursting of starch grains are dealt with in the section 'How Does it Thicken?', while the coagulation of proteins is discussed under that heading at the end of this chapter.

Once these principles are mastered, cooking results can be controlled, and one can vary or invent recipes, knowing that they will work.

### Why Does it Rise?

The rising of breads, cakes and pastries (sometimes called 'leavening') is achieved by splitting the gluten content of the flour into layers and maintaining them in that state until they are set by the heat which is applied during cooking. The whole process relies on the presence of carbon dioxide, air and water vapour, and these in turn are controlled by the ingredients, the method of mixing, the cooking temperature and the raising agent. Once the basics of physical and chemical raising are understood, the principles can be applied to any and every combination of ingredients for baked goods.

1. RAISING AGENTS

*(a) Carbon Dioxide*: This may be formed by two types of raising agent, one chemical, the other biological. In chemical leavening, carbon dioxide is produced from the action of an alkali (generally sodium bicarbonate) with an acid. Used on its own, sodium bicarbonate will produce some carbon dioxide, but the end-product will taste alkaline. By adding an acid (whether a type normally present in such foods as sour milk, treacle and fruit juices, or one contained in baking powder—see below—or in the form of cream of tartar) all the available carbon dioxide is evolved, and any residual alkali is neutralised.

Commercially produced baking powder consists of sodium bicarbonate plus an acid-reacting material, together with a 'stabiliser'. The acid material varies from brand to brand, but the stabiliser is generally cornflour or rice flour, and the whole is thoroughly mixed to give a balanced combination. (See also 'Self-raising Flour', page 10.)

The biological raising agent is yeast, which ferments sugar to produce carbon dioxide. The sugar required for the reaction comes not only from any sugar added initially but also from the 1 per cent present in flour and from starch in the flour, which is broken down to form sugars.

Yeast is obtainable in two forms: dry (an inactive state), which must be blended with sweetened liquid before use, or compressed (baker's) yeast, an active, living organism which must be kept at a low temperature to inhibit activity till needed.

Once the yeast has been added to the flour mixture, this must be allowed to ferment. Moderately high temperatures will give a rapid rise, but temperatures above 32°C will kill the yeast organisms. Low temperatures give a slower rate of fermentation, but when a yeast dough is returned to room temperature and allowed to rise further, excellent results are produced. (Very low temperatures retard fermentation, but do not kill the organism.)

During baking, or other cooking, it is important for the carbon dioxide to be released *before* a crust is formed. Batters and doughs, which are soft and easily stretched when first heated, become firm as the starch content gelatinises and the protein content coagulates, so they must reach their maximum volume before this setting occurs. Once the crust has formed, any further release of carbon dioxide causes cracking and produces low volume, with a firm texture.

(*b*) *Air*: During the creaming process in cake-making the air that is incorporated is held by the fat, forming fat-surrounded air cells. The walls of these cells melt during cooking, being replaced by a structural framework of coagulated protein and gelatinised starch. At the same time, the air bubbles are expanded by heat and enlarged still further by carbon dioxide and steam.

In fatless sponge cakes, the chief raising agent is the air which is incorporated during the whisking of the egg whites. Whisked egg white consists of air bubbles surrounded by protein; these air bubbles expand and the protein coagulates when heat is applied.

In flaky and puff pastries, the air trapped during layering expands on heating, and this contributes to the rising and ultimate flakiness of the product.

Too much air, however—that is, increased air not balanced by proportional increases in egg, flour, etc.—will cause a collapse of the structure, as there is insufficient protein to maintain it.

(*c*) *Steam*: The conversion of liquid into vapour (steam) is important in most baked products. For instance, in choux

Using Garlic 1: When crushing a garlic clove, add a little salt to absorb the juices; add to casseroles, stews, etc. (e.g. Beef Balls en Casserole)

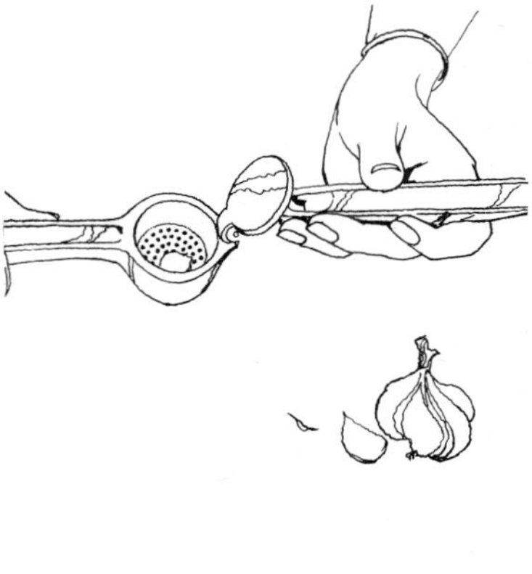

Using Garlic 2: If you have a special garlic press, you can squeeze out the pulp only, to flavour a salad

pastry and Yorkshire pudding, steam is the main raising agent, with the eggs supplying protein to form a framework. Steam, in conjunction with air, is also the raising agent in other pastries; it is derived from well-chilled fat and water. Steam contributes to the raising of most batters, along with carbon dioxide, enlarging the air cells already present.

When steam is the key raising agent, a relatively high temperature is needed at the start of the cooking, for rapid production of steam. But too high a temperature sets the mixture before the protein framework is fully expanded, giving a hard crust and low volume; too low a temperature gives pale, soggy, poorly risen products.

### 2. FLOUR

Flour provides the proteins which, when they come in contact with moisture, supply the gluten needed for the structural framework. In bread-making, strong flours with high protein content are used. Moisture is added, and the dough is kneaded thoroughly to ensure maximum production of gluten, which is required to provide a framework strong enough to withstand the prolonged stretching during proving and to coagulate during cooking.

In cake mixtures, a lower-protein and higher-starch flour is used; here the other coagulated protein, such as egg, helps to form the structural framework, and less strength is required, so sugar and fats, which have a tenderising effect on gluten, can be added.

*Self-raising Flour* is a softer type, thoroughly mixed with an alkali (sodium bicarbonate) and an acid-aerating agent, usually an acid phosphate. Acid phosphate is chosen because it is resistant to decomposition by moisture; this lengthens the flour's storage life, but tends to slow down the initial reaction of the raising agent when heat is applied. The flour and the raising agents are sifted together many times to ensure even distribution.

### 3. FATS

Solid fats (e.g., butter, margarine, cooking fats) are used to 'shorten' products, i.e., to inhibit gluten development. As fat is insoluble in water, it prevents gluten strands from clinging together and forming a solid mass. In cake mixtures, the fat holds much of the air incorporated during mixing, but thorough mixing or emulsifying is needed to ensure even distribution of fat and therefore of air. In pastry, such fine mixing is replaced by rubbing in or otherwise incorporating the fat to form layers between the gluten, to give a crumbly or flaky product.

Oils can also be used in cakes and shortcrust pastry, but adjustments will be necessary to the other ingredients to give a comparable result.

4. MOISTURE CONTENT

Moisture is required for the evolution of steam and the development of gluten. Too much weakens the gluten, causing it to break under the pressure of expanding gas. This in turn makes the cell walls collapse, so that small volume and coarse texture result. Too little moisture, on the other hand, gives a stiff mixture, with gluten that is unable to stretch sufficiently; this, too, results in small volume, and the texture is close and heavy.

5. EGGS

Eggs play a triple rôle as raising agents in cake-making. First, the whites can be whisked to a foam incorporating a large volume of air; this property can, however, be affected by the eggs themselves; if an egg is old, with a thin white, the volume of foam will be low; a viscous white produces a more stable foam. The addition of salt or vinegar stabilises the foam by slightly coagulating the protein; sugar also increases the stability, whereas the presence of fat (as in the egg yolk) inhibits foaming power. The second important factor in eggs is their property of protein coagulation, so forming the structural framework (see page 22). Thirdly, the moisture or water which eggs contain contributes towards the production of steam.

6. SUGAR

This delays the development of gluten and the coagulation of protein, so it is necessary to add more protein, usually eggs, to replace the loss and so provide a structural framework. Cakes which are high in sugar tend to shrink during cooking, giving a layer of collapsed cells at the bottom.

*Exercises*

To illustrate the inter-relationships between raising agents and ingredients, and the effect they have on the end product.

A. Make up 9 batches of basic scone mixture, using the ingredients listed below, but varying the flour and the raising agent as detailed in 1 to 9.

| | |
|---|---|
| 200 g flour (see details below) | 125 ml milk or water to mix |
| A pinch of salt | Raising agent (see below) |
| 25 g butter or margarine | |

Mix to a soft dough and knead lightly. Roll out to a thickness of 1.5 cm, cut into rounds and bake at 232°C (mark 8, 450°F) for 10 minutes.

1. Self-raising flour with no additional raising agent.
2. Plain flour plus 2 level tsp. (10 ml) baking powder.
3. Plain flour plus ½ level tsp. (2.5 ml) bicarbonate of soda and 1 level tsp. (5 ml) cream of tartar.
4. Plain flour plus ½ level tsp. (2.5 ml) each of bicarbonate of soda and cream of tartar; substitute soured milk for fresh.
5. Self-raising flour plus 1 level tsp. (5 ml) baking powder.
6. Self-raising flour plus ¼ level tsp. (1.25 ml) bicarbonate of soda and ½ level tsp. (2.5 ml) cream of tartar.
7. Plain flour plus 3 level tsp. (15 ml) baking powder.
8. Plain flour plus 3 level tsp. (15 ml) baking powder; allow 3 minutes extra baking time.
9. As 4, but omit the cream of tartar.

Compare the results under the following headings: general appearance; colour; flavour; texture.

B. Make up a basic Victoria sandwich mixture, varying both the method of mixing and the raising agent used, as follows:

1. Self-raising flour; cream the margarine and sugar well.
2. Plain flour plus 1 level tsp. (5 ml) baking powder; cream the margarine before creaming in the sugar.
3. Plain flour with ¼ level tsp. (1.25 ml) bicarbonate of soda plus ½ level tsp. (2.5 ml) cream of tartar.
4. Plain flour plus 1 level tsp. (5 ml) baking powder. Don't cream the margarine prior to adding the sugar.
5. Plain flour plus 1 level tsp. (5 ml) baking powder. Cream the margarine and sugar thoroughly and add an extra egg.
6. Plain flour plus 1 level tsp. (5 ml) baking powder; cream incompletely, but add an extra egg.
7. Plain flour. Cream the margarine and sugar mixture thoroughly and use an extra egg.

Note the rise, measuring it carefully; the general appearance; colour; texture; flavour. Which raising agent, if any, is the most effective or most important?

C. Make up a fatless sponge, using 2 eggs, 50 g caster sugar; 50 g plain flour. Vary the method of mixing:

1. Whisk the egg and sugar until stiff; fold in the flour.
2. Whisk the egg and sugar until stiff; beat in the flour.
3. Don't beat the egg and sugar mixture very stiffly before adding the flour.

Compare the results, noting rise; colour; texture; flavour.

Air and steam are the principal raising agents: in what way has the method of mixing affected them?

D. Using a variety of flours, make up (*a*) Yorkshire puddings and (*b*) Puff-type pastries.

Compare the results.

### How Does it Thicken?

Many foods or food constituents, mainly of plant origin, have thickening or setting properties, which are useful in cooking. The chief groups are starches, pectin, gums and also gelatine, which is of animal origin.

#### 1. STARCH

Before the action of starch can be considered, it is necessary to discuss the relationship with the cellulose which composes the main part of plant foods. Cellulose is a complex carbohydrate made up entirely of glucose units, and cannot be readily broken down into its component parts. Much of the cellulose is removed by processing (e.g., the outer layers of the cereal grain, which contain the greatest percentage of cellulose, are removed during milling). The remaining cellulose forms the supporting structure surrounding the starch granules. Moisture softens the cellulose, and eventually penetrates into the cells. The starch then absorbs the water and swells, rupturing the cellulose walls.

The softening of cellulose is thus an essential preliminary to the release of starch and any subsequent thickening.

Starch itself forms the chief food reserve of carbohydrates in plants, enabling them to live and grow. Grains (e.g., wheat) contain up to 70 per cent starch, while roots and tubers (e.g., carrots, potatoes) contain 20–30 per cent. Starch is also found in various fruits, seeds, nuts and the pith of some palm trees (e.g., sago).

The starch is present in the plant cells as granules, and each plant has its characteristic form of granule, differing in shape, size and solubility. Starch granules do not dissolve in cold water, but form a suspension which is cloudy and murky in appearance. When the mixture is heated, the granules swell and burst, releasing their contents, a substance called Granulose. This stage when the granulose is released is known as the point of gelatinisation. The temperature at which it occurs varies with the type of starch. Granulose is soluble, and on further heating it dissolves and the solution becomes more translucent and viscous. With even more heating the viscosity decreases, then increases again on cooling.

If the starch is allowed to swell in a small amount of water, or if it is heated without sufficient stirring, the granules stick together as they swell, forming lumps. Some starches, such as potato and tapioca, form a clearer paste than others, but flour pastes are opaque, due to the presence of components other than starch. The degree of gel depends on the temperature, the concentration of starch, the presence of sugar and acid.

When a high concentration of starch is used, an extended cooking time or increased temperature is needed to avoid a 'raw' taste. Sugar has a marked effect on the gelatinisation of starch. Initially, it gives a more tender and translucent gel, but if added in high proportions, it prevents the formation of a gel by competing with the starch for the available water. Therefore any sugar should be added after the end of the cooking. The presence of acid in low concentration aids gelatinisation, but a high concentration prevents it.

The starches generally used for thickening are flour, potato flour, cornflour, rice flour and arrowroot. They are sometimes known by the French terms, *fécules*. The amount of each needed to produce a similar viscosity in hot liquids varies greatly. (Flour in particular must be used in a higher proportion than pure forms of starch, because of its non-starchy components.) Therefore straight substitution of one thickener for another is not always practicable.

*Flour* is often blended with fat to form a roux or beurre manié, or with water to make a paste.

*Roux* is the most usual method of adding flour for a sauce, etc., and the only one carried out before the start of cooking. Fat and flour are generally used in equal amounts, but a little more fat simplifies the making. Heat the fat until it just melts—don't overheat—and add the flour with the pan off the heat. (This is important, as otherwise the flour loses its thickening powers.) Return the pan to the heat and cook for 1–2 minutes. The liquid should ideally be added while warm but not boiling, and off the heat; stir continuously to ensure a smooth, not granular, texture. Return the mixture to the heat and cook gently—don't boil.

A sauce is not ready immediately it is thick, but must be cooked for at least 5 minutes. Really thick sauces, such as the panada used for binding croquettes and similar mixtures, must be cooked very thoroughly. Bear in mind, when making casseroles and stews, that all-round heat tends to make sauces disintegrate more than base-only heat, so a stew cooked on top of the stove produces a different consistency from one cooked in the oven. And if a dish is cooked too quickly, this may result in the sauce thinning. (See Basic Recipes, at end of book, for proportions for sauces of different consistencies.)

*Beurre Manié*—the professional way of correcting the con-

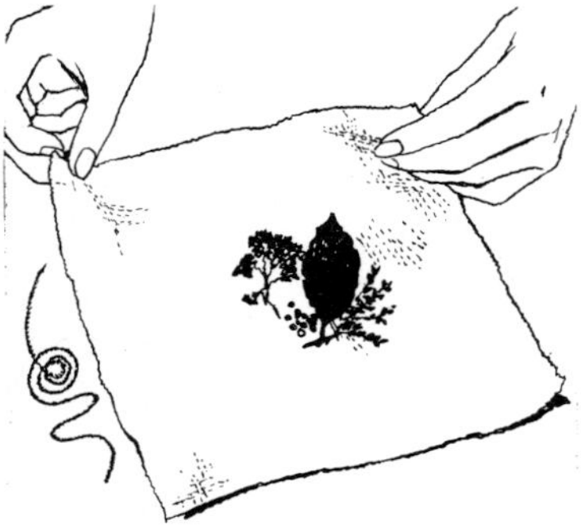

Bouquet Garni 1: Place in a piece of muslin sprigs of fresh herbs, a pinch of dried herbs, a bay leaf, or whatever is asked for in the particular recipe—see for instance Navarin of Lamb

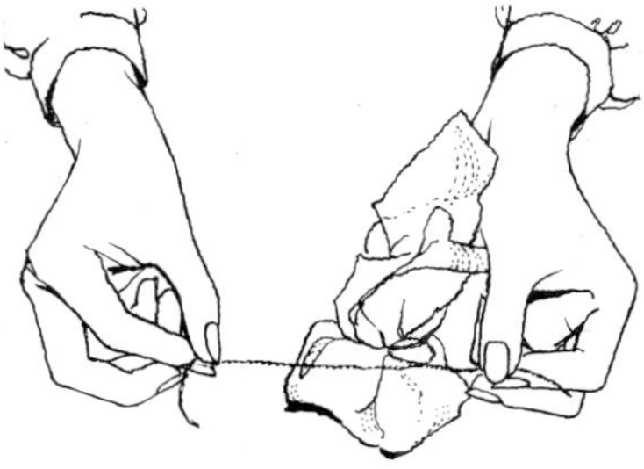

Bouquet Garni 2: Tie the muslin securely with thread or tape, and use the bouquet to flavour a soup, stew, casserole, etc.

sistency of a mixture when cooking is completed and the flavour is right—is used when just a little thickening is needed. It is the way to give body and extra richness to certain sauces and soups, and to give substance to small amounts of concentrated, unthickened fish and meat liquors.

Use equal quantities of butter and flour, or 1 part butter to 2 or 3 parts flour. In a small bowl, work the creamed fat to a paste with the flour. The hot liquid to be thickened should hardly show a bubble; whisk in the beurre manié a little at a time, and simmer just long enough to cook the flour—don't let it go on boiling.

*Note*: Use plain flour for preference—self-raising can be used, but leaves a perceptible taste in the mouth.

*Flour and Water Paste*: Flour is often mixed to a smooth paste with water to use as a thickener which may be added to hot liquids such as soups and stews. It must be mixed in carefully, as the mixture needs continuous stirring to prevent the formation of lumps. The taste of the dish may be affected—the last-minute addition of flour tends to lower the flavour levels.

*Arrowroot*: A dry, powdery starch from the roots of the maranta plant, which is grown in the West Indies. When mixed with water, it swells into a consistent jelly and is used for thickening gravies, etc., and for fruit glazes.

For a light thickening, allow 1 level tsp. (5 ml) to 125 ml liquid; for a thick sauce, to be served warm, use 2 level tsp. (10 ml) to 125 ml liquid. (Fruit glaze is given in the Basic Recipes at the back of the book.) Blend the arrowroot in a pan with twice its quantity of water and then either add the measured liquid cold, bring to the boil while stirring and cook for ½–1 minute, or add boiling liquid to the arrowroot and water and bring just to the boil, stirring: the latter method gives a clearer result.

*Cornflour*: This is ground from maize (Indian corn); it is particularly suitable for sweet milk and fruit sauces, but can also be used for savoury ones. For a glaze it does not give such a clear result as arrowroot or potato flour.

For a pouring sauce, use 3 level tsp. (15 ml) to 250 ml liquid; for gravy, 7 level tsp. (35 ml) to 250 ml liquid; for thickening casseroles, 5 level tsp. (25 ml) to 500 ml liquid; for glaze, 2 level tsp. (10 ml) to 125 ml liquid.

Either blend the cornflour to a cream with a little cold liquid, add some hot liquid, stirring, return the sauce to the pan and boil for 1 minute, or add the blended cornflour to the hot liquid, stirring briskly. The roux method of mixing is also used.

Cornflour mixtures are more viscous after cooking, so adapt the quantities accordingly for cold dishes.

*Rice Flour*: This does not clear when cooked and is therefore not satisfactory for transparent glazes. It needs longer cooking than either potato flour or arrowroot, thickens considerably as it cools, and it absorbs liquids—bear all these points in mind if you use it for thickening re-heated dishes such as casseroles. Its texture, granular rather than smooth-flowing, is suited to purées and hearty soups and for giving substance to stews. For a similar consistency to that produced by arrowroot or potato flour when hot, use twice the quantity. Use the hot liquid method as given under Arrowroot.

*Potato Flour*: The dried powder of the potato after all the water has been extracted. It is used particularly in France and is consequently sometimes known by the French name, *fécule*. It is less expensive than arrowroot, but can be used in the same way, though it should be boiled for a little longer. Added advantages of potato starch are that it thickens at a lower temperature and is not much more viscous when cooled than when it is hot.

## 2. PECTIN

This is a substance occurring in the flesh of most fruits and in the roots and stem pith of many plants. The amount present is especially large in succulent soft tissues and during rapid growth. As the fruit ripens, its pectinic substances absorb water and become gelatinous, and this slightly soluble gelatinous substance is called pectin.

Acid is essential for the release of pectin, and gelling is brought about by the addition of sugar; therefore, for a successful set when jam- and jelly-making, all three ingredients—pectin, acid and sugar—are essential.

The amount of pectin present in a fruit can be estimated as described below: the better the pectin content, the more sugar that can be used in a jam or jelly.

*Pectin Test*: Simmer the fruit until soft and pulpy. Take 1 tsp.

(5 ml) juice and put it into a cup or glass with 3 tsp. (15 ml) methylated spirit, stir together, then note the jelly-like clotting.

Good pectin content is shown by a large jelly-like lump.
Fair pectin content is shown by two or three lumps of jelly.
Poor pectin content is shown by a clot of jelly broken into small pieces.

From the point of view of making jam or jelly, fruits can be classified according to their acid/pectin content:

(*a*) Adequate acid and pectin: apples (tart), blackberries, sour cherries, crab apples, cranberries, black and red currants, gooseberries, grapefruit, lemons, limes, loganberries, oranges (Seville), plums, raspberries.
(*b*) Adequate pectin, low acid: bananas (unripe), cherries (sweet), figs (unripe), melon, quinces.
(*c*) Low pectin, adequate acid: apricots, rhubarb, strawberries.
(*d*) Low pectin, low acid: figs (ripe), peaches, pears.

There are various ways of overcoming the deficiencies. A combination of fruits may be used so that one counteracts another's defects. Acid can be added in the form of lemon or lime juice, citric acid or tartaric acid; commercial pectin or home-made pectin stock (see below) may be added.

*Pectin Stock*: Any sour cooking apples may be used, including windfalls, apple peel, cores and crab apples.

Wash 900 g fruit, and cut it up; cover with 700 ml water and stew gently for about ¾ hour, until well pulped; strain through a jelly bag.

To preserve the stock, re-boil the juice, put into heated jars, seal and sterilise for 5 minutes.

To use, allow 85 ml per 1 kilo of fruit.

Gooseberries and red currants can also be used to make pectin stock: use only 550 ml water to 900 g fruit, and stew for ½ hour before straining.

*Pectin and Sugar*: The amount and quality of the pectin govern the amount of sugar used to precipitate the gelling action in jams and jellies. With added pectin more sugar can be used, giving a greater yield for the basic amount of fruit; however, preserves made without added pectin are less sweet and have a more fruity flavour.

3. GUMS

These are amorphous, transparent substances which are widely distributed in plants. They are partly soluble, but their general action is to absorb water and swell to form a gel. Because gums are both odourless and tasteless, they are widely used in commercial food manufacture as thickeners—in soups, jellies, fish pastes, ice cream—and as emulsifying agents and stabilisers, to maintain the consistency of various products.

4. GELATINE

Although this is of animal and not vegetable origin, it has many properties in common with plant gums. It is a pure and odourless extract from bones, tendons and hide waste. Gelatine is insoluble in cold water, but will absorb many times its own weight of water to form a solid gel. It should not be heated above 60° to 70°C, or there is progressive destruction of the gelling powers.

5. CREAM, BLOOD: See under 'Coagulation'.

### What is meant by the Coagulation of Proteins?

Proteins can be classified, according to their origin, as:

*Animal Protein*: further divided into:

(*a*) Fibrous protein, which supplies strength, elasticity and protection; found in the muscle tissue of meat.

(*b*) Globular protein, dispersed in the tissue fluids, particularly in blood, milk, egg whites, etc.

*Plant Protein*: present to some extent in all plants, but of particular dietary importance in the wheat used in bread-making.

The coagulation of the proteins can be brought about by heat, exposure to ultra-violet light, pressure, mechanical shaking and the action of chemicals—acids, alkalis, salts and alcohols. It takes place in two steps:

1. *Denaturisation*: This is the modifying of the actual structure of the proteins, leading to a change in their reactions—solubility is decreased, they are more susceptible to enzyme action, and they become more viscous.

2. *Coagulation*: The insoluble denatured protein is precipitated—this change is irreversible.

*Meat*

The muscle tissue of meat is made up of microscopic fibres held together by connective tissue, and the whole muscle is surrounded by a sheath of connective tissue. The proportion of connective tissue varies with the activity of the muscle—the more active this is, the greater the amount.

Each of the microscopic fibres contains water, in which there are dissolved protein and mineral salts. The protein clots when the animal is killed and the body cools. This hardening of the muscle fibres is called *rigor mortis*, and it is essential that meat should be hung until this stiffness has passed off. The coagulated protein then liquefies, due to the action of enzymes and the formation of acids.

Connective tissue is made up of two proteins—Elastin, which is very tough and little altered by heating, and Collagen, which although insoluble in water, is converted by the action of moist heat into gelatine, thus making the meat tissue more tender. Connective tissue can be mechanically tenderised by pounding: this breaks the sheath surrounding the muscle fibres and allows the digestive juices to reach and break down the protein more quickly. The use of a weak acid solution (e.g., by marinading meat in a wine or vinegar solution) also increases the solubility of the protein, thus aiding in the breakdown of connective tissue and consequent tenderness.

When meat is cooked, this first of all denatures the protein: the changes are slight at 40°C, but by 60°C to 65°C the connective tissue is converted into gelatine.

*Fish*

Fish muscle tissue also contains collagen, but without the tough elastin. Therefore cooking is readily completed by the conversion of the collagen into gelatine and the coagulation of the protein. Beyond this point, the flesh of fish becomes dry and crumbly and tends to toughen.

*Milk*

The main protein present is casein, and this is not usually coagulated by heat, unless the milk is slightly acid, or a very high temperature is used. Homogenised milk, however, will coagulate quickly on heating, because the process has reduced the stability of the proteins to both reagents and temperature. Natural coagulation occurs when milk sours; the milk sugar (lactose) is converted to lactic acid, and this coagulates the casein.

CHEESE: The coagulation of casein is of major importance in the manufacture of cheese. The protein is precipitated by the addition of acid or of Rennin, forming a continuous mass which breaks down into curds when agitated, releasing the whey. The curd is then modified by heat, pressure, ripening, etc., to give the characteristic kind of cheese.

If cheese is subjected to excess heat, the protein will toughen, forming strings, while the fat necessary for the consistency and tenderness of the product will separate out.

*Cream*

The fact that the casein, a protein, coagulates when heated enables cream to be used as a thickening agent for rich gravies and pan juices.

The occasional unwanted coagulation that occurs when cream is added to coffee is due to the sensitivity of the casein to the high mineral content, or the slight acidity, of the coffee.

*Blood*

Blood can be used as a thickening agent, as in the traditional

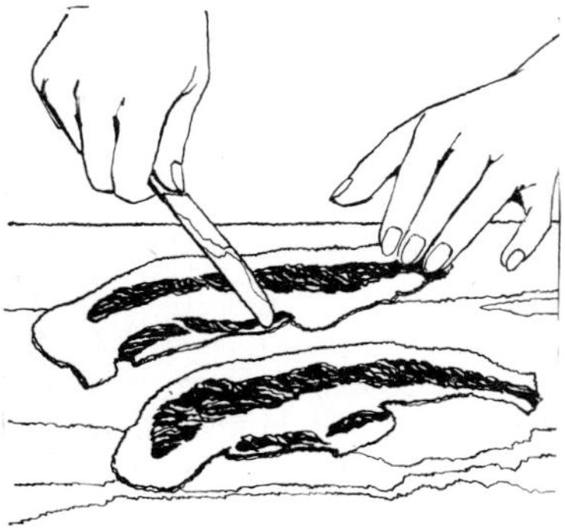

Preparing Rashers for Bacon Rolls: Rind the bacon, then flatten and stretch it with a knife blade before rolling it up and fixing on a skewer. (See Roast Chicken recipe)

Individual Raised Pies: Mould a portion of hot-water crust pastry round the base of a jam jar to give the shape. (See Raised Veal and Ham Pies)

dish, Jugged Hare; the protein present in the blood coagulates, thus giving the mixture a thicker consistency. Blood is also the essential ingredient of Black Pudding, where it binds together the fat and groats.

When used as a thickening agent, blood should be added at the end of the cooking time; combine it with a small amount of the hot liquid before gently mixing it with the rest; re-heat to simmering point, but don't re-boil.

*Eggs*

A large proportion of egg white is made up of protein albumens suspended in water. The jelly-like consistency is due to fibres of carbohydrate which provide a structural framework that holds the liquid albumen. The yolk also contains albumen, along with other proteins. The proteins coagulate when heated, beginning at about 60°C. At 65°C the egg will no longer flow, and at 70°C it will be firm but tender. Beyond this point the egg white will become a very tough, solid mass and the yolk crumbly or almost powdery, due to the shortening effect of the fat.

The way egg coagulates makes it a useful binding agent. When it is mixed with dry or loose ingredients, subsequent heating coagulates the protein so that it holds or binds all the ingredients together. In baking, the eggs provide structural protein.

Eggs can also be used as a thickening agent, but need to be treated carefully; they must be cooked only just enough to coagulate the protein—excessive heat causes over-coagulation, the structure becomes porous and the sauce or custard begins to separate out and curdle. Further heating will cause evaporation and shrinkage.

The coagulation of proteins in egg white make it important as a raising agent. The whites can be beaten to form a foam, which scientifically speaking is a colloid of bubbles of air surrounded by albumen. Mechanical denaturisation (i.e., beating) makes some of the albumen insoluble, thus stiffening and stabilising the foam. Over-beating, on the other hand, incorporates too much air, thus stretching the albumen to the extreme, so that it becomes thin. A certain degree of elasticity is, however, vital, especially if the foam is to be baked, so that before the albumen is coagulated by heat, the air incorporated can expand without breaking the cell walls.

*Wheat*

Wheat flour contains two proteins which, when mixed with water combine to form the protein Gluten, an essential ingredient in bread-making. The character of wheat flour depends on the proportion of both protein and starch that it contains. The more gluten that is developed by the absorption of water, the higher the rise and yield of the finished mixture. As the gluten content decreases, the starch content rises. Flours that are low in gluten and high in starch are the so-called 'soft' flours, which are ideal for cake-making.

For bread-making, we need a flour that is high in protein content, to give the gluten that is vital for the structure of the bread; it holds the other constituents such as starch and the leavening gases as they are formed, and it also maintains the structure as the protein coagulates.

The protein content of the flour must also be of the correct quality. Some wheat glutens formed are so tough that they are incapable of stretching, but special strains of wheat have been developed that provide both the right quality and sufficient quantity of gluten; flours made from these grains are termed 'strong'. Strong flours have the high water-absorption

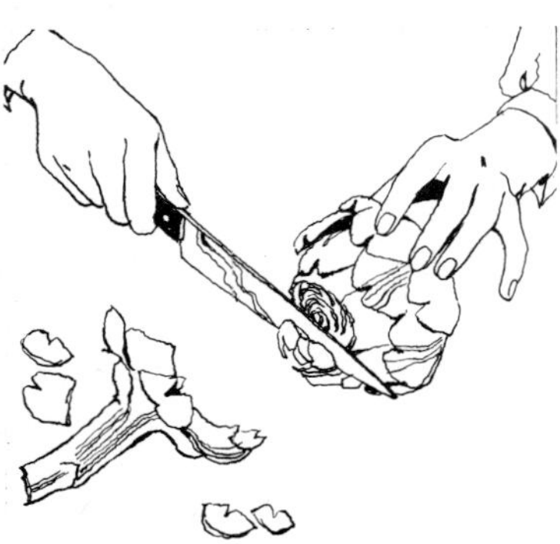

Globe Artichokes 1: Cut off stalk, then cut off tips of top leaves with a knife

Globe Artichokes 2: Use kitchen scissors to trim off tips of side leaves. Tie with string to cook, but remove string before serving

capacity necessary for the formation of gluten, though thorough mixing and kneading are required to develop the elasticity. This elastic gluten stretches greatly as the steam within it expands, and when heated it coagulates to form the structure of the product.

*Other Grains*: Rye contains only a small amount of gluten, so when it is used for bread it gives a characteristic heavy texture. Oats, barley, maize and rice contain no gluten and cannot be used to make true bread.

*Exercises in protein coagulation*

A. Make up a basic yeast dough mixture, but vary the flour, using (*a*) plain flour, (*b*) strong flour, (*c*) cornflour.
Compare the results, noting rise, texture and flavour.

B. Make up a basic meringue mixture, but vary the whisking times:

1. Beat to form a light foam before adding the sugar.
2. Beat to a stiff foam so that the whites will stand up in peaks before adding the sugar.
3. Beat until the egg white looks dry and flaky before adding the sugar.

Compare results, noting the number of meringues made from each batch and the volume and texture.

C. Study the effect of heat on coagulating proteins. Make baked egg custards, but vary the cooking temperatures and the times:

1. 177°C (mark 4, 350°F) for 40 minutes.
2. 177°C (mark 4, 350°F) for 1 hour 15 minutes.
3. 204°C (mark 6, 400°F) for 40 minutes.
4. 232°C (mark 8, 450°F) for 40 minutes.

D. Choose one of the following dishes and note in detail the physical and chemical changes that occur at each stage from mixing, through baking, up to the final serving: Soufflé; Rough Puff Pastry; Victoria Sandwich.

## CHAPTER 2

# THE SCIENCE OF FOOD CARE

For every organic molecule produced in nature, there is a natural method of decomposition. When therefore we try to preserve foods, we are working counter to nature, and setting ourselves some complicated problems.

### Spoilage Agents

There are three main types: Microbial, Enzyme and Oxidation.

1. MICROBIAL AGENTS

(*a*) *Yeasts*: These are microscopic, generally uni-cellular organisms that reproduce rapidly by budding, and spread by contact. They grow well in acid conditions and are very active in the fermentation of sugars. Most species are readily destroyed by exposure to a heat of not less than 60°C for a few minutes, but foods can easily be re-contaminated unless adequately protected. Yeasts are inactivated by cold, and deep freezing will destroy some kinds.

(*b*) *Moulds and Fungi*: These organisms, unlike ordinary plants, do not possess chlorophyll and are therefore unable to assimilate carbon dioxide by the process of photosynthesis. Thus, they need a host to provide nutrients.

Moulds can be large and complex structures; a mould starts as a thin thread, and under favourable conditions develops rapidly to form a network with the appearance of cottonwool. In later stages there is some coloration, due to the formation of the reproductive spores. The majority are sensitive to heat and fairly readily destroyed. They are inactivated but not destroyed by freezing.

Fungi of various kinds are found growing on all sorts of environments, but in general each lives on only the one kind of host, though there are a few fungi that may attack several hosts. For all, a prime requisite for growth is a very damp but warm environment. Common fungi are toadstools and mildews.

(*c*) *Bacteria*: These are the most widespread and active of the micro-organisms. They are minute and uni-cellular, capable of rapid multiplication by simple cell division. Bacteria can form spores which are very resistant to adverse conditions, and to destroy these requires extreme heat under pressure. Refrigeration slows down bacterial action, and deep freezing inhibits it completely, but neither has any permanent effect on the actual organisms present, so they will again multiply when returned to a favourable temperature.

The commonest bacteria causing food poisoning are *Salmonella*, *Staphylococci*, *Streptococci* and *Clostridium botulinum*. They are especially dangerous because their presence cannot always be detected by smell or taste.

### 2. ENZYMES

Enzymes are complex structures present in all living cells; when the cells die, enzymes are able to act on the proteins and fats present and break them down. During the storage of food, therefore, there can be extensive damage. Enzymes are permanently inactivated by extreme heat, while moderate temperatures accelerate their activity. Extreme cold prevents their action temporarily, but has no effect once the temperature rises again. One enzyme which is important in food storage is Lipase, which attacks fats, shows great resistance to freezing and remains active at temperatures as low as −25°C. It is therefore capable of producing changes in meats and poultry both during processing by freezing and during storage. Cows' milk also contains an enzyme that is troublesome: it is inactive at body temperatures, but is activated by cooling to 20°C. Homogenisation, by decreasing the size of fat globules and dispersing them, accentuates this problem. However, by pasteurising prior to homogenisation, this difficulty can be overcome.

The action of enzymes is also important in the commercial production of dehydrated foods, where the moisture content is low enough to prevent bacterial growth, but not low enough to inhibit the enzymes; it is therefore essential to blanch foods before dehydration.

### 3. OXIDATION

Oxidation occurs spontaneously, and rancidity occurs when any food containing fat is exposed to the air. The rate of reaction depends on the type of fat, the temperature and the light. Atmospheric oxidation can be controlled by limiting access to oxygen during processing, by packing foods tightly in their containers, with the minimum air-space, by vacuum packing, and by constant low storage temperatures. Care must be taken to preserve any naturally occurring anti-oxidants present in the food; anti-oxidants can also be added during processing.

Spoilage from oxidation begins with the absorption of odours, and foods with a high fat content and mild flavour are particularly susceptible. Absorption of odours is slower when the fat is hard rather than soft, and when the temperature is low, while high temperatures accelerate absorption. It is essential, then, that susceptible foods should be kept away from any tainting material, by being stored in separate containers or wrapped in some form of impermeable material (such as plastic film, foil, greaseproof paper, etc.) and kept in a very cool place, preferably a refrigerator.

The presence of oxygen also causes browning in some foods, particularly certain fruits (e.g., bananas, apples, pears); the effect is due to the interaction of enzymes and oxygen.

### Conditions Affecting Spoilage

These are both varied and inter-related. They include temperature, humidity, the presence or absence of oxygen, the acidity or alkalinity (pH) of the environment, and the concentration of the medium.

1. TEMPERATURE: Microbes may be divided into three main groups, according to the temperature at which they live.

(*a*) Low-temperature group (*cryophilic* microbes). The optimum temperature—the temperature at which the microbes grow best—is around 20°C. These microbes occur naturally in air, soil and water. They can grow below freezing point, provided the medium does not freeze completely. Therefore this group is of key importance in the preservation of food by freezing. Some bacteria will still grow and multiply just below the temperature at which the food begins to freeze, i.e., at −2°C. For yeasts the figure is −5°C and for moulds −7°C.

(*b*) Moderate-temperature group (*mesophilic* microbes), with an optimum temperature of around 37°C. The microbes in this group live on warm-blooded animals, and ultimately find their way to the soil. They generally fail to grow at a temperature below 5–10°C. This group contains the organisms harmful to human health.

(*c*) High-temperature group (*thermophilic* microbes), with an optimum temperature of around 60°C. Many of them fail to grow at all at normal temperatures, but are of particular importance in food canning, as they are very resistant to destruction, even at high temperatures.

2. HUMIDITY: All microbes are greatly influenced by the amount of moisture available. Bacteria must get their nutrients in a soluble form, therefore water must be present. Moulds are able to grow on products containing little water, provided there is sufficient moisture present in the atmosphere. The rate of growth is directly related to atmospheric humidity, being most rapid when humidity is high, and falling off as humidity decreases. Both bacteria and fungi require a high humidity, moulds need drier conditions, and the yeasts are intermediate.

3. EFFECTS OF OXYGEN: Microbes can be divided into two main groups according to their reaction to oxygen:
*Aerobes* are microbes that cannot develop *without* the presence of oxygen.
*Anaerobes* are microbes that cannot develop *in* the presence of oxygen.

Most moulds are aerobic. Yeasts grow well only in the presence of air, although they are able to ferment material without it. Some bacteria are aerobic, some anaerobic.

4. ACIDITY OR ALKALINITY—pH—OF MEDIA: Most bacteria grow in a neutral or slightly alkaline medium, but the yeasts and lactic acid bacteria develop in a medium of low acidity, while the moulds are acid-tolerant and can develop in a medium of relatively high acidity. The addition of acid or alkali to the medium will therefore affect the growth rate of the various organisms living on it.

5. CONCENTRATION OF ADDITIVES: The presence or absence of various additives and the degree of concentration affect the microbial growth.

(*a*) Salt: Some bacteria are sensitive to salt and will not grow on a medium containing more than a very low percentage, while other bacteria thrive on a saturated salt solution. The higher the percentage of salt, the smaller the amount of water that is available to the micro-organisms.

(*b*) Nitrates and Nitrites: These substances have an inhibiting effect on microbial growth, and are therefore widely used in the commercial preservation of meats. Enzymes activate these chemicals so that they act as oxidising agents and the medium, normally anaerobic, becomes aerobic. A great many organisms require anaerobic conditions, so if these chemicals are added, the growth of such organisms is restricted and controlled.

(*c*) Sugar: This can be added in such high proportions that organisms are hindered from growing; there is no water available to them and this excludes all but perhaps those moulds which can survive a dry medium, provided the atmosphere is damp.

*Exercises*

The following experiments give some idea of what is involved in food spoilage; they should if possible be carried out in conjunction with the Science Department, as the facilities there may be more suitable.

A. Prepare *five* plates of agar solution and leave them exposed to the air for 24 hours. Cover them, then leave each in a different set of circumstances.

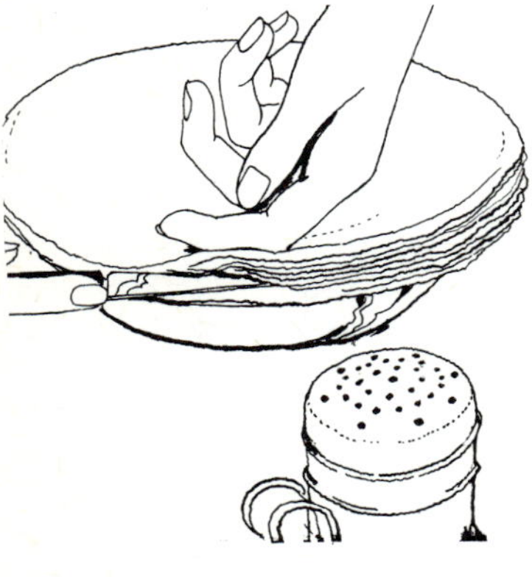

Pie Edgings 1: To 'knock up' the edge of a pie, use the back of the knife blade, placing the forefinger as shown. (See Spicy Apple Pie)

Pie Edgings 2: Crimp or scallop the edge with little knife cuts, holding the pastry down with the thumb. (See Spicy Apple Pie)

*Plate 1*: (control plate): Leave at room temperature.
*Plate 2*: Place in refrigerator; record the temperature.
*Plate 3*: Leave in a hot, dry place, e.g., an airing cupboard or incubator, if available; record the temperature.
*Plate 4*: Place somewhere warm and damp; record temperature.
*Plate 5*: Leave at room temperature, in an airtight tin or other container.

B. Prepare *three* plates of agar solution. To one add a few drops of vinegar, to the second a few drops of dissolved bicarbonate of soda. Add nothing to the third, which is the control plate.

Expose all the plates to the air for 24 hours, then cover and leave in warm, damp conditions for at least a further 24 hours.

C. Observe the growth of the agar subjected to the various conditions. If a powerful microscope is available, prepare slides, compare the different growths microscopically and note the difference between the colonies of yeasts, moulds, fungi and bacteria. Which predominate?

What effect have the various conditions had on the growth pattern, as compared with that on the control plates left at room temperature? What conclusions can you draw?

## Effects of Spoilage

I. ON CARBOHYDRATES

With foods rich in carbohydrates, bacteria cause fermentation, especially of sugars. Acids and alcohol are produced and carbon dioxide is released. If in this process air is excluded, acids will develop to a point where further growth of the organism is inhibited. This 'limiting acidity' is determined by the concentration of the sugar. If the concentration of the sugar is high enough, then sufficient acid will be formed to limit any further changes; if the sugar concentrations are low, then the food will not be preserved by this acid fermentation. Acids produced by fermentation will not be stable if there is ready access to air, since air removes the preserving acids by oxidation. Some bacteria are able to attack both sugars and proteins, but usually the concentration of sugar will prevent attacks on proteins.

2. ON PROTEINS

Bacterial decomposition of protein causes greater detriment than the decomposition of carbohydrates. The changes are complex: protein is broken down into its component parts, and further attacks on the amino acids liberate acids, alcohols and hydrocarbons. These are further fermented to produce simple acids, alcohols and gases. The liberation of ammonia is noticeable in the advanced stages of the process, but even in the initial stages of protein decomposition there are noticeable 'off' smells.

Moulds are inhibited by acids and sugars, but even if these are present, the moulds will still attack proteins. Acids are partly neutralised by the liberation of ammonia through the action of moulds on protein; this process gradually accelerates until the medium becomes near neutral—the ideal breeding ground for many bacteria.

3. ON FATS

Fats are less susceptible than proteins and carbohydrates to decomposition by micro-organisms, but there are still extensive changes. Micro-organisms containing enzymes cause a breakdown of the fat tissue, and these products can be fermented in the same way as carbohydrates. Fats may go rancid due to the action of microbes, but this is rare, and is more likely to be due to the action of oxidation.

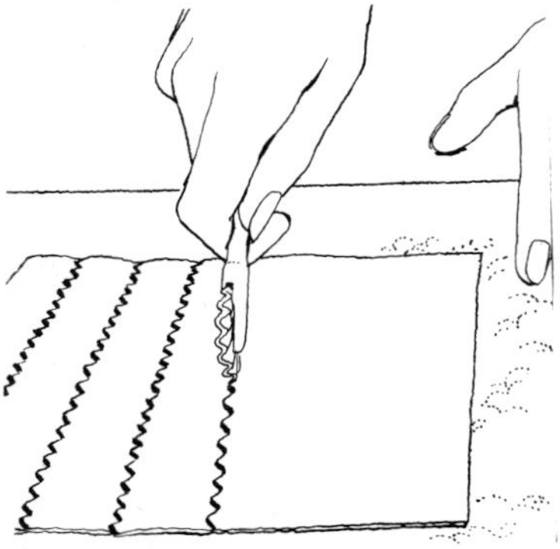

Cutting Pastry Strips (e.g. for Mincemeat Tranche): Use a pastry wheel to give a neat serrated edge

Pastry Leaves: Cut a narrow strip of pastry, then cut across with diagonal lines, to give diamond shapes; mark veins with a knife, and use to decorate pies, e.g. Salmon Shells

**Preservation of Food**

When any food is preserved, it is essential not only to destroy the spoilage agents, but also (where no preservative is added) to prevent later re-contamination.

All food to be preserved should be in prime condition, free from blemishes, imperfections or infections.

There are four main methods of food preservation—heating, freezing, dehydration and addition of preservatives.

1. HEATING

This is the most convenient method and therefore the one most widely used, chiefly by means of commercial canning and bottling (though a good deal of fruit bottling is still carried out at home). Bacteria, moulds and yeasts are generally destroyed by heat, but the cans or bottles used must be perfectly sealed to exclude further entry of air and subsequent re-contamination.

Methods used to preserve food by heating are designed to ensure adequate destruction of micro-organisms while retaining the best possible flavour and appearance.

*Fruit Canning and Bottling*: Successful preservation of fruit depends on efficient sterilisation. The surfaces of fruit normally have yeasts and moulds present, and these micro-organisms, always present in the atmosphere, cause the fruit to ferment and go mouldy when it becomes over-ripe. Enzymes, responsible for the ripening process, ultimately cause rotting. Therefore, to preserve fruit these surface moulds and yeasts must be killed and the enzymes inactivated by sterilisation; to prevent re-contamination the sterilised containers must be completely sealed.

(See end of chapter for notes on the technique of home fruit bottling.)

*Vegetable Canning and Bottling*: Preservation of vegetables in these ways is very much more difficult than for fruit, and nowadays little home vegetable preservation is carried out. All vegetables are prone to contamination by microbes present in the soil, and these are likely to include spore-forming bacteria which are very resistant to sterilisation. *If the product is incompletely sterilised, these micro-organisms will continue to develop in the can or jar, producing a toxin very harmful to man.* Unfortunately, this toxin can be produced without any apparent signs of spoilage. Unlike fruits, which contain acids that prevent the production of bacterial organisms, *vegetables are non-acid and must therefore be subjected to a high temperature under pressure*. However, if the medium is made acid, as with pickles, then the vegetables can be successfully preserved without pressure sterilisation.

*Meat, Poultry and Fish* are canned and bottled commercially.

### 2. FREEZING

Freezing is the removal of heat so that the temperature drops sufficiently to ensure the preservation of food by completely inhibiting the growth of moulds, yeasts and bacteria. The enzymes present, however, must if possible first be destroyed by blanching the foods.

All foods contain water, and as the temperature drops during freezing, this water is converted into ice crystals. If the process takes place slowly, then the crystals formed are large, damaging the structure of the cells and causing loss of nutrients. The quicker the actual freezing, the less the damage that occurs to the cells and the nutrients; also the time taken to pass through the temperature range capable of supporting microbial growth is shortened to the absolute minimum.

(See end of chapter for notes on home freezing.)

### 3. DEHYDRATION

Dehydration is the removal of water. Without water most of the micro-organisms and enzymes which cause food spoilage cannot live. The practice of drying foods in the sun or wind is probably the oldest method of food preservation; it has been applied to fish, meat (biltong, pemmican, etc.), herbs and fruit (e.g., dates, apricots, prunes). The main advantage of drying is that it produces food which is light in weight and, if correctly packaged and stored, will keep indefinitely.

The principle of dehydration is to transfer sufficient heat into the food to cause the water content to evaporate. Commercially, this is done by a hot air system; the food is kept in motion while in contact with the hot air, and this increases the rate of drying. Other methods are drum drying, where the food is passed over heated rollers (used in making potato flakes, instant breakfast cereals) and spray drying, where food is dispersed as small droplets into the drying air (instant milks, coffees).

It is important that the dried foods should be able to take up water again, so as to return them as nearly as possible to their original state for eating, i.e., they must absorb water quickly on soaking or cooking.

*Accelerated Freeze Drying*: Water can exist in three states—solid, liquid or gas (steam or vapour). In normal drying processes, the water content of food is evaporated from its liquid state. During Accelerated Freeze Drying the food is first frozen, then subjected to a mild heat treatment under a high vacuum, which causes the ice to evaporate directly. The freezing operation is carried out very quickly, to prevent the formation of large crystals, and because the heat treatment is mild, there is no alteration to the structure of the food, so that when it rehydrates it is very close to its original form. However, there is the problem of oxidation, for unless packaging and handling are adequate, the dried product is prone to break, which increases the danger of air penetration.

*Exercise on preserving by drying:*
Using as a guide the book *Home Preservation of Fruit and Vegetables* (see end of chapter), dry a selection of fresh herbs and store them for winter use.

4. ADDITIVES
(*a*) *Salt*: Food preserved by the addition of salt is often referred to as 'cured'. Adding salt causes the water in the food to be drawn out of the cells; finally, the point is reached where no more water can be drawn from the cells, and at this stage the spoilage micro-organisms can no longer grow and multiply, thus the food is preserved.

For fish, ham and bacon, salt is often used in conjunction with smoking, which gives added flavour. The food is salted and the brine formed is drained away after 2–3 weeks. At this stage the salt has saturated all the remaining juices, making the water unavailable for microbial growth. Then the food is smoked, to give the characteristic flavour.

Home-made pickles also make use of the special properties of salt, in conjunction with vinegar (see below).

*Exercise on use of salt in preserving:*
Using as a guide *Home Preservation of Fruit and Vegetables*, salt some runner beans and store for winter use.

(*b*) *Vinegar*: When foods are saturated with an acid solution, the growth of micro-organisms and the activities of enzymes are inhibited. Generally, this is used in conjunction with salt, to produce pickles, etc. —salt draws water from the food so that there is insufficient water remaining to dilute the acid.

(*c*) *Sugar*: Has the same preservative effect as salt, drawing the moisture from the cells: this is the principle used in the crystallising of fruit.

(*d*) *Chemical Additives*: These are varied, but their use is controlled by strict specifications and they are constantly under review. Legally, a chemical additive must be harmless, give a useful degree of stability, be readily dispersible in the food and not impart any foreign odour, flavour or colour, even during long storage.

### Technique of Bottling Fruit

THE JARS OR BOTTLES: These are wide-necked glass jars, each covered with a metal sealing disc or a heat-resisting glass disc with a rubber ring, and with a screw-band to hold the disc firmly in place. They can be obtained in two sizes, holding approx. 500 g and 1 kilo (1 and 2 lb.). Both jars and screw-bands can be re-used, but a new rubber band for the glass disc, or a new metal sealing disc, must be used every time.

All jars should be checked, to make sure they can be made quite airtight and that they and the fittings are free from flaws.

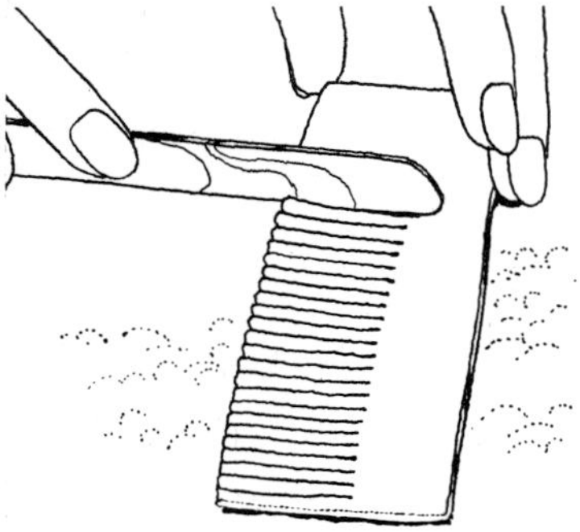

Making a Pastry Tassel 1: (e.g. for Raised Veal and Ham Pies): Cut an oblong pastry strip and cut at close intervals, leaving an uncut band along one edge

Making a Pastry Tassel 2: Roll up the strip and damp the end of the uncut part to make it stick. Before fixing to the savoury pie, separate out the fringe as seen

They must be scrupulously clean, so wash them and rinse in clean, hot water.

SYRUP FOR BOTTLING: Fruit may be preserved in either syrup or water, but syrup certainly gives a better flavour and colour. The usual proportion is 225 g sugar to 570 ml water, but the amount may be varied according to the sweetness of the particular fruit. Use granulated sugar, dissolve it in half the required amount of water, bring to the boil and boil for 1 minute, then add the remainder of the water. (This method cuts the time required for the syrup to cool.) If the syrup is to be used while still boiling (i.e., for oven sterilisation), keep a lid on the pan to stop evaporation, which alters the strength.

PACKING THE FRUIT: Put the prepared fruit into bottling jars layer by layer, using a packing spoon or a wooden spoon handle. When a jar is full, the fruit should be firmly and securely wedged in place, without bruising or squashing; the more closely it is packed, the less chance there is of the fruit rising after processing, when it will have shrunk to some extent. Add the liquid as described under the particular method of sterilisation.

When the bottles have been filled with fruit and liquid, dispel all air bubbles by jarring each bottle on the palm of the hand; alternatively, pack the fruit and add liquid alternately until the bottle is full. Fill to the brim before putting on the fittings. With wet-pack methods it is essential to loosen the screw-bands by a quarter-turn before processing, to allow steam and air to escape, or the bottles may burst.

PROCESSING AND TESTING: Sterilise the fruit by one of the methods described below, then test it as follows: lift the bottles one at a time on to a wooden surface and screw the band on firmly. When the bottles are cold, test for correct sealing by removing the screw-band and trying to lift the bottle by the sealing disc. If the disc holds firm, this shows that a vacuum formed as the jar cooled, and it is now hermetically sealed. If the disc comes off, there is probably a flaw in the rim of the jar or on the cap. If, however, several bottles are unsealed, the processing procedure may have been faulty. The fruit from such jars should be used up at once, or transferred to perfect jars and re-processed without delay (though this unfortunately results in over-cooking).

STERILISING: There are two main methods—in a water bath (slow or quick method) or in the oven (wet or dry pack).

WATER BATH METHOD: This is considered to be the more exact method, but it does require some special equipment:

(*a*) A large vessel 6–8 cm deeper than the height of the bottling jars—e.g., a very large saucepan, a zinc bath or a zinc bucket. It must have a false bottom such as a metal grid, strips of wood nailed together in a trellis fashion, or even a folded coarse cloth.

(*b*) A thermometer (a sugar-boiling one will do).

(*c*) Bottling tongs—not essential, but they make the job of removing the bottles from the bath much easier.

SLOW WATER BATH: Pack the bottles with the fruit, then:

1. Fill up the bottles with cold syrup.
2. Put the rubber rings and metal discs or heat-resisting glass discs and the screw-bands in place, then turn the screw-bands back a quarter-turn.
3. Place the bottles in the large vessel and cover with cold water, immersing them completely, if possible, but at least up to the necks.
4. Heat gently on top of the cooker, checking the temperature of the water regularly; raise to 54°C in 1 hour, then take a further ½ hour to raise to the processing temperature given in the chart below.
5. Maintain temperature for time given in chart overleaf.

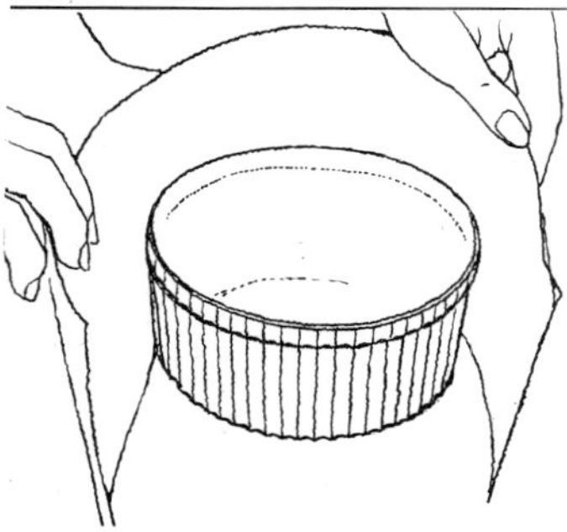

Preparing a Soufflé Dish 1 (e.g. for Lemon Soufflé): Cut a strip of greaseproof or non-stick paper long enough to go round dish and overlap slightly; make it deep enough to come about 5 cm above the top of the dish

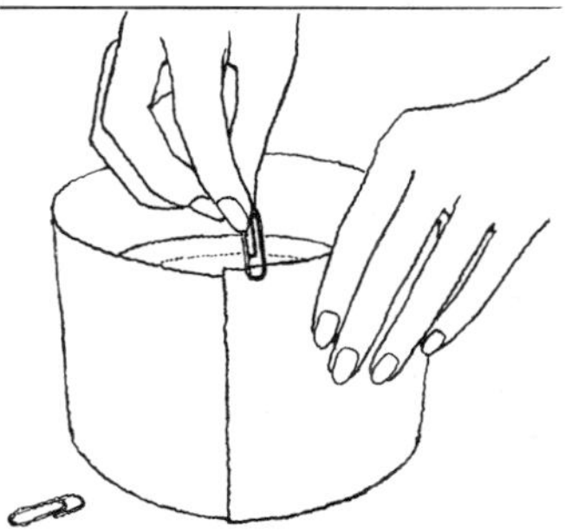

Soufflé Dish 2: Place paper band round outside of dish, keeping it a good shape, and secure with paperclips at top and bottom of overlapped portion

6. Remove the bottles with the tongs (or bale out enough water to remove them with the aid of an oven cloth).
7. Place the bottles on a wooden surface one at a time and tighten the screw-bands straight away.

QUICK WATER BATH: If you have no thermometer, this is a good alternative method. Fill the packed bottles with hot (not boiling) syrup, cover and place in the vessel of warm water. Bring the water to simmering point in 25–30 minutes and keep simmering for the time stated in the chart.

*Times for Water Bath Method*

| | *Slow method*<br>Raise from cold to temperature given in 90 mins., and maintain as below | *Quick method*<br>Raise from warm (38°C) to simmering (88°C) in 25–30 mins. and maintain as below |
|---|---|---|
| *Soft fruit:*<br>*Normal packs*<br>Blackberries<br>Raspberries<br>Loganberries<br>Mulberries<br>Currants<br>Gooseberries and Rhubarb for made-up dishes<br>Apples, sliced | 74°C for 10 mins. | 2 mins. |
| *Soft fruit*<br>*Tight packs*<br>As above, including Gooseberries and Rhubarb to serve as stewed fruit | 82°C for 15 mins. | 10 mins. |
| *Stone fruit*<br>Whole Apricots, Cherries, Gages, Plums, Damsons | As above | As above |
| *Miscellaneous*<br>Apricots, Peaches, Nectarines, halved<br>Pineapple<br>Plums, halved | 82°C for 15 mins. | 20 mins. |
| Figs, Pears<br>Tomatoes, whole | 88°C for 30 mins. | 40 mins. |

OVEN METHOD: This is preferred by many people because quite a number of bottles can be done at one time and—except for the jars—no special equipment is needed. The oven method is not quite so exact as the water bath one, as it is not so easy to maintain a constant temperature, and it is easier to over-cook the fruit.

When following this method, use only one shelf of the oven, placed in the middle, and don't overcrowd the bottles on it, or the heat will not penetrate the fruit evenly.

WET PACK: Heat the oven to 150°C (marks 1–2, approx. 300°F). Fill the packed jars with boiling syrup to within 2 cm of the top and put on the rubber rings and the heat-resisting glass discs, if used, but *not* metal discs. Don't put the screw-bands in position. Place the jars 5–6 cm apart on a solid baking sheet, lined with newspaper to catch any liquid which may boil over. Put in the centre of the oven and cook for the time stated in the table. Remove the jars one by one, put on the metal discs, screw the bands tightly in place and leave to cool.

DRY PACK: Heat the oven to 120°C (mark $\frac{1}{4}$, approx. 250°F). Pack the bottles with the fruit but don't add any liquid. Cover with the heat-resisting glass discs but *not* the rubber rings or metal discs, if used, and place 5–6 cm apart on a baking sheet lined as above. Cook for the time stated in the table, then remove the jars one at a time (not all together). Use the contents of one jar to top up the others if the fruit has shrunk in the cooking. Fill up at once with boiling syrup and place the rubber bands and metal discs or heat-resisting glass discs in position, then screw the bands on tightly. Leave to cool.

### *Times for Oven Method of Sterilising*

The following are the temperatures and processing times recommended by the Long Ashton Research Station. It is assumed that jars holding approx. 500 g (1 lb.) will be used.

*Note*: The dry pack oven method is not recommended for fruits which discolour in the air, such as apricots, apples, pears, plums, peaches, etc. With both oven methods the time required varies not only with the type of fruit, but also with the tightness of the pack and the total load in the oven at one time, the load being calculated according to the total capacity (reckoned in g or lb.) of the jars.

| | *Wet Pack* | *Dry Pack* |
|---|---|---|
| | Pre-heat oven to 150°C (mark 1, approx. 300°F); process as follows: | Pre-heat oven to 120°C (mark ¼, approx. 250°F); process as follows: |
| *Soft fruit* *Normal packs* Blackberries Currants Loganberries Mulberries Raspberries Gooseberries and Rhubarb (for made-up dishes) Apples, sliced | 1–4 jars for 30–40 mins.; 5–10 jars for 45–60 mins. | 1–4 jars for 45–55 mins.; 5–10 jars for 60–75 mins. *Not recommended for Apples* |
| *Soft fruit* *Tight packs* As above, including Gooseberries and Rhubarb (for use as stewed fruit) | 1–4 jars for 40–50 mins.; 5–10 jars for 55–70 mins. | 1–4 jars for 55–70 mins.; 5–10 jars for 75–90 mins. |
| *Stone fruit, dark* Whole Cherries Damsons, Plums | 1–4 jars for 40–50 mins.; 5–10 jars for 55–70 mins. | 1–4 jars for 55–70 mins.; 5–10 jars for 75–90 mins. |
| *Stone fruit, light* Whole Apricots Cherries, Gages Plums | 1–4 jars for 40–50 mins.; 5–10 jars for 55–70 mins. | *Not recommended for light fruit* |
| *Miscellaneous* Apricots, halved Nectarines Peaches Pineapple Plums, halved | 1–4 jars for 50–60 mins.; 5–10 jars for 65–80 mins. | *Not recommended for these fruits* |
| Figs | 1–4 jars for 60–70 mins.; 5–10 jars for 75–90 mins. | 1–4 jars for 80–100 mins.; 5–10 jars for 105–125 mins. |
| Pears Tomatoes | 1–4 jars for 60–70 mins.; 5–10 jars for 75–90 mins. | *Not recommended for pears or tomatoes* |

**Technique of Freezing**

FRUIT: *Maximum storage time, 12 months*
Small soft fruits will freeze very quickly; they do not require cooking prior to freezing, and can be packed in any of the three ways given below. Other fruits are prone to discoloration due to oxidation, so care is required in the preparation and thawing procedure.

Wash the fruit in ice-cold water if really necessary, and drain on absorbent paper. Fruit which discolours should be kept during preparation in a lemon juice solution—use 1 lemon to 1 litre water.

Pack the fruit in one of these ways:

*Dry Pack*: Suitable for fruit such as gooseberries, blackcurrants, raspberries, etc., which are whole, small and not prone to discoloration. Pack in a rigid container, so that there is no damage during handling.

Baking Blind (used when making case for Lemon Meringue Pie, Quiches, etc.) 1. Put flan ring on baking sheet and line with pastry; trim edges by passing rolling pin over them. 2. Cover surface of pastry with greaseproof paper. 3. Put in uncooked dried beans, etc., to weight paper and keep shape of flan. Remove paper and beans 5–10 mins. before end of cooking time; return case to oven to finish baking

*In Sugar*: Suitable for soft fruit, e.g., raspberries, strawberries. Layer the fruit with the dry sugar (preferably caster) and pack in a rigid container.

*In Syrup*: For non-juicy fruits and for those that discolour during preparation (see page 41). Allow about 280 ml syrup per 450 g fruit.

The strength of the syrup depends on the fruit:

Mild fruits such as apples require only a light syrup (115 g to 570 ml water). Soft fruits require a heavy syrup (225 g to 570 ml water, or 280 g sugar to 285 ml water). Stone fruits require a moderate strength syrup (170 g sugar to 570 ml water). To make the syrup, dissolve the sugar in the water, bring to the boil, cover, then cool.

*To Use Frozen Fruit*: Thaw it slowly in the unopened container in a cool place. If it is to be eaten raw, serve it while it is still chilled. If further cooking is required, thaw it only until the pieces can be separated. Gooseberries and other small fruits to be used in pies, etc., keep their shape better if placed in the pie-dish in their solid state, topped with pastry and cooked at the temperature required for pastry

VEGETABLES: *Maximum storage time, 12 months*

Choose young, tender vegetables, and for best results freeze within a few hours of picking. Vegetables should be scalded or blanched prior to freezing, to halt enzyme action and to improve the colour. Allow at least 3.5 litres of water per 500 g vegetables; the time will vary with the size and shape of the vegetables; plunge them into ice-cold water to prevent further cooking and to cool them as quickly as possible. After cooling, drain thoroughly and pack straight into containers.

*To Use Frozen Vegetables*: There is no need to thaw them. Place in the minimum amount of boiling salted water and cook quickly until just tender.

MEAT: *Maximum storage times*: *beef, lamb, 12 months*; *pork, 9 months*; *veal, 3–6 months*; *offal, 2 months*

It is not worth freezing meat if it has to be bought retail—to make it an economical proposition, it must be bought wholesale or direct from a farmer.

Meat can readily be frozen in a home freezer, but results are variable, and it is usually better to buy it ready frozen and just store it. It must be of really top quality, with some, but not too much, fat.

*To Use Frozen Meats*: Both beef and lamb can be successfully cooked directly from the frozen state and this has the advantage of reducing weight loss and retaining the flavour. However, if it is more convenient for them to be thawed before cooking, the actual texture will be excellent, although there tends to be less flavour.

To cook beef from the frozen state, place the joint in a cold oven, set to 190°C (mark 5, approx. 375°F) and allow 30 minutes per 500 g, plus 30 minutes, from the time the oven reaches the correct temperature (about 30 minutes). When cooking a thawed joint, treat it as fresh meat.

For frozen lamb, allow 25 minutes per 500 g plus 20 minutes from the time the oven reaches the correct temperature.

Pork, veal and offal should be thawed completely, then cooked as for fresh meat.

POULTRY: *Maximum storage times: chicken, 12 months; duck, 6 months; giblets, 3 months*

Freeze only young, tender birds (if possible starved for 24 hours before killing). Hang the bird in a cool place for 1 day, then draw and clean in the normal way. Joint it if desired, but do not stuff.

*To Use Frozen Poultry*: Poultry must be thawed completely prior to cooking, as it is essential that the internal temperature of 88°C (190°F) should be reached. If this sterilising temperature is not reached during cooking, bacterial infection and food poisoning can result. To thaw it in the refrigerator, allow enough time—a leg joint will take about 6 hours to thaw completely, and a whole bird 12–15 hours. Thawing at room temperature will require about half that time.

FISH: *Maximum storage time, 3 months*

Freeze only very fresh fish, within 24 hours of catching. Leave small fish whole, but cut larger ones into fillets or steaks. Non-oily fish should be dipped into a brine solution (225 g salt to 2.5 litres cold water) for about 30 seconds before being drained and frozen.

To use, thaw large pieces in the package; steaks and fillets can be cooked directly from the frozen state.

COOKED DISHES

One of the great advantages of a home freezer is that made-up dishes can be prepared, frozen and stored until required. There are a few foods that can't successfully be frozen—hard-boiled eggs go rubbery; milk puddings and mayonnaise curdle; rice, spaghetti and potatoes tend to go mushy; sauces thickened with flour tend to separate out (use cornflour instead); onion, garlic and herbs should be used with discretion, as over a long period they may develop a musty taste.

*Exercise*

Explain how the activity of micro-organisms can be turned to our advantage in: (*a*) The hanging of game. (*b*) The fermentation of wines.

**Recommended Reading**

On applied food preservation: *Home Preservation of Fruit and Vegetables*; Ministry of Agriculture, Fisheries and Food publication, from HMSO, price 47½p.

On home freezing, *Choosing and Using a Home Freezer*, by Good Housekeeping Institute; available by post from the Institute at Chestergate House, Vauxhall Bridge Road, London, S.W.1, price 10p (please also send a stamped addressed envelope). *Deep Freezing*, by Pat M. Cox, published by Faber & Faber, price £4·20.

On commercial freezing, *Food Preservation*, Unilever publication, available free (as class sets) from Unilever Education Section, Unilever House, Blackfriars, London, E.C.4. *Deep Freeze Cookery*, by Marika Hanbury-Tenison, published by MacGibbon & Kee, price £3·20.

## CHAPTER 3

# THE SCIENCE OF MEAL PLANNING

No diet is good unless it supplies the body with all the nutrients necessary for health. There are six major nutrients: carbohydrates, fats, proteins, minerals, vitamins, water. They can be divided into two main groups, according to their functions:

*The Protective Foods*, of two kinds:
(*a*) Body-building—proteins and minerals. These repair old tissues and build new ones.
(*b*) Regulating—minerals, vitamins, water. These control the body systems and functions.

*Supplementary Energy Foods*—fats and carbohydrates. These supply heat and energy.

**Proteins**

Proteins are essential constituents of both plant and animal cells. Plants are able to build up their own proteins from inorganic materials obtained from the soil and the air, but animals are unable to do this and therefore depend on ready-formed protein. This is digested and broken down into its component amino acids, which are absorbed into the blood stream and re-formed into body proteins. There are 22 amino acids, and all but 8–10 of them can be synthesised or produced in the body at a fast enough rate to keep up with the demands of the tissues. It is important however that those 8–10 amino acids should be supplied to the body in the required amounts. Foods that are rich in these particular 8–10 acids are known as complete proteins (also termed first-class or animal proteins); they include all animal protein with the exception of gelatine. Foods low in the particular amino acids are known as incomplete proteins (also called second-class or vegetable proteins); this group includes all vegetable protein, plus gelatine, though this is of animal origin.

*Sources*: *Rich*—fish, meat, eggs, cheese, milk, poultry.
*Fair*—legumes (peas, beans, lentils, etc.), bread, cereals, nuts.

**Minerals**

These form part of the body structure and aid in the regulation of normal body functions; they are widely distributed in foods. The most familiar ones are:

1. CALCIUM
*Sources*: *Rich*—milk, cheese; *Fair*—eggs, green and root vegetables, cauliflower, celery.

2. PHOSPHORUS
*Sources*: *Rich*—fish, cheese, eggs, milk, meat.
*Fair*—cereals, green vegetables, root vegetables, legumes and nuts.

3. IRON
*Sources*: *Rich*—liver, kidney, heart, eggs, whole-grain cereals.
*Fair*—meat, fish, legumes, green vegetables, potatoes.

4. IODINE
*Sources*: iodised salt, fish, vegetables (amount depending on iodine content of the soil).

5. FLUORINE
*Sources*: tea, possibly drinking water (depending on area).

6. SODIUM
*Sources*: widely available as Sodium Chloride (i.e., salt, as used at table and in cooking), which is a very useful part of our diet, since the chloride is also essential for the formation of the gastric juices; found in bread, many cheeses, Bovril, Marmite, corned beef, ham, vegetables.

7. POTASSIUM
*Sources*: *Rich*—globe and Jerusalem artichokes, bananas, butter beans, milk, potatoes, spinach, tomatoes.
*Fair*—apples, cauliflower, fish, meat, orange juice.

**Vitamins**

These are substances that are required in small amounts in our foods in order to promote the body's general health. With the exception of vitamin D, they can normally be obtained in a good mixed diet of natural foods, so it is hardly relevant to specify 'rich' and 'fair' sources. The human body cannot synthesise these essential nutrients, and they must be obtained from food, so it is necessary to know which ones to include in the diet to ensure an adequate supply.

Vitamins are divided into two main groups:
(*a*) Fat-soluble—vitamins A, D, E, K.
(*b*) Water-soluble—vitamins B, C.

1. VITAMIN A

*Sources*: Fully formed vitamin A is found only in foods of animal origin—fish liver oils, liver, butter, milk, eggs, cheese, canned salmon, sardines and tuna. However, there is a substance called Carotene, present in green vegetables, yellow vegetables and some fruits, which is converted to vitamin A within the intestines. Thus foods rich in carotene are a valuable asset: they are—carrots, spinach, kale, tomatoes, cabbage, apricots, beans, peas, Brussels sprouts, oranges.

2. VITAMIN D

*Sources*: Sunlight is the chief source—the ultra-violet rays convert a substance present in the skin into the vitamin. Vitamin D is rarely found in plants and never in high concentration. Some is found in fish, especially in the liver, so cod-liver oil and halibut-liver oil are the most important natural food source of vitamin D. However, it is also present in small amounts in butter, cheese, milk and eggs and as an additive in margarine, and these bring the overall intake up to the required level.

3. VITAMIN E

*Sources*: Vegetable oils, whole-grain cereals, milk, butter, margarine, eggs, liver, legumes, green vegetables.

4. VITAMIN K

*Sources*: Spinach, cabbage, kale, cauliflower. Vitamin K is also synthesised in the intestines by bacterial action.

5. VITAMIN B COMPLEX

(*a*) Thiamine (Vit. $B_1$)

*Sources*: Widely distributed, since all animal and plant tissue contains thiamine; found, for example, in whole-grain cereals, bran, nuts, ham, pork, liver, peas, fish, Marmite.

(*b*) Riboflavin
*Sources*: Milk, liver, kidney, eggs, pork, chicken, yeast, beef, bacon, cheese, wholemeal bread, green vegetables, Bovril.

*Note*: This vitamin is destroyed by light, so milk, which is an important source, should be stored in a dark, cool place.

(*c*) Nicotinic Acid and Nicotinamide
*Sources*: Liver, salmon, pork, poultry, bran, kidney, wholemeal flour, peanuts, beef, mutton, yeast, Marmite.

(*d*) Vitamin $B_{12}$
*Sources*: Liver, kidney, meat, fish, milk.

*Note*: Several other factors can also be included in the Vitamin B complex, but in general, offal such as liver and kidney, and a mixed diet of natural foods, provide sufficient of each.

6. VITAMIN C (ASCORBIC ACID)
*Sources*: Rich ones are rose-hips, blackcurrants, Chinese gooseberries, citrus fruits. Fresh vegetables are a valuable source, but care in cooking is essential to retain its full value; the vegetables should be prepared at the last minute, placed in a minimal amount of boiling salted water and cooked for

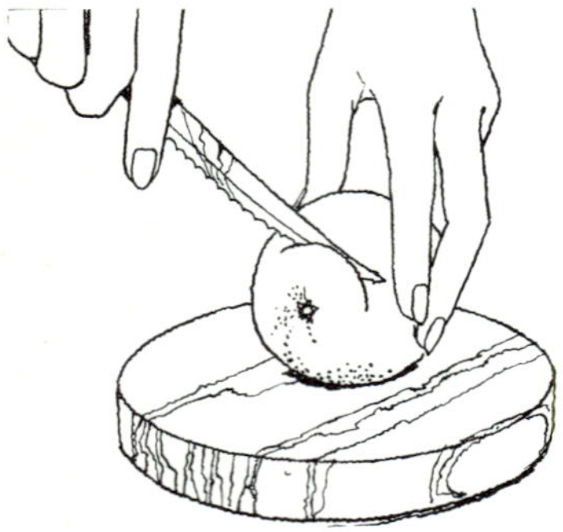

To Section an Orange, Lemon or Grapefruit 1: (e.g. for Fruit Salad or to garnish Roast Duck): Slice off the bottom of the fruit thinly

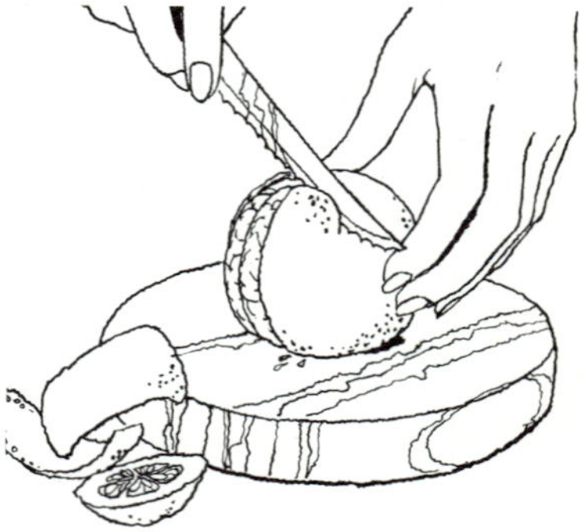

To Section an Orange 2: Stand fruit cut side down on a wooden board. Insert a small sharp-pointed knife into the top of the fruit and cut the peel away in sections, together with all the white pith; use a sawing motion

the shortest possible time, until just tender, and they should be served at once. If green vegetables are scarce, remember that potatoes retain their maximum vitamin C content when cooked in their skins; if you don't like the skins, peel them *after* cooking.

Salads are a readily acceptable source of vitamin C, but in practice a greater intake of the vitamin is ensured by eating correctly cooked vegetables, since we consume a much greater total of cooked as opposed to raw vegetables.

*Note*: Never add bicarbonate of soda to the water when cooking green vegetables, as this destroys the vitamin.

**Water**

This is a vital constituent of all body cells.
*Sources*: Beverages, water contained in solid foods and that obtained by oxidation of the hydrogen in proteins, carbohydrates and fats.

**Fats**

Fatty, waxy or oily substances are found in both plant and animal tissues. The difference in physical state (whether solid or liquid) is due to the component fatty acids.

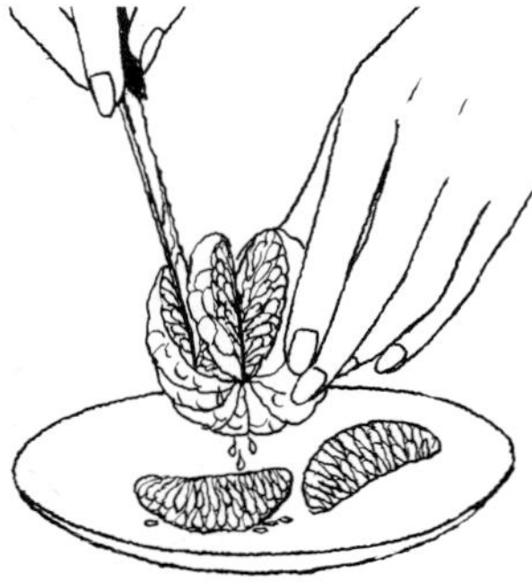

To Section an Orange 3: Cut between the segments close to the membranes, working over a dish to catch all the juice

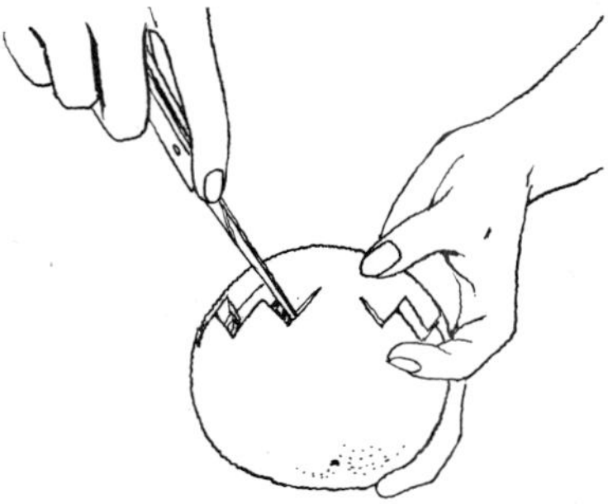

To Zigzag Grapefruit: Use small, sharp-pointed knife to make a series of short cuts at an angle to each other right round the fruit. Push the knife in quite deeply, so that when the two parts of the fruit are pulled apart they have vandyked edges. (See Spicy Hot Grapefruit)

*Sources*: Butter, margarine, lard, dripping, vegetable fats and oils, fish oils, meats, especially pork, full-cream cheeses, cream, bacon, eggs, full-cream milk.

### Carbohydrates

Some 50 to 60 per cent of our total Calorie intake is supplied by carbohydrates. These are the sugars, starches, dextrins and cellulose; all of them are simple sugars linked together. Carbohydrates are generally broken down into simple sugars for absorption by the body; cellulose, however, cannot be broken down in this way and passes unaltered through the digestive tract. Dextrins, which are intermediate in the breakdown of starches to sugar, are formed by the action of dry heat on starch; they are found when bread is toasted, in the crust that forms on loaves as they are baked, and when potato skins crisp as they are baked.

*Sources*: *Rich*—wholemeal flours and breads, whole-grain cereals, legumes, nuts, potatoes.

*Fair* (use in the diet with discrimination)—highly refined flours, polished rice, puffed or flaked cereals, sugar, jam, biscuits, cakes, etc.

### Daily Dietary Pattern

To calculate the necessary nutrients for each meal would be tedious. It is better to work to a daily meal pattern, with average requirements, which will meet the body's needs, yet allow for variety. The plan below applies to all age groups, the variation being in the amounts eaten.

| | |
|---|---|
| *Milk* | Pre-school children: 850 ml—1 litre.<br>Schoolchildren, adolescents—minimum 850 ml.<br>Adults—570 ml.<br>Expectant and nursing mothers—1 litre. |
| *Cheese* | 25–30 g. |
| *Eggs* | 1 daily, if possible; at any rate, 3–5 weekly. |
| *Meat, Fish* | Generous serving; serve liver or kidney once weekly, if possible. |
| *Potatoes* | Daily serving, especially for adolescents. |
| *Vegetables* | Generous daily servings, cooked and raw. |
| *Fruit* | Raw fruit or tomatoes daily. |
| *Fats* | Pre-school children—need little.<br>Adolescents, heavy manual workers—about 40 g. |

Other adults (who should restrain their appetite for fatty foods)—25 g.
*Note*: Figures include all butter, margarine, oils, etc., in cooking, as spreads and so on.

*Bread* 30–55 g.

*Sugar* This is a cheap, easily digested energy food, but lacks every nutrient bar carbohydrate, so it should be used with restraint. The danger is that sugar tends to replace the more nutritious foods, and excessive amounts lead to obesity.

### Slimming

Overweight and obesity are all too common, and it is wise to tackle the problem as early as possible. Overweight is seldom due to glandular disorders or to heredity, but is more likely to be influenced by environment and the eating pattern, so check the amount you eat each day against the chart given above. Are you taking too high a proportion of carbohydrates and fats?

Anyone seriously anxious to lose weight should first check with the family doctor, then limit the daily food intake to that given in the chart, cutting out between-meal snacks and sugar (if necessary, substitute saccharin). For a limited period, skimmed milk can replace full-cream, and low-fat spreads can replace butter or margarine. The total intake of fats can be reduced to 15 g daily, and carbohydrates to 25–30 g bread and 110 g potatoes (or 25–30 g rice).

Once the desired weight has been reached, the daily fat intake may rise to a total 30 g and bread to about 50 g.

Weight loss, if it is to be permanent, should be achieved slowly—aim at losing only about 1–1½ kilos per week, and do avoid crash dieting, since, for active people, this creates great 'energy gaps', with the temptation to nibble.

Calculation of Calories is not entirely straightforward arithmetic. Thus 28 g peppermint sweets contain 111 Calories, while 28 g beef contain 92 Calories. The difference of 19 Calories doesn't look big enough to be important, but pause to consider the other aspects of the matter.

The two 28-g portions contain:

| | *Protein* | *Fat* | *Carbohydrate* | *Vitamins* |
|---|---|---|---|---|
| Peppermints | 0.1 g | 0.2 g | 29 g | 0 |
| Beef | 6.9 g | 6.8 g | 0 | B group |

And even those insignificant 19 Calories do matter—just a few taken in excess of requirements each day mount up over the years to many kilos. So, as a general rule, keep to a varied diet that is low in starches and sugars.

**Vegetarians**

True vegetarians, known as Vegans, eat no food of animal origin—no meat, fish, poultry, cheese, eggs or even milk. However, the majority of Vegetarians, known as Lacto-vegetarians, include milk, cheese and possibly eggs in their diet. There would appear to be a wide nutritional gap on such a restricted régime, but with careful planning all the essential nutrients can be included in the daily diet. Vitamin $B_{12}$, the 'animal protein factor', can now be manufactured commercially, and is available in pill form, or, like many of the other B vitamins normally provided by organ meats, can be specially prepared and incorporated into various health foods.

Catering for vegetarians and vegans does require care, but if it is for only one meal or for a short period, there are no real problems—soups, salads, pizzas and any number of vegetable dishes can be presented. But if you do vegetarian

Melon Balls: Use a special scoop cutter to gouge out small balls of flesh from the melon, after removing the seeds from the centre. (See Melon and Grape Cocktail)

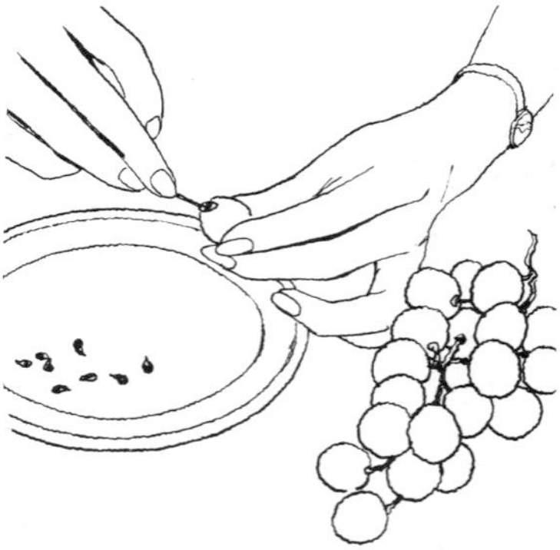

Seeding Grapes: Use a large darning needle to hook out the seeds from the washed grapes. If time is short, halve grapes first. (See Melon and Grape Cocktail)

catering for a prolonged period, it is advisable to contact a Vegetarian Society or to obtain books on the subject, to enable you to provide a nutritionally adequate series of meals, well presented, and in accordance with your guest's convictions.

### Diabetics

Diabetes is a disease in which, because of an inadequate supply of insulin, the body is unable to utilise carbohydrates in the normal way for the release of energy within the body cells. Normally, carbohydrate is converted during digestion into glucose, which is absorbed into the blood stream and transported to the tissues. There, with the aid of insulin, it is burnt to give energy for muscular contractions, etc. If the glucose is not burnt up, it remains in the blood (giving high blood-sugar levels) and is finally passed out via the kidneys.

Some diabetics are able to produce some insulin, but not sufficient to cope with a diet that is rich in carbohydrate. However, if the carbohydrate content is controlled, these people can lead a normal active life. Generally, a high-protein diet is prescribed, with modifications to the fat intake, and carbohydrates are kept very low.

A diabetic who has to have insulin injections is very much more restricted. The diet must be modified to suit the individual requirements; the exact amount of carbohydrate for each meal will be prescribed, and the timing of the meals will also be prescribed.

In general, eliminate all sugar, using saccharin where necessary; limit flour, and don't thicken soups, stews, gravies, etc. Use eggs rather than custard powder to make custard. Grill rather than fry foods. Include minimal amounts of starchy vegetables such as beans, peas, carrots, swedes, parsnips, potatoes and onions.

CHAPTER 4

# THE ART OF MEAL PLANNING

Many people leave the planning of a meal until an hour or so beforehand, so depend on what's to hand or what can easily be bought. This seldom leads to a really successful meal. Menus should be planned at least a day or so in advance, and the ideal is to work out a whole week's menus at a time. This helps to avoid repetition and gives a better nutritional balance; in conjunction with careful shopping (see the separate chapter) it also saves money. For instance, cooking a large bacon joint—more than you need for one meal—means a proportionately smaller weight loss and a saving in time when preparing the second meal.

The time of year and the weather will influence your choice of menu, but don't be too hidebound—salads, for instance, can be enjoyed all the year round for the colour, texture and variety they bring to a meal. The number of people to be served, as well as the equipment and facilities you have, must to some extent dictate your choice (it's a brave woman who embarks on fritters or pancakes for a dozen guests!). Remember the importance of presentation, and let appropriate garnishes give eye appeal and perhaps food value at the same time. (See 'The Food on the Table'.)

### Menu Planning Principles

*Flavour*: Aim at a good combination of flavours, balancing strong ones with milder tastes. Avoid serving a series of courses which echo each other, such as Grapefruit and Orange Cocktail, a main course with an Hollandaise Sauce, and finally Lemon Soufflé. Remember that acid foods sharpen the appetite, while sweet ones tend to dull it.

*Texture*: All meals should provide a variety of texture, some soft, some crisp or chewy. A casserole, for instance, can be served with jacket potatoes and a tossed salad, rather than with creamed potatoes and spinach. Similarly, serve croûtons with soup, a sauce or savoury butter with the drier or more plainly cooked foods—for example, parsley butter balls with grilled fish fillets, savoury tomato sauce with meat loaf.

*Colour*: A meal is judged largely by its initial appearance, so try to visualise how it will look on the table—does it look wan and drab, or gay and colourful? Which of these menus would look more tempting?

| | |
|---|---|
| Chicken Fricassee | Chicken Fricassee |
| Creamed potatoes | Parsleyed potatoes |
| Leeks | Carrots |

*Form or Shape*: As a rule, food is best presented in its natural state or shape, except perhaps for such occasions as children's parties, where novelty is required. But do check to see that there is some variety of shape. Rissoles and potatoes look a lot more interesting with long-shaped carrots and broccoli rather than with peas and whole-kernel corn echoing the rounded shapes.

*Method of Cooking*: On the one hand, facilities and cooking equipment have to be fully used—no-one wants to put on the oven for just one dish—but on the other hand, a meal cooked entirely by the same method is monotonous. Probably no-one would offer steamed fish, steamed potatoes, steamed carrots and steamed jam pudding, but quite a few might serve up fried fish and chips, followed by apple fritters.

Aim at contrast in shapes, as on right-hand plate

**Planning a Time-table**

One of the great problems for beginners when planning a meal is to dovetail the preparation, etc., so as to have the whole course ready at the same time, with the following courses ready in their turn. The best thing is to decide first on the time the meal is to be served, then work backwards, noting what preparation, if any, can be done in advance. Take this meal as an example, assuming it is to be served at 1 p.m.:

Tomato soup
Roast lamb    Mint sauce
Roast potatoes
Runner beans    Carrots
Lemon meringue pie

*Notes*:

(*a*) The soup may be home-made, or canned or packet type. If home-made, it can be prepared, blended or sieved the day before and kept in a covered container in the refrigerator.
(*b*) The lamb must be weighed to assess the cooking time.
(*c*) The potatoes require par-boiling.
(*d*) All vegetables must be prepared, but not left soaking.
(*e*) The Lemon Meringue Pie takes time, but the pastry case can be made the day before and stored in an airtight tin.

*Time-table (working backwards)*

1.00 Serve meal.
12.55 Dish up meat and potatoes; make gravy.
12.53 Drain beans and carrots, place in serving dishes and keep warm.
12.51 Add vinegar to mint and pour into sauce-boat.
12.48 Put soup on to heat and plates to warm.
12.45 Put beans into boiling salted water.
12.35 Wash all preparation dishes. Put water for beans on to boil.
12.30 Put carrots into boiling salted water.
12.25 Put water for carrots on to boil. Slice beans.
12.20 Chop mint with sugar and put into basin with 1 tsp. boiling water.
12.15 Put par-boiled potatoes into roasting dish and baste. Prepare carrots.
12.00 Wash and peel potatoes, place in boiling salted water and boil for 5–10 minutes, then drain.

11.58 Place pie in oven for 10 minutes, or until lightly tipped with brown.
11.50 Prepare meringue and pipe onto pie filling.
11.35 Prepare pie filling and fill case.
11.30 Put lamb into oven.
11.15 Assemble equipment and ingredients. Set oven to 218°C (mark 7, 425°F) and turn on.

**Planning the Day's Meals**

If you follow the general menu pattern outlined here, you will ensure well-balanced meals, with all the essential nutrients that are needed each day. Naturally, any particular group of people may need to modify the pattern, and if the income is very low, this may enforce some changes.

BREAKFAST

This very important start to the day should never be missed out. A well-balanced breakfast, providing protein, vitamins, minerals, fats and carbohydrates, prevents tiredness and hunger during the morning and makes sure that your working capacity doesn't wane. Breakfast is especially important to slimmers—it does away with that dangerous longing to

Breakfast should include fruit or fruit juice and a protein main course

'nibble' halfway through the morning. Fortunately, it can be quite easily prepared, taking little time and effort.

Fruit should always be served in some form—raw, cooked or as juice. A protein dish should follow—egg, fish, bacon, etc. A cereal, prepared or cooked, is sometimes taken as well, or it may replace the protein dish; however, since sugar is used somewhat liberally with cereals, it is really best to alternate them with cooked breakfast dishes. To finish off, have a slice of bread or toast, with butter or margarine, meat or yeast extract, honey or marmalade. Plus of course a drink of some kind.

*Fruit Juice*: Choose one with a sharp, refreshing taste, not one of the sweet 'nectars'. Favourites are orange or grapefruit, apple or an apple/orange blend, and tomato.

*Raw Fruit in Season*: Pears, apples, peaches, grapefruit, oranges, etc. Serve prepared, i.e., sliced or segmented.

*Cooked Fruit*: Stew and serve chilled.

*Ready-to-serve Cereals*: Serve with fruit and milk.

*Cooked Cereals*: Oatmeal or rolled oats, porridge, etc., are often served with hot milk or cream in the colder months.

*Main Course*: This is the essential feature, and should ideally consist of a combination of foods that are plainly cooked and served—usually chosen from the following:

Eggs, cooked in a variety of ways—poached or scrambled, on toast; coddled; boiled; fried; baked; as a plain omelette.

Fish—fried or grilled fresh fish; poached smoked fish; fish fingers, fish cakes.

Bacon, grilled or fried, and teamed with eggs, kidneys, sausages, tomatoes, apple rings, etc.

Sausages, grilled or fried—served as for bacon, and particularly good with tomatoes or apple sauce.

Other meats—liver, mince, etc.—are more likely to be welcomed by people doing a heavy job.

*Bread*: ring the changes on sliced white and brown bread, toast, rolls, crispbread and so on.

*Beverage*: a hot drink, usually tea or coffee, should be served; teenagers and younger children may prefer milk.

### LUNCH OR SUPPER

This is the lighter of the two main meals, and when you serve it depends on whether you have the dinner, or chief meal, at mid-day or in the evening. (For high tea, see p. 60). The make-up of the meal varies considerably, according to the tastes and activities of the family, but there is a basic general pattern.

*Main Course*: This must include a protein such as meat, fish, eggs or cheese, which may be served in innumerable ways. Vegetables may be an integral part of the dish, or served separately. If a salad is to be served as the main course, this should include a generous amount of protein. The main possibilities are:

(*a*) Savoury meat dishes, which are often based on those meats not so suitable for use in the dinner meal, such as kidneys, sweetbreads and so on; quite often the meat dish will be a means of using up leftovers, for example, Cottage Pie, Meat Croquettes, Stuffed Marrow.

(*b*) Cold meats, with chutneys and salads in hot weather, and with such things as hot salads and jacket potatoes in the colder months.

(*c*) Bacon—grilled or fried, and served with a variety of other foods, such as kidneys, liver, scalloped vegetables.

(*d*) Fish, cooked in a number of ways—fried, grilled, baked, poached, soused, or made up into a range of dishes. Accompaniments and presentation may be very varied.

(*e*) Eggs—often combined with stronger-flavoured foods in more or less elaborate dishes, for instance: baked eggs with a savoury sauce; omelettes with herb, cheese, bacon or other filling; soufflés made with fish, corn, cheese, and so on; quiches including cheese, bacon or other additions.

(*f*) Cheese dishes: cheese is a concentrated and flavourful food that can be used in many dishes—in soufflés, baked fondues, omelettes, rarebits, quiches, pasta dishes and so on. Generally, cheese dishes have a soft texture and require a crisp accompaniment.

(*g*) Substantial soups, chowders: these can make an all-in-one main course, with just toast or salad as accompaniment. A lighter, thinner soup makes a very pleasant beginning to a rather more leisurely meal; it should be followed by a fairly substantial main course, such as an omelette or a cheese or meat dish.

(*h*) Vegetables: Many vegetables form the basis for the main course of a lunch or supper, though they generally need supplementing with a protein-rich food to make them sustaining, as in baked beans with bacon; cauliflower with cheese sauce; creamed vegetables with ham; corn and ham fritters.

*Breads*, as for breakfast, should be varied; choose from the plain breads, French bread, rolls, scones, quickbreads, muffins, toast, Melba toast, crispbread and so on.

*Second Course*: This is not absolutely necessary, but it usually takes the form of fresh fruit, stewed fruit or a light sweet, or alternatively, cheese and biscuits—perhaps served with watercress, celery or radishes.

*Beverage*: as for breakfast.

### HIGH TEA

In very many families the evening meal takes this form. For the main part, any of the dishes suggested under (*a*) to (*f*) on the preceding page may be served; bread and butter is the usual accompaniment, but try also to include tomatoes, lettuce or other salad. To follow, the most usual choice is cakes, with perhaps bread and jam or paste, and often canned or preferably fresh fruit.

### LUNCHES FOR SPECIAL CASES

The housewife at home by herself is rather inclined not to bother with a mid-day meal, but lunch is in fact just as important for her as for any other member of the family. Any 'under-fives' need their most important meal of the day at mid-day, since it should be completely digested by their bedtime at about 6 p.m. With careful planning, all the different interests can be studied, so that some of the preparation for the grown-ups' evening meal can be achieved while the midday meal for the children and their mother is being cooked. For example:

*Mid-day lunch for mother and child*

Steamed cod Parsley sauce
Carrots and steamed potatoes
Baked egg custard with fresh fruit

*Adults' evening meal*

Fish pie (using fish, sauce and potatoes remaining from lunch)
Green bean and carrot salad
Fresh fruit

Packed lunches can be both tempting and nutritionally sensible

PACKED LUNCHES

These need intelligent planning if they are not to be monotonous and badly balanced. There is no reason why a packed meal shouldn't contain as much nourishment as a sit-down one—in fact, ideally a packed lunch and a sit-down one should be interchangeable.

Sandwiches, the commonest basis for a packed lunch, are simply prepared and easily carried, but they do tend to become hackneyed, so add as much variety as possible by means of salads, packed in small plastic containers, introduce soups (hot or cold), carried in a vacuum flask, and include such things as Scotch eggs, sliced pork pie, cold meat, chicken, etc., or a small quiche, accompanied by salad greens. Here is one sample menu: Tomato Soup, followed by Scotch Eggs and Cole Slaw, topped off by fresh fruit.

*Exercises*

A. Plan a preparation schedule for the following two-course meal to be served at 7 p.m. (Read the notes first.)

Spaghetti alla Paesana
Tossed green salad
Marshmallow sweet

*Notes*:

(*a*) Salad vegetables must all be washed and placed in the refrigerator to crisp.

(*b*) Oil and vinegar dressing can be mixed and kept for several days in a covered jar or bottle; it simply requires shaking up before being used as required.

(*c*) Spaghetti must be cooked in boiling salted water, drained and served at once.

(*d*) The marshmallow sweet may be made the day before and then 'dressed up' not more than 2 hours before it is served.

B. 1. Plan a three-course dinner menu for four people.
2. Make out a preparation schedule for the meal.
3. List your own notes.

C. Plan a tray supper to be eaten by yourself and three friends while watching TV.

### DINNER

Whether taken at midday or in the evening, dinner is the main meal of the day, when the whole family is together. Nutritionally, it should dovetail with the other meals, bringing the intake of various foods to the required level.

The meal is usually built around the meat course, which is accompanied by potatoes and two other vegetables (one green one and perhaps a root vegetable). Soup may be served to introduce the meal, and a dessert may follow the main course—though those with a weight problem shouldn't take dessert, but have fresh fruit or cheese and biscuits.

*Soup*: Choose a light kind, to stimulate rather than satisfy the appetite. Crisp toast shapes, small rolls or bread may be offered with it.

*Meat*: Selected from joints, or smaller cuts, of beef, lamb, pork, veal or poultry. As there is little nutritional difference between one cut and another, based on an equal weight of flesh, the less expensive meats are in no way inferior to the more expensive ones. The cooking method will vary according to the cut, and this will in turn influence the choice of vegetables and their method of cooking.

*Vegetables*: Because of their nutritive value, potatoes should be eaten most days—but do vary the method of cooking. Pasta and rice make useful alternatives.

Everyday boiled potatoes and party-special Duchesse potatoes

Green vegetables include cabbage, Brussels sprouts, broccoli, cauliflower, spinach, green and yellow beans, peas, and asparagus. Other vegetables to choose from include artichokes, broad beans, beetroot, carrots, celery, sweet corn, aubergines, leeks, onions, marrow, parsnips, turnips, swedes and pumpkin. There is no excuse for repetition—if carrots, for example, appear in a stew, don't also serve them as an accompaniment.

Lattice potatoes, chips and crisps—more attractive variations. Fry lattice potatoes and crisps in deep fat (190°C, 375°F) for about 2 mins.; drain well. For chips, see *Cooking is Fun*

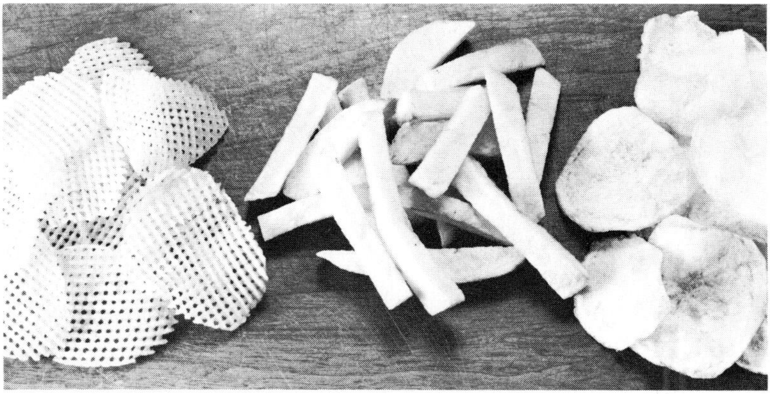

*Dessert*: Pleasant finish though this is to a family meal, it is by no means a necessity.

FORMAL DINNERS

For a very formal occasion, the menu includes more courses, and this is the traditional order:

Soup
Hors d'oeuvre
Fish
Entrée
Sorbet
Roast
Dessert and fruit
Cheese

*Exercises*

A. Plan a day's meals for a family consisting of mother, father, son aged 3 and grandmother.

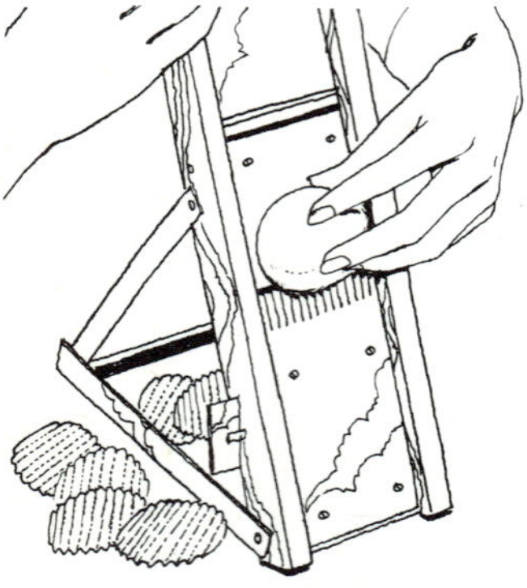

Lattice Potatoes: Press the peeled potato with a downward motion against fluted blade of mandolin. Before making next cut, turn potato itself half-way round, so that on the two surfaces of each slice the ridges go in opposite directions, making the 'lattice' effect. Deep-fry the slices. (See photograph on p. 63)

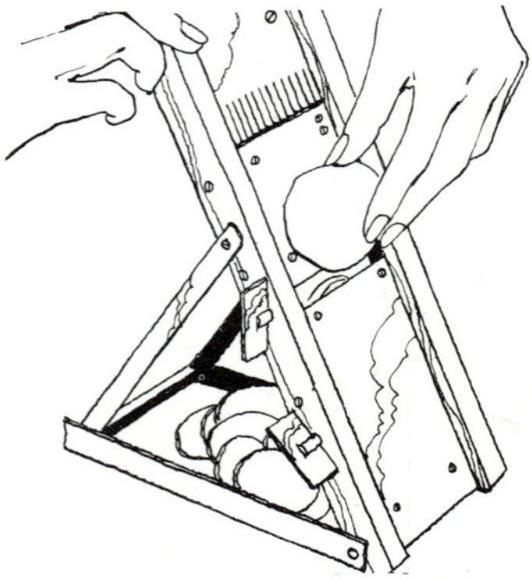

Potato Crisps: Press the peeled potato with a downward motion against the plain blade of the mandolin, giving thin, smooth slices, which are then deep-fried. (See photograph on p. 63)

B. Plan a day's meals for a family of four—mother, father and two teenage daughters—starting a holiday with an 8-hour drive—i.e., plan for breakfast (no leftovers), packed lunch and meal on arrival.
C. Plan a day's meals for two teenage boys who are camping with limited cooking facilities—a couple of Calor-gas burners.
D. Plan 4 day's meals—breakfast, lunch and dinner—for a family of 4 consisting of mother, father, son of 12 and daughter of 16 (father out for lunch except at weekend). Set out the meals in tabulated form.
E. Plan the meals for a weekend for the family of 4 as above, plus a visiting family of 2 adults and a child of 8. Make out a shopping list, with quantities required.

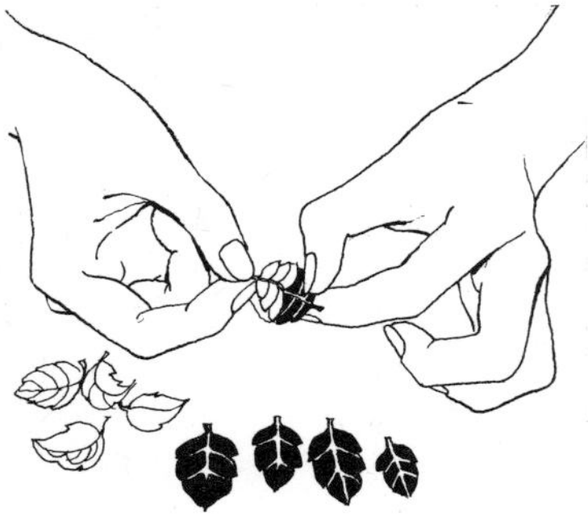

Chocolate Leaves: Melt some chocolate in a basin over hot water. Choose various-sized rose leaves, with a stem. Using tweezers, draw the underside of each leaf across the melted chocolate. Leave on waxed paper, chocolate side up, until set. Peel off the leaf from the stem end, carefully easing it away. Keep the leaves in a cool place until required to decorate a cake or cold sweet such as Mousse

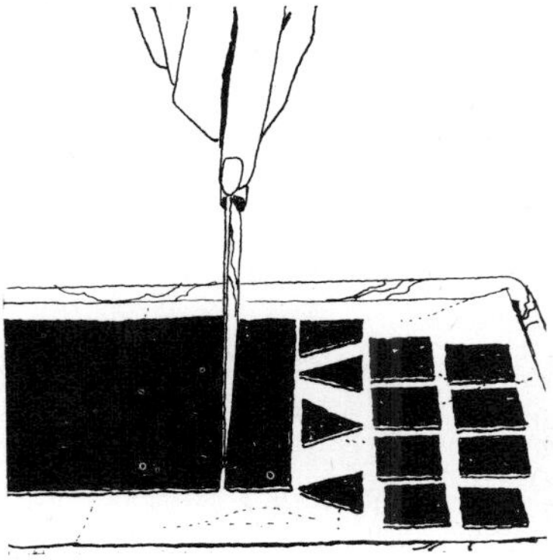

Chocolate Squares and Triangles: Pour melted chocolate in a thin layer on to non-stick paper placed on a baking tray; when it is set, cut with a sharp knife to give small shapes which can be used to decorate cold sweets and cakes such as Fairy Cakes

F. Plan the day's meals for a Sunday to cope with the following family engagements:
Mother: out visiting in the afternoon.
Father: golf from 10 a.m. till 2.30 p.m.
Son: Squash at 2.00 p.m.
Daughter: Sunday School class in morning, home in afternoon.

### Planning Special-occasion Meals

The usual basic principles apply here, but you have to balance carefully the numbers being catered for, the equipment and facilities to hand and the time you can spare. Don't be too ambitious at first—let simplicity be the keynote, with the accent on attractive presentation.

These notes should help you with the planning of a dozen or so different kinds of party.

#### RECORD OR TV EVENING

Quite the easiest kind of party for the inexperienced, as it's completely informal—just a general get-together with your friends, to flip through a few records or watch television in company, with interludes for chat when the programmes become less interesting. Everyone gets hungry, of course, but no-one is dedicated enough or has time to spare for any elaborate meal-getting. So make a variety of quiches or pizzas early in the day; add some open sandwiches, which can be put together just before the guests arrive and left covered with polythene; alternatively, lay out all the ingredients on a table and let people make their own sandwiches. Scoop out the inside from some bread rolls, fill with a super savoury mixture and serve piping hot.

Offer mugs of hot coffee, cocoa or soup, or if you are celebrating, why not mull some cider? If dancing is the order of the day, an iced punch or fruit cup will be popular.

#### BARBECUES

Outdoor barbecues spell informality, and nothing can rival the smoky charcoal flavour of food cooked and eaten in the open air—always provided the weather is co-operating.

Barbecue parties should not be too ambitious, since catering for large numbers can mean tedious waits. Food amounts are best calculated on the generous side—outdoor living often increases an otherwise birdlike appetite.

Simple grills are usually the basis of the menu—chops, steaks, sausages, frankfurters, chicken joints and so on, with a lavish supply of 'burger buns or French bread. For the more experienced, or those with sophisticated equipment, chickens may be spit-roasted. Supply a good variety of sauces, pickles and relishes, bottled or home-made. Potatoes can be baked in the embers of the fire, and corn-on-the-cob can be wrapped in buttered foil and cooked on the grid (turn the cobs frequently and allow about 25 minutes). Offer a choice of super salads—for example, cole slaw, potato, curried rice and banana, pepper and pineapple, tomato and cucumber, Waldorf salad. Desserts aren't necessary, but have some fresh fruit ready. If the evening is cool, a great pot of soup will make a welcome starter.

Paper plates save the cleaning and washing up once the fun is over, and plenty of paper napkins should be available. Barbecues are essentially gay, informal and 'do-it-yourself' occasions.

### CHEESE AND WINE PARTY

This is suitable for entertaining in a fairly informal way a

Choose a variety of contrasting cheeses for a Wine and Cheese Party, or for a cheeseboard included in a main meal

large number of guests, when time, energy, facilities and funds are all somewhat limited. Since a cheese and wine party is not intended to replace a main meal, it is usually timed for late morning or early evening.

Provide a good selection of cheeses, which should of course vary in texture, flavour and appearance. Some readily available foreign and British cheeses to remember are: Port Salut, Tomme de Raisin, Danish Blue, Brie, Edam, Stilton, Emmenthal, Gruyère, Caerphilly, Cheddar and Cheshire. Allow about 80 g cheese per person.

Supply plenty of crusty rolls or slices of French bread and plain biscuits, with perhaps a variety of cheese dips accompanied by biscuit or salad dunks. A large bowl of fruit looks attractive and makes a pleasant finale.

Provide bread and butter plates, knives and paper napkins, and set the whole out simply, arranging things so that people are able to help themselves with the least possible effort and confusion.

The wine may be served from a separate table. Have a few trays available so that some drinks can be handed round. If you are using easily-handled standard-sized bottles, pour straight from them; otherwise you may find it convenient to decant the wine into large china or glass jugs. For refills the jugs or bottles may be circulated, if this leads to less moving about.

### BUFFET PARTIES

When you are entertaining more than a handful of people, a help-yourself party is ideal. Simple or elaborate, success comes with planning. Arrange a menu you can handle with comparative ease, using the days and hours beforehand to full advantage, so that as little effort as possible is required once your guests have arrived. Chicken salad is a good example of the kind of dish that is popular and lends itself to advance preparation; recipes for this and some other dishes in large-scale form are given at the end of the chapter.

For serving arrangements, we suggest a main table for the cold savoury dishes, with plates, knives, forks and napkins set in separate piles for guests to help themselves; cheese pastries and other nibbles can be distributed at several points round the room. Provide heatproof mats or if possible plate-warmers, so that the hot casseroles or curries left standing for some time will remain tempting.

Desserts can be put ready on another table or on a trolley which can be wheeled in when required. A separate drinks trolley, table or sideboard is also needed. Serve coffee or tea to drink later.

COCKTAIL AND/OR SHERRY PARTY

This sort of party is usually held at mid-day or in the early evening, and enables one to cope with a relatively large number of people without having to provide a full meal. The choice of drinks may be limited to just three or four—gin, vermouth, whisky and sherry—or if desired, the range may be extended to include Dubonnet, Campari, Pimms and so on. Do have to hand fruit juices and other soft drinks for those who prefer them. Serve the drinks from a table or trolley set along one side of the room, and particularly avoid tucking the drinks table into a corner, as this leads to congestion. Pass ready mixed drinks around on trays, and have ready a stock of ice cubes, thin lemon slices, cocktail cherries and olives. For a sherry party, provide medium and dry sherries, slightly chilled, and sweet sherry served at room temperature.

The food should be 'bite-size'. You can include the usual range of small savoury titbits—cocktail sausages, scampi on sticks, cocktail onions, cheese straws, olives, gherkins, salted nuts, and savoury dips with a variety of dunks. Hot savouries can also be served—such things as prunes or oysters wrapped in bacon, savoury éclairs, cheese tartlets and so on. Arrange the food attractively on trays and platters, and distribute these round the room, so that all the guests can easily help themselves.

DINNER PARTIES—FORMAL OR INFORMAL?

A formal dinner party may consist of anything from three to five courses, with a different wine served with each course. However, entertaining on this scale is seldom attempted unless some form of help is available to cope with the cooking, serving, waitressing, etc., or unless caterers are hired for the occasion.

The informal dinner party, on the other hand, is one of the most popular ways of entertaining. If the hostess is to enjoy herself, then the party does need to be sensibly planned and plenty of time should be allowed for preparation. Since the hostess must double as cook, it is essential that the menu should be relatively simple. Three courses, followed by a cheese-board and coffee, are quite sufficient.

Avoid any dish that requires last-minute preparation or split-second timing—this means such things as hot soufflés, omelettes, fried foods and so on—and if you are not very experienced, avoid also any dish that demands a large number of accessories, such as traditional roast turkey with all the trimmings.

Once the menu has been decided, make sure that everything is not only well cooked, but well presented, with the appropriate accompaniment. Here is one example:

Smoked trout with lemon wedges
Brown bread and butter
Crown roast of lamb   Mint sauce   Gravy
Minted potatoes   Diced mixed vegetables
Cherry-topped Pavlova

FONDUE DINNER PARTY

One of the most informal kinds of home entertaining is the cook-it-yourself meal based on, say, Fondue Bourguignonne. If you are at all unsure how well your guests will get on with each other, this is a sure-fire method of bringing them together—no-one can stand-off at such a party. A fondue dish of hot oil is placed centrally on the table, and the guests have individual dishes of raw cubed steak which they cook themselves.

Have about three dips to accompany the steak: (1) Horseradish cream; (2) Curry: for this, mix 3 tbsp. (45 ml) each of mayonnaise and whipped cream, 1 level tsp. (5 ml) curry powder, 1 tsp. (5 ml) chutney sauce; (3) Paprika: beat 75 g cream cheese until soft, combine with 4 tbsp. (60 ml) mayonnaise, 1 level tsp. (5 ml) paprika and 3 gherkins, finely chopped.

Serve crusty French bread and a choice of salads as accompaniments. A hot soup may be served as starter, and a cold dessert to finish the meal.

Alternatively, serve a Cheese Fondue, with cubes of bread to dunk in the mixture.

PROGRESSIVE DINNER

An amusing way of catering for fairly large numbers, if you can organise a group of friends to co-operate, each electing to prepare and help serve a different course of the predetermined menu. Each course is served at a different home, and the guests travel from place to place. This divides the work load, and all the guests have a chance to enjoy themselves. It might work out like this:

*House 1*: Drinks and small snacks.

*House 2*: Starters. It's wise to serve cold ones—melon wedges, prawn cocktails, Salade Niçoise, etc. However, if an automatic oven is available, then any hot starter could be offered, depending on the rest of the meal. Soup is generally welcome, and can be left ready in vacuum flasks.

*House 3*: Main course. A casserole is a good choice, as any delays en route will not then cause a gastronomic catastrophe. Serve with oven-cooked rice and a variety of salads.

*House 4*: Dessert. A cold one is ideal, since it can be prepared beforehand and served in individual glasses. Flans are also very good: have a number, varying in flavour and appearance, if possible.

*House 5*: Coffee, with, if you wish, liqueurs, a cheeseboard and a selection of petits fours.

### COFFEE MORNING OR EVENING

Inviting friends round for 'elevenses' is a pleasant and simple way of entertaining for those with a certain amount of leisure time. The coffee must be well-made and piping hot, accompanied by hot (but not boiled) milk. Whichever method of making you use—and there's a wide variety—the coffee itself, when bought, should be both freshly roasted and freshly ground. Allow 45 g coffee to 570 ml water.

Food for a coffee party should be simple, and tending towards the savoury rather than the sweet. Offer scones, plain or savoury, croissants or brioche (served warm), plus biscuits and small cakes or buns.

### TEA PARTY

A tea party may be a social occasion, or it may arise because a committee is meeting or some other activity is taking place in your home. Only very light refreshments are required—small sandwiches, scones or asparagus rolls, accompanied by small tea cakes or a gâteau (be sure to have cake forks to hand). Provide both China and Indian tea, with milk and sugar, and with thin slices of lemon for those who prefer it.

### CHILDREN'S PARTIES

The highlight of a young child's year is his or her own party. Children's parties don't run themselves, but must be most carefully organised. Make a longish list of games (better prepare too many than not enough), and alternate the quiet ones with the rowdier ones; have small prizes to hand out.

Serve the food in a separate room from the one where the games are being played. Select easy-to-eat foods, keeping everything as simple as possible. Choose a special theme for the celebration cake, if possible—perhaps the child has a hobby or interest that could be successfully illustrated in some way. Failing this, the birthday cake can take the form of, say, a yacht, a cat, a house, a gingerbread man—something novel will delight all the children. Most children love savoury foods such as sandwiches, cocktail sausages, sausage rolls and potato crisps. Little iced cakes are appealing, especially when decorated with the initials of each guest, or with small sweets. Meringues, éclairs and rich fruit cakes are best reserved for older children. Jellies and ice cream can also be served.

### THEATRE PARTY

A theatre or concert outing with a party of friends is always enjoyable, and the meal can be planned to fit in with the times of the show.

If the performance is early, then drinks and snacks can be served beforehand, followed by supper after the show. The snacks should be fairly satisfying: arrange a variety of appetising morsels on cocktail sticks and skewer these into a grapefruit, apples or a small cabbage. Good titbits are blue cheese

Jacket potatoes can be left to cook themselves for a late supper

and celery; cocktail sausages wrapped in a slice of cucumber; prawns and cucumber cubes; stoned prunes stuffed with cheese; stuffed olives; cheese and pineapple cubes; gherkins, radishes and such like. Serve small club or open sandwiches, and if the weather is cool, hot savouries.

The supper to be served on your return requires some skilful organisation, and you must avoid having anything too heavy so late in the evening. Casseroles requiring long, slow cooking are ideal. If soup is served, this can be kept hot in a vacuum flask. Large jacket potatoes (p. 91) can be left to cook over a long period; salads can be left ready to be dressed at the last minute. For dessert there are innumerable sweets that can be made up the day before. Cold starters also present no problems.

If the show is late, then the meal to be served beforehand must be exactly timed, but the selection of dishes to be served is more or less unrestricted, provided you keep to things that are simple to serve and eat. Don't bother with coffee after the meal—it can be ordered at the theatre.

INSTANT PARTIES, USING WHAT'S AVAILABLE

Today's wealth of store-cupboard foods makes impromptu entertaining easy and simplifies planned party-giving, too. Adding just a touch of ingenuity to the contents of a can or packet, or presenting it straight, but attractively garnished, may be all that's needed. When people drop in for drinks at short notice, whip up a dip to serve with biscuits or salad dunks, depending on what you have to hand. A good savoury that can easily be concocted is Cheese and Almond Balls. Finely grate 200 g Cheddar cheese, mix with 1 tbsp. (15 ml) lemon juice and 3 tbsp. (45 ml) hot milk, then beat until smooth and creamy; add 50 g finely chopped ham and 8–10 chopped stuffed olives. Roll into balls and coat these with toasted nibbed almonds; spear with cocktail sticks and serve with buttered biscuits.

For a rather more substantial kind of instant meal, see the notes and suggested menus in the Convenience Foods section of the 'Sensible Shopping' chapter.

## Drinks, Everyday and Party

The beverages we drink in this country are very varied; they range from tea, coffee and chocolate (steaming hot most of the year, iced in summer-time), through soft drinks—a term used to cover the many natural juices, squashes, crushes and carbonated drinks—to such things as fruit cups and party punches and the straight alcoholic drinks, including of course beer, ale, cider and wines.

Milk is often regarded as more of a food than a beverage, yet chilled milk and hot milk can both be most welcome at the right moment. Younger children who don't like them straight may delight in milk shakes and ice cream sodas. When mixed in an electric blender, fresh fruit and other shakes take on a really smooth, creamy texture—experiment with a whole range of flavours.

Fresh fruit juices are becoming more and more popular, at breakfast time, as a starter course for a main meal and as a between-meals drink. Mixed together in varying proportions, or combined with other ingredients, citrus juices provide an infinite choice of winter cockle-warmers and summer coolers.

### COOL AND PRETTY—CUPS, COOLERS AND JULEPS

Presentation plays an important part with these drinks. Borage, the attractive herb with tiny blue-mauve flowers, imparts a delicate flavour to many fruit and wine cups; when it is not available, use sliced cucumber. Lemon balm, sorrel and mint can also be used. Fruit makes an eye-catching decoration, but must be used with discretion. Try orange, lemon and lime slices, or twists and spirals of the thinly pared rind; fresh or Maraschino cherries; whole or sliced strawberries; slices of peach; apple, thinly sliced with the skin left on; grapes, whole or halved and seeded; red currants frosted with sugar and hung in tiny clusters on the rim of the glass.

Ice cubes can be coloured or flavoured to blend with the drink, and look particularly attractive with small pieces of fruit set in them. To give a party look to a pretty drink, try frosting the rim of the glass; dip about 1 cm of it in egg white or water, then dip at once in the same depth of granulated sugar; leave upright to dry.

Handy for sweetening cold drinks is a concentrated sugar syrup made by dissolving 450 g caster or granulated sugar in 285 ml water over a low heat; when the sugar has dissolved, bring just to the boil; leave to cool, then store, covered, in the refrigerator.

For cool drinks, chill the unopened bottles of soda, wine, etc., before using—don't do it by adding large quantities of ice, which will merely dilute the drink.

*Handy Measures*: A 'split' of ginger ale or soda is approx. 160 ml; a 'measure' is $2\frac{1}{2}$ tbsp. (38 ml). Wineglasses hold about 125 ml, goblets and tall glasses about 150 ml; tumblers 250 ml, and liqueur glasses $1\frac{2}{3}$ tbsp. (26 ml).

PUNCHES AND MULLS

Spicy, warming, reviving punch is especially welcome during the Christmas festive season. Tea is included in many recipes as a balancer and harmoniser of flavours. The traditional lemon or orange slice is more than just a garnish—it adds its essential oil to the flavouring of the brew.

The advantage of serving mulled wines rather than punches is that they are not only easier to make, but also less expensive. Any sound red wine—even if rather coarse or rough—will do, but tell the wine merchant what you want it for.

Recipes are merely a general guide—if you are out of one ingredient, substitute something similar—orange or pineapple instead of lemon, or an alternative spice. No punch or mull is better than the palate of the person making it. Taste therefore as you go along, and remember that the object is to achieve a mellow blend.

Punches and mulls should never be allowed to boil—the heat should be applied gently and gradually, or it will cause the spirit or wine to lose its flavour. The drink should however be served piping hot. One way to keep it warm is to pour it into the warmed bottles and to stand these in hot water.

## A Taste for Wine

Whatever the jargon used about it, the attraction of wine undeniably lies in three factors—colour, aroma and taste. All wines have the first and the last, but aroma, or bouquet, is found in less than a quarter of all wines.

HOW TO BUY WINE: The reliable wine merchant with a reputation to lose is the best adviser you can have, if you don't know much about wines. However, it can't be emphasised too often that the best wine for *you* is the one that most pleases your taste, at the price you want to pay—and by experimental wine tastings, the merchant can aid you in finding it.

For parties, good savings can be made by buying cheerful *vins ordinaires* (red, white or rosé) in jars or other large containers. Once opened (so long as you replace the cork or cap firmly), the wine will remain in drinkable condition for a week, but not longer.

*Amounts*: See the chart at the end of this chapter.

HOW TO SERVE WINE: A great deal is written on this subject, but here are the most important points:

1. All white wines should be served chilled, but not iced. Don't put ice into them.
2. Red wines are best served at room temperature, but since room temperatures vary, let them stand for a couple of hours in the warm part of a room at around 16° to 19°C. Don't, however, stand the bottle in front of a fire, or plunge it into hot water. Uncork red wines an hour or so before serving.
3. Decant as necessary. The object of this is to separate the wine from its lees (i.e., sediment) and with a red wine, to let it 'take the air'. However, it is not always necessary to decant red wine. So long as the bottle has stood still for an hour or so before serving, and you take the glasses to the bottle and pour carefully, thus giving it the minimum disturbance, it should be perfectly clear in the glass. With some of the cheaper red wines, you can decant them into a carafe that has been thoroughly heated with hot water and then leave at room temperature for a couple of hours – the wine will noticeably mature and taste better.
4. Glasses for wine should be clear, colourless and thin, preferably with a bowl that narrows somewhat towards the rim, so as to hold the wine's bouquet. Stemmed glasses are much more pleasant than tumblers. And some of the reasonably-priced 'public-house' stemmed glasses can be used for everyday serving of any wine.
5. Don't overfill wineglasses – there should be room enough left in the glass for it to be rotated so that you can get the aroma of the wine without spilling it.

Glasses for Different Wines: Top row, left to right: Hock, Champagne, Sherry. Bottom row: Aperitif or Liqueur, large 'all-purpose' wineglass and small glass for sweet wines with dessert

HOW TO STORE WINE: Place the bottles horizontally, so that the wine keeps the cork moist. They may be stored in anything from a 12-bottle carton to bins or racks. Keep them in a cool, dark place, never in the fridge or airing cupboard.
THE WINE FOR THE FOOD: The classic and formal order is:
With Soup: Pale Sherry or Dry Madeira
With Fish: Dry White Wines or Dry Champagne. (These are also suitable with oysters and other shellfish)
With Entrées: Claret
With Roasts or Game: Red Burgundy
With Sweets: Sauternes
With Cheese: Port, Brown Sherry or Madeira

When only one wine is served throughout, then it should be the one most appropriate for the main course.

*Wines for a Crowd*

Providing drinks for an elastic number of guests, or for a party like an informal buffet, is no trouble so far as the quantities are concerned. With the sale-or-return service offered by most wine merchants (who will usually also lend glasses free of charge) you can order quite generously.

FOR A BUFFET PARTY: White wine is often the one most enjoyed, but a red wine, too, would not be amiss. You can, of course, start with sherry or apéritifs (reckon on 2 glasses per guest) and then serve the wine (on average, half a bottle per person).

FOR A DINNER PARTY: Reckon that 3 bottles of table wine will serve 6 generously, or just suffice for 8 people.

---

The drawing shows, from left to right, bottles commonly used for Claret, Sherry and Port; Burgundy; Fortified wines not bottled in their country of origin; German wines from Franconia; Moselles and Hocks; Hungarian wines; Champagne; Italian Chianti

FOR A SUMMER NIGHT BARBECUE: A punch, a cider cup and ice-cold lager make the sort of choice to offer.

FOR A WINE AND CHEESE PARTY: You can offer two styles of white wine (perhaps a white Burgundy and a Hock) and two red (say a Portuguese or Spanish and an Italian). White wines specially suit the creamy cheeses, while reds suit the English types and the Continental 'blues'.

*Recommended Books*
Allan Sichel's *Penguin Book of Wines* (Penguin, 30p); Robin Don's *Teach Yourself Wine* (English University Press, 52½p); Hugh Johnson's *Wine* (Sphere Books, 75p).

**Recipes for Drinks**

Here is a small selection of useful party drinks.

## Spicy Fruit Punch

- 150 g caster sugar
- 500 ml water
- 500 ml fresh or canned unsweetened orange juice
- 250 ml canned pineapple juice
- Juice and thinly pared rind of 1 lemon
- 6 cloves
- ½ level tsp. (2.5 ml) ground nutmeg
- ½ level tsp. (2.5 ml) ground mixed spice
- 6 splits Canada Dry ginger ale, chilled
- Crushed ice
- Lemon or orange rind twist for garnish

*Serves 20*

Dissolve the sugar in the water over a low heat, then cool. Blend together the fruit juices, lemon rind and spices, and add the sugar syrup. Chill and strain. Add the ginger ale and crushed ice just before serving, and garnish.

## White Wine Cup

- Fresh fruit in season, e.g., strawberries, peaches, apricots
- 1 level tbsp. (15 ml) sugar
- 4 tbsp. (60 ml) Kirsch or Maraschino
- 1 bottle of medium-dry white wine
- 1 bottle of sparkling hock

*Serves 12*

Slice the fruit and place in the bottom of a bowl. Sprinkle with sugar, pour on the Kirsch or Maraschino and leave for

½ hour. Pour on the still white wine and chill for a further ½ hour. Meanwhile, chill the sparkling hock. Add the hock to the cup, and serve at once.

## Lemon Cider Cup

3 lemons
100 g caster sugar
1 cinnamon stick
500 ml boiling water
1 litre cider, chilled
1 split of soda water, chilled

*Serves 12*

Peel 2 of the lemons very thinly, free of any white pith. Place the peel, juice, sugar and cinnamon stick in a jug, pour on the boiling water and stir until the sugar is dissolved. Allow to cool, then strain the mixture into a bowl. Just before serving, add the cider and soda water. Decorate with sliced lemon.

## Sangria

1 bottle of Spanish or Portuguese red wine, chilled
Fizzy lemonade, chilled
A slice of lemon
Slices of apple and orange
Caster sugar

*Serves 6*

This is a happy reminder of sunny holidays!

Chill the wine, in the bottle, and an equal amount of lemonade. Before serving, mix together and add the slice of lemon, the sliced apple and orange and caster sugar to taste—Sangria, to be refreshing, should never be too sweet.

## Christmas Eve Mull

Thinly peeled rind of 1 lemon and 1 orange
4 level tbsp. (60 ml) Demerara sugar
125 ml water
½ level tsp. (2.5 ml) powdered cinnamon
1 level tsp. (2.5 ml) grated nutmeg
2 bottles of Portuguese red wine such as Vila Real
6 tbsp. (90 ml) rum or cherry brandy (optional)

*Serves 10*

Make sure that the lemon and orange rinds are quite free of white pith; simmer them with the sugar, water and spices to extract the full flavour. Add the wine and the spirit (if used).

Heat gently until the mixture is hot but not boiling, then strain it into a heat-resistant punch bowl or pitcher.

## Glühwein

12 sugar lumps
4 slices of lemon
4 slices of orange
4 cloves
2 bottles of claret
A piece of cinnamon stick

*Serves 8*

This traditional drink, well-known to all those who have enjoyed an Austrian ski-ing holiday, is very easy to make. Put all the ingredients into a saucepan and slowly bring almost but not quite to boiling point. Remove from the heat, strain and serve at once.

## Frosted Orange Cream

250 ml fresh orange juice
2 individual bricks of vanilla ice cream
1 level tsp. (5 ml) caster sugar

*Serves 2*

Blend all the ingredients together in the goblet of an electric blender or liquidiser for 30 seconds. Serve at once in tumblers, with straws.

## Blackcurrant Shake

500 ml cold milk
2 tbsp. (30 ml) cream
6 tbsp. (90 ml) blackcurrant syrup

*Serves 2*

Place all the ingredients in the goblet of a blender or liquidiser and blend for 30 seconds. Pour into tall glasses.

## Coffee Shake

500 ml milk, chilled
3 individual blocks of vanilla ice cream
4 tbsp (60 ml) coffee essence

*Serves 2*

Put all the ingredients in the goblet of a blender or liquidiser and blend for 20 seconds. Pour into tall glasses.

*Note*: If you prefer, replace the coffee essence by 2 level tbsp. (30 ml) instant coffee, dissolved in 1 tbsp. (15 ml) water, plus 1 level tbsp. (15 ml) sugar.

## Iced Tea and Coffee

See chart at end of chapter.

### How Much? How Many?—Drinks and Food for Parties

LONG AND SHORT DRINKS

Drinking habits vary so much that any guide can only be quite general.

*Buffet Parties*: Allow per person 1 to 2 shorts and 3 to 6 longer drinks, plus coffee.

*Drop-in-for-Drinks*: Reckon on 3 to 5 short drinks per person, and 4 to 6 small savouries, plus the usual olives and nuts.

*Drinks by the Bottle*: Sherry, port, straight vermouths, 12 to 16 glasses per bottle. Spirits and vermouths in single 'nips' for cocktails, yield just over 30 per bottle. Reckon on 16 to 20 drinks of spirits from a bottle when serving them with soda, tonic water or other minerals.

A split of soda or tonic gives 2 to 3 drinks.

Table wines give about 5 to 6 glasses per bottle.

A $19\frac{1}{2}$-oz. (approx. 550 g) can of tomato juice can give 4 to 6 drinks.

A bottle of fruit cordial diluted with 4 litres water gives 20 to 25 drinks.

## QUANTITIES FOR SMALL SAVOURIES

| | *Ingredients* | *Portions* | *Notes* |
|---|---|---|---|
| Sausage rolls | 680 g shortcrust or flaky pastry<br>1 kilo sausage-meat | 30 medium or 50 small | Pastry based on 680 g flour, 340–450 g fat |
| Bouchées | 450 g puff pastry<br>570 ml thick white sauce<br>300 g prepared filling | 50 | Pastry based on 450 g flour, 340 g butter<br>Fillings: chopped ham, chicken, egg, shrimps, mushrooms |
| Cheese straws | 225 g cheese pastry | 100 | Pastry made with 225 g flour, 110 g fat, 110 g cheese |

## QUANTITIES FOR STARTERS, MAIN COURSE, ETC.

| | *1 portion* | *24–26 portions* | *Notes* |
|---|---|---|---|
| Soup: cream, clear or iced | 190 ml | 4.75 litres | Serve, garnished, in mugs or cups |
| Fish cocktail: shrimp, prawn, tuna or crab | 25–30 g | 680 g fish<br>2–3 lettuces<br>850 ml sauce | In stemmed glasses, garnished with a shrimp or prawn |
| Meat with bone | 140 g | 3–3.5 kilos | Cold roasts, barbecue chops |
| Meat, boneless | 85–110 g | 2.25–2.75 kilos | Casseroles, meat balls, sausages, barbecue steaks |
| Turkey, boneless | 85–110 g | 7 kilos (dressed) | Served hot or cold |
| Chicken | 1 joint (140–220 g) | 6 birds about 1.125–1.350 kilos (dressed) | Served hot or cold |

QUANTITIES FOR STARTERS, MAIN COURSE, ETC.

| | *1 portion* | *24–26 portions* | *Notes* |
|---|---|---|---|
| Ham or tongue | 85–110 g | 2.25–2.75 kilos | Halve amounts if making stuffed 'cornets' |
| Pâté for wine-and-pâté party | 85–110 g | 2.25–2.75 kilos | Halve amounts if serving pâté as starter course |
| Salad Vegetables: | | | |
| *lettuce* | $\frac{1}{6}$ approx. | 3–4 lettuces | Dress at last minute |
| *cucumber* | 3 cm | 2 cucumbers | |
| *tomatoes* | 1–2 tomatoes | 1.350 kilos | |
| *white cabbage* | 30 g | 700 g | For winter salads |
| *boiled potatoes* | 60 g | 1.350 kilos | For potato salads |
| Rice or pasta | 40 g (uncooked) | 1 kilo | Can be cooked a day ahead, re-heated 5 mins. in boiling water |
| Cheese (with biscuits) | 30–40 g | 680 g–1 kilo<br>450 g butter<br>1 kilo biscuits | Larger amounts for assorted cheese board |
| Cheese for wine-and-cheese party | 80 g | 2–2.250 kilos, at least 4 types | More if a cheese dip is also being served |

## QUANTITIES FOR MADE-UP DISHES

| | *Portions* | *Ingredients* | | *Notes* |
|---|---|---|---|---|
| Spaghetti Paesana | 20 | 10 onions<br>1 kilo back bacon rashers<br>5 14-oz. (approx. 400-g) cans of tomatoes<br>500 g mushrooms<br>2 green peppers<br>250 g butter | 5 tbsp. (75 ml) tomato paste<br>2 chicken stock cubes<br>2½ level tsp. (12.5 ml) basil<br>5 level tbsp. (75 ml) cornflour<br>1½ kilos spaghetti | Follow recipe in Meat section.<br>Serve garnished with grated Parmesan cheese |
| Chicken Salad (Most suitable for summer parties) | 20–25 | 5 1½-kilo oven-ready chickens, roasted<br>1 kilo long-grain rice<br>Salt and pepper<br>15 bananas<br>15 oranges<br>625 ml mayonnaise | French dressing made from:<br>10 tbsp. (150 ml) salad oil<br>5 tbsp. (75 ml) vinegar<br>Salt and pepper to taste | Follow recipe in Poultry section.<br>Serve garnished with chopped parsley and almonds |
| Beef Goulash | 20 | 2¼ kilos stewing steak<br>10 medium-sized onions<br>2 green peppers<br>200 g fat<br>10 level tsp. (50 ml) paprika | 3 tbsp. (45 ml) tomato paste<br>Salt and pepper<br>225 g flour<br>1.25 litres beer stock<br>10 large tomatoes<br>A bouquet garni | Prepare as for a basic casserole recipe.<br>Heat oven to 163°C (mark 3, 325°F) and bake mixture in 5 casseroles (or cook on top of stove in thick, heavy pans for 2 hrs.) |

### QUANTITIES FOR SWEETS

| | Portions | Ingredients | | Notes |
|---|---|---|---|---|
| Meringues | 50 small shells | 6 egg whites<br>340 g caster sugar | 425 ml whipped cream | 2 halves if with cream; 1 with fruit, ice cream |
| Trifle | 25 | 2.25–2.5 litres custard | 25 sponge fingers<br>1 large can fruit | Decorate with cream, glacé cherries, nuts |
| Fruit Salad | 25 | 1.75–2.25 litres sugar syrup | 3 kilos fruit<br>850 ml cream | Prepared fruit (except bananas) may be left in syrup for 24 hrs. |

### QUANTITIES FOR COFFEE AND TEA (allowing 190 ml per serving)

| | Ingredients, 24–26 servings | | Notes |
|---|---|---|---|
| *Coffee* | | | |
| Ground, hot | 250–300 g coffee<br>3.5 litres water | 1.75 litres milk<br>450 g sugar | If made in advance, strain after infusion. Re-heat without boiling |
| Ground, iced (serve in glasses) | 340 g coffee<br>3.5 litres water | 1.75 litres milk<br>Sugar to taste | Make coffee, half sweetened, half not; strain and chill. Mix with chilled milk |
| Instant, hot | 55–85 g coffee<br>3.5 litres water | 1.125 litres milk<br>450 g sugar | Make in jugs as required. Serve sugar separately |
| Instant, iced (serve in glasses) | 85 g coffee<br>1.125 litres water | 3.5 litres milk<br>Sugar to taste | Make coffee, half sweetened, half not; chill, mix with chilled milk |
| *Tea* | | | |
| Indian, hot | 60 g tea<br>4.5 litres water | 850 ml milk<br>450 g sugar | Better to use several pots than one outsize one |
| Indian, iced (serve in glasses) | 85 g tea<br>4 litres water | 1.125 litres milk<br>Sugar to taste | Strain tea directly it infuses; sweeten half. Chill; serve with chilled creamy milk |
| China | 60 g tea<br>5.125 litres water | 3 lemons<br>450 g sugar | Infuse tea 2–3 mins. only or it loses fragrance. Put thin lemon slice in each cup before pouring. |

## CHAPTER 5
# SENSIBLE SHOPPING

Whether food shopping is a pleasant task or just a necessary bore depends on your temperament and skill. Those housewives who are bored by it are most likely the ones who have only a limited cooking repertoire and who are too conservative to try anything new.

It usually pays to go along to the shops yourself, either to get to know the shopkeepers or, in the supermarkets, to spend a few minutes strolling along to see what's new. Provided time isn't at a premium, shop around, for you can save money by not buying the first thing you see.

Go shopping with a detailed list, but don't stick to it too rigidly, if you see anything unexpectedly tempting and good value for money. Having a list will however make sure you don't forget vital things like butter or sugar.

When making your list, check your store cupboard to see what is wanted. Consult your week's menus, if you have worked them out (see later), and buy according to the dishes planned and the number of people to be catered for. If you go out to business, get in basic stores during the weekend, either each week or fortnightly. Get green and salad vegetables as required, since their flavour and vitamin content diminish with storage.

*Cooking for Today and Tomorrow—with Planned-overs*: If the time-and-motion men moved into our homes, they'd prescribe a lot more planning and fewer bouts of cooking. It's all very well being a marvellous cook, but not much fun for your children and husband if you're always cutting, peeling, beating, stirring, baking. Provided you've a refrigerator (an investment that pays handsomely in time and money saved), planned cooking is the answer.

Whereas leftovers just happen, planned-overs result from being wise before the event, from intentionally cooking in quantities for two or three meals. A good beef stew, for instance, can be prepared, cooked immediately, and then refrigerated in three different dishes, so that any one lot is never re-heated more than once. A lamb casserole can be divided into two portions, one being enriched with say pearl barley, the other flavoured with tomato, garlic and herbs. The important thing to remember is that all cooked meat must be re-heated slowly but very thoroughly in stock or gravy and simmered for at least 15 minutes.

Mince is equally versatile: serve it as Hamburger Holstein (with fried egg on top), or as a baked meat loaf with jacket potatoes, or as 'burgers with tomato sauce and noodles. Only you will realise that they all stem from the same mince, onion and egg mixture.

When you are buying a joint, think ahead: why not, for instance, get a bacon joint big enough to give you meat for a hot and a cold meal, leaving the end bits, which don't slice well, to be chopped into omelettes or mixed with chicken remainders and peas into a white sauce, or to put into vol-au-vent cases, for a third meal. Just remember not to be *too* generous with the helping first time round, and you'll have enough left for later use.

The ideal is to rough out a week of menus (as many working wives do), so that your planning, shopping, preparing and cooking can all be co-ordinated. Part of the fun of working in this way is that you cook with concentrated enjoyment when the creative urge comes upon you. And in any case you get the double satisfaction of producing a lot of lovely food at one go, with just one great kitchen clean-up, and a peaceful few days to follow.

### Food Budgeting

When you start housekeeping there will be plenty of people ready to tell you exactly how much you ought to spend every week on milk or meat or vegetables. The trouble is that no two advisers agree about the amounts. You'll find it much easier if for the first few weeks you keep a simple account book and an open mind. Buy what you think you'll need and put it all down, and very soon you will see how the money is going and whether you are buying too little milk or too much bread. Then you can decide on a reasonable basic housekeeping allowance and begin to tailor your spending to fit.

As a nation, we spend on average between a quarter and a third of our income on food; usually it's the largest single item in our budget, so it needs careful consideration. Given plenty of money, there's no problem about catering and shopping well—it's shopping economically that demands the thought. Discuss the question in class: examine the suggestions given here and see what other ways of saving money will emerge.

Don't imagine that money-saving meals must be austere or stodgy. A little thought, and they add up to good and exciting eating, with new dishes you'll be proud of. And don't forget that simple things like bread, cheese and celery, with a glass of milk, make an excellent square meal.

*Thinking Ahead*: It pays off in hard cash, as well as in variety and balanced eating, to scheme out the main meals for a few days in advance, as we suggested. You can then look at each item and question its cost and food value.

*Knowing where it Goes*: Price-mark your shopping list—not forgetting to add in any 'impulse buys'.

*Buying from Plenty*: Make the most of fresh fruit, vegetables and fish when they're at their seasonal peaks. No fear of monotony, since there are always new ways of preparing most foods to give variety in taste, texture and appearance. Buy the ingredients for jams, marmalades, jellies, sauces and pickles at glut times, cutting your spending on those things for the months ahead.

Coating Meatballs: Put the breadcrumbs in a shallow tray, add the meatballs and shake the tray with a to-and-fro motion, so that the balls keep their shape and are evenly coated

*Deciding How Much*: Buying correct quantities saves money. Economy-size packs are no economy if half the stuff goes stale before you use it. General guide-lines for amounts to buy for each person for one meal are:
225 g meat on bone; 175 g boneless meat (without much fat); 85–110 g cooked sliced meat or sausage; 85 g meat for made-up dishes; 225–250 g chicken; 110 g liver; 225 g whole fish; 150 g fish fillets; 150 g root vegetables; 150 g runner beans; 150–200 g sprouts or cabbage; 300 g peas in pod; 350 g fresh spinach; 40 g pasta, rice, lentils, dried peas and beans; 100–125 g fruit in pies, puddings or compotes; 125 ml milk in milk puddings, moulds, jellies.

*Buying Brands*: Don't be mesmerised by just one brand name. Try other brands two or three times, and you may come to like them better. And if it's a cheaper brand, the odd pence saved mount up surprisingly over the months.

*Making it Yourself*: Why buy things you can cook more cheaply at home? Your own cakes, scones, tarts, pies and pasties will be more to your taste and usually work out cheaper. It pays to make your own fish cakes and hamburgers, too.

*Stocking Wisely*: Store-cupboard sense cuts costs. Stock, for instance, the less expensive canned fish—sardines, herrings, pilchards, tuna—which make many light lunch and supper dishes. Evaporated milk is a good standby, too: it can be chilled, whipped and flavoured with essence to replace cream. Dried skim milk will save on fresh milk for cooking.

'*Waste Not . . .*': Bread which has dried out too much, if it is already sliced, can be briefly dipped in milk or water and then toasted or fried. Or dip it in beaten egg, drain and fry it, to serve with melted jam or powdered cinnamon and sugar, as the delightful sweet called Poor Knight. Or cube the bread, then fry or oven-dry it to make croûtons, or crumble it for use as crumbs. Dry sponge or plain cake can be used up in crumble-top fruit pies.

## Good Buys

*Cereals, Pulses*: Rice, semolina, porridge oats, dried beans, lentils, etc., and the various pastas (not made-up canned sorts) belong in an eating-better-for-less budget. The pastas are excellent with meat or smoked fish for main meals. Pearl barley and lentils give body to soups. Rice, tapioca and semolina make delicious and pretty sweets.

*Eggs*: Always good value for money, eggs make excellent low-cost main dishes even for the most formal occasions — soufflés, savoury or sweet, and omelettes with imaginative savoury fillings, or with jam or fruit. Crème caramel and other egg custards make attractive party sweets.

Dishes like Welsh rarebit, baked beans and spaghetti make economical and nourishing main courses when topped with a poached or fried egg, plus some crisp bacon.

*Fresh Meat*: The cheapest cuts of meat have the same food value as the dearest. But work out how much actual meat you are getting, in proportion to bone and fat. Cheaper but quick-to-cook meats include mince, best end of neck, slices of belly pork. Economical but needing longer cooking are shin of beef, brisket, scrag end of mutton, breast of lamb (stuffed for roasting or done flat in a casserole), blade bone and spare rib of pork.

*Bacon*: Joints—collar, forehock, knuckle, for instance—make marvellous main meals and are usually cheaper than fresh meat joints. Boiled forehock, bony but lean, gives a fine hot family meal, then a cold one, as well as soup.

*Poultry and Game*: Chicken joints are sometimes more economical than a whole bird. If you are near a country-town market, you may be able to buy wild pigeons at a few pence per bird, and they make good pies.

*Offal*: Cheap 'variety' meats like the coarser kinds of liver, kidneys and tripe can be enjoyed in so many ways. Half a head of calf or pig is a real bargain; cook the half pig's head with bay leaf and cloves, serve it with a vinaigrette sauce, call it *Tête de Porc Vinaigrette*, and you have a gourmet dish—with plenty of meat left for another meal.

*Fish*: Take a plunge, buy the cheapest, and you may be amazed—rock salmon or whiting in a well-flavoured batter is delicious. Fresh herrings, hot or cold, are as flavourful and adaptable as the most expensive fish; so is haddock, fresh or smoked.

*Root Vegetables*: Parsnips, carrots, swedes and turnips can make a good course in their own right. Try whole beetroot served hot with crumbly bacon and a cheese or Béchamel sauce.

*Cabbage*: Crisp raw winter cabbage, finely shredded, is a good base for different salads when lettuce is dear. It is also wonderfully tasty when cooked with a little chopped onion, seasoning and butter, and it makes a light and satisfying dish if topped with a poached egg or slice of bacon.

*Tomatoes*: Very ripe ones may be a good buy if you can cook them the same day. Mis-shapen tomatoes are usually cheap but good.

**A Matter of Convenience**

Look into almost any shopping basket, and you'll notice the can, the packet and the deep-freeze item that make for today's time-saving but appetising meals.

For obvious reasons, no-one would advocate relying completely on 'can-opener cookery', but it has a definite place in our lives. It means that you can always produce various quick dishes and, provided you carry a stock of certain flavourings, etc., those dishes can be made pleasantly different. It pays to collect menus for some 'instant' meals and to tack the list to the inside of the store-cupboard door, with alongside each menu the foods required. To start your quick-and-easy-menu collection, we've planned one which is just right for a twosome, another for an everyday family occasion and a third that is a little more sophisticated. (See pp. 93–95).

Try to keep the store cupboard equipped with things that will in an emergency eke out or enhance any fresh foods you

Jacket Potatoes 1: Cut a cross in top of scrubbed raw potato

Jacket Potatoes 2: Squeeze cooked potato so that cuts open up, showing fluffy cooked inside part. (For Stuffed Jacket Potatoes, see Vegetables chapter)

may have available. Apart from the invaluable cans of soup, fish, meat, fruit and beans (kidney and butter beans as well as the famous baked ones), the instant potatoes, rice and pasta, keep an adventurous selection of dried herbs, spices and condiments, dried sliced onions, celery flakes, dehydrated mushrooms, red and green pepper bits and 'Lazy Garlic' or garlic chips. Ready-made sauce mixes and condensed soups supply a balance of flavours often difficult to achieve when you're cooking in a hurry. 'Jiffy' lemons and P.L.J. supply juice without any waste (though P.L.J., once opened, should be used up within 3–4 weeks). Horseradish cream or relish gives uplift to many quick dishes. Concentrated tomato purée and canned tomatoes always come in handy. Soy and Worcestershire sauces enliven many dishes (a dash of either is wonderful in the cheese sauce for cauliflower, and enhances the flavour of mushrooms).

Short-cuts with vegetables are helpful. For quick boiled potatoes, choose large old ones, slice thinly, boil gently for 10 minutes, then drain well and if you wish, mash them. Canned new potatoes may be sautéed whole until golden, with a little chopped onion in the pan. Good fresh, firm cabbage cooks in minutes if you shred it finely into the minimum amount of boiling salted water and drain it when it's just tender but still crisp; add a knob of butter and a dusting of nutmeg. Halved tomatoes are sustaining and delicious if topped with thyme-and-parsley or sage-and-onion stuffing mix and a little melted butter before they are grilled; add grated cheese if you like.

Some reminders on essential nutrients are given in another chapter, but here are notes on the food values of processed foods, to help you achieve balanced menus. Proteins and fats seem to be only slightly affected in nutritional value. Carbohydrates suffer from oxidation reactions encouraged by heat. Vitamins are more adversely affected than any other nutrients by all methods of preservation. This is particularly true of the water-soluble vitamin C and to some extent the B group and Riboflavin. Vitamin A survives better than any other. However, to obtain a realistic picture, offset these losses in vitamin content against those which occur when fresh vegetables are transported and marketed. Also, since preserved vegetables are cooked for a shorter time, any losses at this stage are less than in the cooking of fresh vegetables. By the time they are eaten, the preserved vegetables have probably suffered no more than fresh products cooked in the home. So far as minerals are concerned, little is known of the effects of preservation methods on them.

**A few Quickies and Store-cupboard Meals**

1. Ham slices wrapped round canned celery hearts, par-cooked chicory, canned asparagus or frozen broccoli, then coated with cheese sauce and 'bubbled' under the grill.
2. Pancakes with a filling of bacon, onion, tomato and Worcestershire sauce, or of creamed corn, cheese and chives, or of sardines with a hint of onion and canned pimiento.
3. Canned salmon, drained and flaked, mingled with cooked macaroni, cheese sauce, a dash of lemon juice, a topping of breadcrumbs, heated and crisped under the grill.
4. To serve on toast—sardines or brisling with well-drained canned whole tomatoes, a pinch of basil and a dusting of Parmesan cheese. Or flaked salmon or tuna heated in white sauce with a little cream, lemon juice and diced cucumber.

*Two-some Menu*:

Tomato soup
Haddock and sweet pepper sauté
Chicory and corn salad
Soufflé omelette

*Soup*: Heat the canned tomato soup. Toast 2 thick slices of bread and cut into cubes; put into cups and add the soup.

*Haddock and Sweet Pepper Sauté*: Follow the recipe in the Fish chapter, but replace the fresh pepper by the contents of a small can of pimientos; drain and slice them thinly.

*Salad*: Wash a head of chicory, separate the leaves and finely slice the small ones. Arrange the larger leaves on flat scallop shells. Open a 7-oz. (approx. 200-g) can of sweet corn kernels, and mix the drained corn with the sliced chicory, then marinade for a short time in a lemon-flavoured French dressing or mayonnaise. Spoon the mixture into the lined shells and garnish with snipped chives.

*Soufflé Omelette*: Beat 3 egg yolks with 25 g caster sugar until thick; fold in 3 stiffly whisked egg whites. Turn the mixture into a large frying pan in which a large knob of butter has been melted. Cook till the underside is golden; quickly put under a grill to set the top lightly. Pour warmed apricot brandy jam over half the surface, mark the omelette across the middle, lift one half over to form a crescent and turn out on to a warm plate. Dust with sugar.

*Family Menu for Four*:

Tomato juice
Meatball recipe—see exercise below
Celery, apple and walnut salad
Pineapple whip

*Tomato Juice*: Sharpen some chilled canned juice with a little lemon juice or Worcestershire sauce.

*Exercise—Meatball Recipe*: Given the following items, work out a recipe for 4 people (for instance, a variation on Shepherd's Pie) and write out in recipe style. A 15¾-oz. (approx. 450-g) can of meatballs in brown onion gravy, a 14-oz. (approx. 400-g) can of baby carrots, 100 g mushrooms (fresh or canned), a 6-oz. (approx. 170-g) packet of instant potato powder, about 3 tbsp. (45 ml) red wine, plus butter, etc.

*Pineapple Whip*: Make up a 1-pint (568-ml) lemon jelly with half the stated amount of water, used boiling; stir to dissolve. When beginning to set, turn it into the goblet of a blender, and add contents of a 15-oz. (approx. 425-ml) can of pineapple and of a 4-oz. (115-g) can of cream. Blend till puréed, then put into 4 stemmed glasses. Leave until chilled and lightly set; decorate with pineapple—canned, crystallised, or fresh.

*Guest Menu for Four*:

Asparagus
Liver Stroganoff Broad bean and tomato salad
Ambrosia

*Asparagus*: Either frozen (thawed) or canned asparagus may be served cold with lemon mayonnaise, or hot with melted butter sauce and thinly cut brown bread and butter.

*Liver Stroganoff*: Follow the recipe in the Meat chapter, but replace the stock by dry white wine, if available. As an alternative to savoury rice, served sautéed potato cubes (1 kilo potatoes), which may be piled round the edge of the liver serving dish and garnished with snipped parsley.

*Salad*: Cook a 1-lb. (approx. 450-g) pkt. frozen broad beans as directed on the packet; drain, run cold water over the beans to cool them, then remove the skins. Skin 225 g tomatoes, remove the seeds and quarter the flesh. Mix the beans, tomato and a French dressing flavoured with mustard.

*Ambrosia*: Place in a serving bowl the contents of an 11-oz. (approx. 310-g) can of orange segments in syrup. Add 2 sliced bananas and 2 tbsp. (30 ml) long-thread desiccated coconut. Chill well.

**Which Shops, and Why?**

Look for the shops with a brisk trade and good turnover, as they generally also have the best storage facilities and therefore the freshest foods. Prices vary enormously, so watch them, and take advantage of any special offers and reduced prices on the goods you really use.

*Specialist Shops* such as the butcher, the baker and the grocer, offer personal service, which will often include advice and help that may be lacking in the supermarkets.

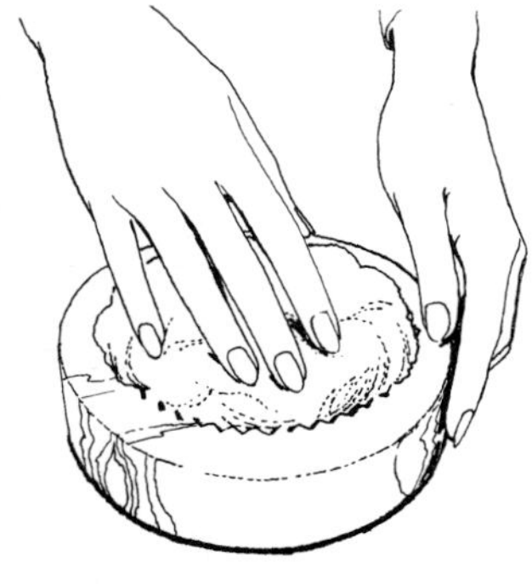

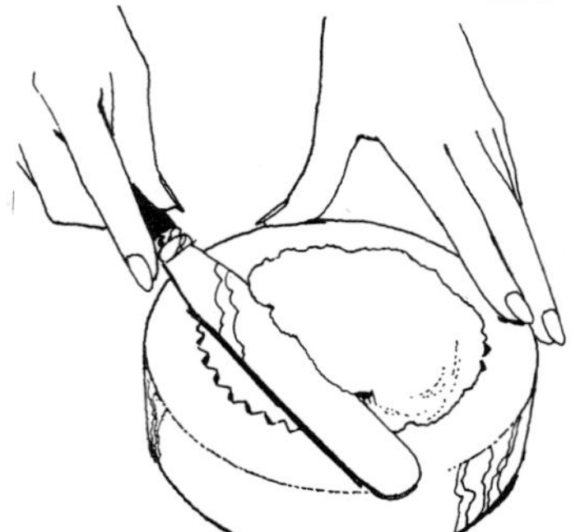

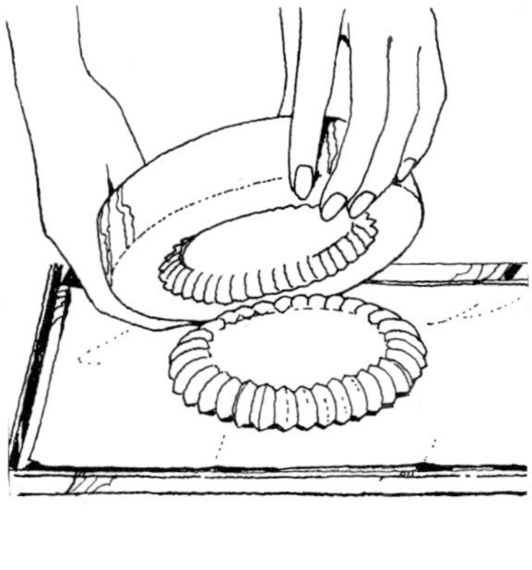

Using a mould to make Shortbread: 1. Dust out mould with rice flour, then put in mixture, pressing well into the scallops. 2. Remove surplus dough by shaving off a thin slice with a knife. 3. Turn shortbread out on to baking tray and bake for required time. (For recipe, see *Cooking is Fun*)

*Multiple and Chain Stores, Supermarkets*: These are the firms with branches in every High Street. You can expect good value for money because of the economies of large-scale operation and a system of centralised buying. Choice may not be as wide as in some shops, the stock being pre-selected and including many 'own brands'; there may be no services like credit or delivery.

*Co-operative Stores*: On the same lines as the multiple stores. Customers can become members of the Co-operative Society. The choice of brands is somewhat limited.

*Street Markets and Barrows*: Prices are as a rule—though not always—lower than in shops. If you use your eyes, you can do exceptionally well with them.

*Mail Order*: This is not a general way of doing food shopping, but at Christmas-time, for instance, good speciality lines are often advertised. There is a tendency nowadays for individuals to set up home cooking services with postal delivery, but make sure, if you use them, that perishable or semi-perishable food is not despatched over the weekend or at holiday times.

*Bulk Buying, Discount Buying*: These can be money-savers. Three dozen of the same item can result in a substantial economy—provided you can store and use them all, or share with friends. Cash-and-carry stores (a form of discount buying) are growing, too. Prices are lower, since you are not paying for expensive services or overheads.

*Shop-to-Door*: Here we have the milkman and baker and a number of local mobile shops, generally restricted to fast-selling lines. Rather similar are the vans selling potatoes and so on, straight from the wholesaler.

## Your Rights and Legal Position

Nowadays you are much less likely to be cheated by the occasional dishonest or careless retailer, for as a shopper you are protected and legally backed by five Acts of Parliament—the Sales of Goods Act, 1893; Trade Descriptions Act, 1968; Food and Drugs Act, 1955; Labelling of Food Regulations, 1970; and the Weights and Measures Act, 1963.

Briefly, the functions of the Acts are as follows:

### SALE OF GOODS ACT

This gives the individual shopper rights against the seller so far as description, merchantable quality and fitness for purpose are concerned.

TRADE DESCRIPTIONS ACT

Prohibits the use of fake or misleading trade descriptions about goods, false representation about the supply of goods and reckless or knowingly false statements about services, accommodation or facilities. Many of the time-honoured old 'dodges' are caught by this Act.

In the old days, advertisements were exempt from the law's rigours. The 'false trade description' had to be actually on the wrapping or, at least, specifically to refer to that particular purchase—for instance, on an invoice. Now even the most general advertisement, if it makes a specific claim about the product, must be accurate.

FOOD AND DRUGS ACT

This Act is particularly applicable to the daily food shopper, so we outline its provisions in more detail:

1. The addition of any substance to food, or the abstraction of any constituent from food, so as to render the food injurious to health, is prohibited.
2. It is an offence to sell to the prejudice of the purchaser food which is not of the nature, substance or quality demanded.
3. The use of a label or advertisement which falsely describes a food or misleads as to its nature, substance or quality, including its nutritional or dietary value, is prohibited.
4. It is an offence to sell unsound food.
5. Food pre-packed for retail sale must be labelled with a statement as to *(a)* the name and business address of the packer or labeller, or a registered trade mark (with the words 'registered trade mark' appearing in close proximity to the mark), and *(b)* in the case of a food of one ingredient, the appropriate designation of the ingredient, or in the case of a food consisting of two or more ingredients, the common or usual name (if any) of the food and the appropriate designation of each ingredient. Unless the quantity or proportion of each ingredient is stated, they must be shown in descending order according to the proportion, by weight, in which each is used. (Water need not be declared as an ingredient.) An appropriate designation means a specific and not a generic name or description—e.g., 'raspberries', not just 'fruit'.
6. It is an offence to import into the U.K. any food which is unfit for human consumption. Imported goods bearing

the name or trade mark of a manufacturer, or the name of any place in the U.K., must be accompanied by an indication of origin. Orders in Council have also been made under the Merchandise Marks Acts, which remain in force until 30th November, 1971, laying down special requirements as to indication of origin in respect of the following imported foodstuffs: bacon and ham; butter; currants, sultanas and raisins; dried eggs; eggs in shell; fresh apples; honey; malt products; margarine; meat and poultry; oat products; raw cucumber; raw tomatoes; frozen or chilled salmon or sea trout.

The duty to enforce the Act lies with the local authorities (and other authorities). If you suspect that an offence has been committed; tell the Public Health Department if you live in a town; otherwise, tell the Weights and Measures Department of your local authority.

### LABELLING OF FOOD REGULATIONS

One of the main provisions of these Regulations (most of which will come into effect in 1973) is to make the wording and type-size of labels, etc., clearer and less likely to mislead.

### WEIGHTS AND MEASURES ACT

This covers things like short weight and measure. Many goods, if pre-packed, have to be marked with their quantities. Some goods, if pre-packed, can be sold only in specified quantities.

### TO SUM UP

In general, if you are dissatisfied with a food purchase—for example, with its fitness for consumption or with the description or weight, you should complain first to the shop, and then, if necessary, to the Public Health Department or Weights and Measures Department. If you think an offence has been committed under the Trades Descriptions Act, you should get in touch with your Weights and Measures Inspector.

CHAPTER 6

# FOOD STORAGE

In this chapter we see how best to store food under domestic conditions, in order to protect it against the spoilage agents already discussed.

## Storage in a Refrigerator

A refrigerator provides satisfactory storage for perishable foods, the growth of micro-organisms is discouraged and enzyme action retarded. Temperatures inside the cabinet are between 1°C and 7°C, and inside the freezing compartment between −18°C and −6°C, depending on the 'star rating'; these will keep the foods in good condition for varying times, depending on the food and where it is stored.

*Exercise*: To find out the variations in refrigerator temperatures and how they compare with the outside temperature.

Pour 45 ml water into each of 6 shallow containers. Put one container in each of the following parts of the refrigerator: freezing compartment; chiller tray; middle shelf of cabinet; crisper tray; door shelf. Place the remaining sample in the larder. Leave for some hours, preferably overnight. Take the temperature of each of the samples and plot the results in chart form, with information on which foods to store where (see following notes).

### USING A REFRIGERATOR

1. All foods must be covered (see later).
2. Allow hot dishes to cool before storing them, or the ice-making compartment will quickly become covered with frost, and this insulating layer will make it difficult for the air to be satisfactorily cooled.
3. Put in correct part of the refrigerator:

(*a*) Raw foods such as meat, bacon, poultry and fish should be kept directly under the frozen food compartment, in the coldest part of the refrigerator.

(*b*) Cooked meat, made-up dishes can go on middle shelves.

(*c*) Vegetables, salad ingredients and bread go at the bottom, vegetables and salads in the crisper, if any.

(*d*) There is usually a compartment inside the door for butter, where it will not become too hard.

4. The 'edge' is taken off the flavour of many foods when they are chilled, so if possible remove such items as cheese, cold meats, salads, sandwiches, etc., from the refrigerator a little while before using them—the time depends on the room temperature. From the cooking angle, eggs and fats should be warmed up before baking time.
5. Wipe up any spilt foods at once, before they harden, and check the contents of the shelves regularly.
6. Defrost the refrigerator regularly, and clean it, using a weak solution of bicarbonate of soda in warm water.

## REFRIGERATOR STORAGE TIMES

| *Food* | *How to store* | *Days* |
|---|---|---|
| *Meat, raw* | | |
| Joints | Rinse blood away; wipe dry, | 3–5 |
| Chops, cut meat | cover with polythene or foil | 2–4 |
| Minced meat, offal | Cover as above | 1–2 |
| Sausages | Cover as above | 3 |
| Bacon | Wrap in foil or polythene, or put in plastic container | 7 |
| *Meat, cooked* | | |
| Joints | In tightly wrapped foil or poly- | 3–5 |
| Sliced ham | thene, or in lidded container | 2–3 |
| Continental sausages | In tightly wrapped foil or polythene, or in lidded container | 3–5 |
| Casseroles | In tightly wrapped foil or polythene, or in lidded container | 2–3 |
| *Poultry, raw* | | |
| Whole or joints | Draw, wash, wipe dry. Wrap in polythene or foil | 2–3 |
| *Poultry, cooked* | | |
| Whole or joints | Remove stuffing; when cool, wrap or cover as for cooked meats | 2–3 |
| Made-up dishes | Cover when cool | 1 |
| *Fish, raw* (white, oily, smoked) | Cover loosely in foil or polythene | 1–2 |
| *Fish, cooked* | As above, or in covered container | 2 |
| *Shellfish* | Eat the day it is bought—don't store | |

| *Food* | *How to store* | *Days* |
|---|---|---|
| *Vegetables, salads* | | |
| Prepared green and root vegetables, green beans, celery, courgettes, aubergines, peppers | In crisper drawer, or in plastic container, or wrapped in polythene | 5–8 |
| Sweet corn, mushrooms, tomatoes, radishes, spring onions | Clean or wipe as necessary; store in covered container | 5–7 |
| Lettuce, cucumber, cut onions, cut peppers, parsley | Clean or wipe as necessary; store in covered container | 4–6 |
| Cress, watercress | Clean or wipe as necessary; store in covered container | 2 |
| *Fresh fruit* | | |
| Cut oranges, grapefruit, lemons | In covered container | 3–4 |
| Strawberries, redcurrants, raspberries, peaches | In covered container | 1–3 |
| Grapes, cherries, gooseberries, cut melon | In covered container | 5–7 |
| Rhubarb, cleaned | In covered container | 6–10 |
| *Eggs* | | |
| Fresh, in shell | In rack, pointed end down | 14 |
| Yolks | In lidded plastic container | 2–3 |
| Whites | In lidded plastic container | 3–4 |
| Hard-boiled, in shell | Uncovered | up to 7 |
| *Fats* | | |
| Butter, margarine | In original wrapper, in special compartment of refrigerator | 14–21 |
| Cooking fats | In original wrapper, in special compartment of refrigerator | 28 |
| *Milk, etc* | | |
| Milk | In original container, closed | 3–4 |
| Cream | In original container, closed | 2–4 |
| Soured cream, buttermilk, yogurt | In original container, closed | 7 |
| Milk sweets, custards | Lightly covered with foil or film | 2 |
| *Cheese* | | |
| Parmesan, in piece | In film, foil or airtight container | 21–28 |

| *Food* | *How to store* | *Days* |
|---|---|---|
| Hard cheeses | In film, foil or airtight container | 7–14 |
| Semi-hard cheeses | In film, foil or airtight container | 7–10 |
| Soft (cream or curd) cheeses | In film, foil or airtight container | 5–7 |
| *Bread, rolls, etc.* | | |
| Any type bread | In original waxed paper or polythene wrapper, or in foil | 7 |
| Sandwiches | (Provided no mayonnaise in filling.) Wrap in foil or use tightly lidded plastic box | 1–2 |
| *Leftovers* | | |
| Casseroles, pies, vegetables, cooked fruit | In original dish, tightly covered, or in plastic container | 2–4 |
| Canned foods, opened | Leave in can but cover; fruits and fruit juices, which tend to alter slightly in flavour, are best put in another container | As for freshly cooked foods |
| *Standbys* | | |
| Batter, uncooked | In covered jug or plastic container | 1–2 |
| Pancakes, cooked | Interleaved with greaseproof paper and foil-wrapped | 7 |
| Dry pastry mix | In screw-top jar or plastic container | up to 14 |
| Pastry, raw | Wrapped in foil | 2–3 |
| Grated cheese | In lidded jar or plastic container | up to 14 |
| Stock, soup | In covered jug | 1–2 |

**Storage in a Larder or Store-cupboard**

A larder, if cool and ventilated, gives the next best storage after a refrigerator—indeed, for some foods it is preferable—but many homes nowadays have only non-ventilated food storage cupboards, which are of more limited usefulness.

The temperature inside a larder or ventilated food cupboard naturally varies according to aspect and weather, but it should be no higher than 10°C for temporary storage of perishables. An open gauze-covered window permits the essential cool air circulation, while excluding germ-spreading flies. The door should be kept shut as much as possible, to prevent the entry of warmer air.

All food stored in larder or cupboard should be kept in

covered containers or suitable wrappings. Containers with closely fitting lids are recommended for non-perishable foods, especially those of a granular or powdery texture, which clog in moist conditions. Airtight containers are essential for commodities whose flavour is vital, such as coffee and spices, and for crisp-textured biscuits, etc.

Foods for long-term larder storage should be placed on the higher or less accessible shelves, while perishables and regularly-used foods should be close at hand. Use foods in the order in which they were bought, putting new purchases at the back of the shelves.

Food bought in packets, e.g., flour, sugar, may be stored in that way until opened; then the contents should be transferred to airtight containers. Labelling is important, especially when the foods look alike.

Quick-dried foods, such as peas, packet soups, and some packaged foods, deteriorate when exposed to air, heat and moisture, but may be stored satisfactorily in the unopened packet or airtight jar if kept in a dry, cool place.

Canned foods should have the date of purchase marked on the label and should be used in rotation. Discard any 'blown' can, shown by bulged ends and leaking seams. If, however,

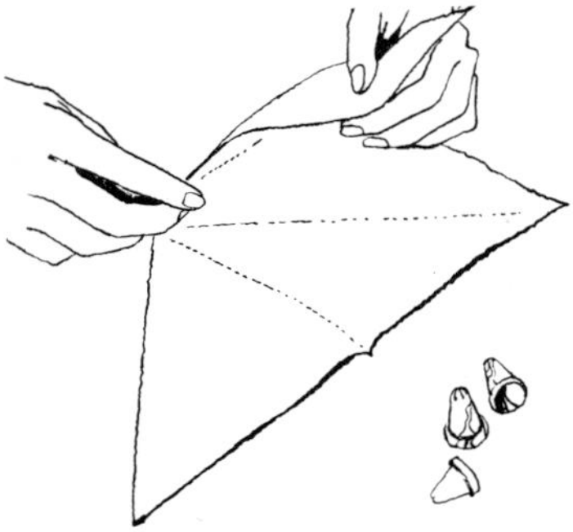

Making a Paper Forcing Bag 1: Fold a 25-cm square of greaseproof paper into a triangle. Roll over one of the folded corners to meet the right angle, then roll the other corner over and round, so that it meets the first one at the back of the bag; adjust until there is a point at tip of bag

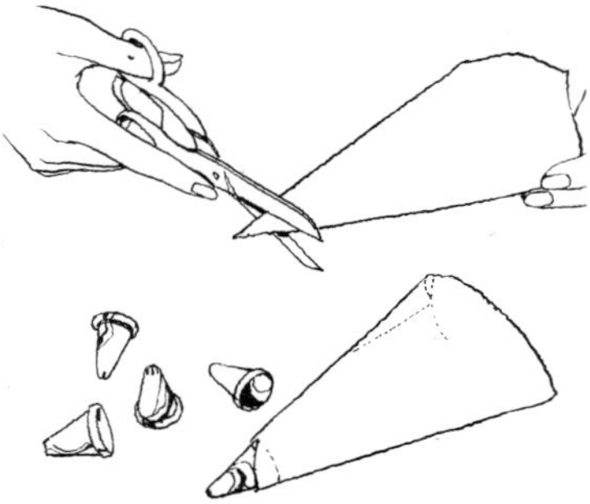

Making a Paper Forcing Bag 2: Fold over the corners several times, to hold them firmly in place. Cut a small piece from the tip of the bag and drop in a metal nozzle

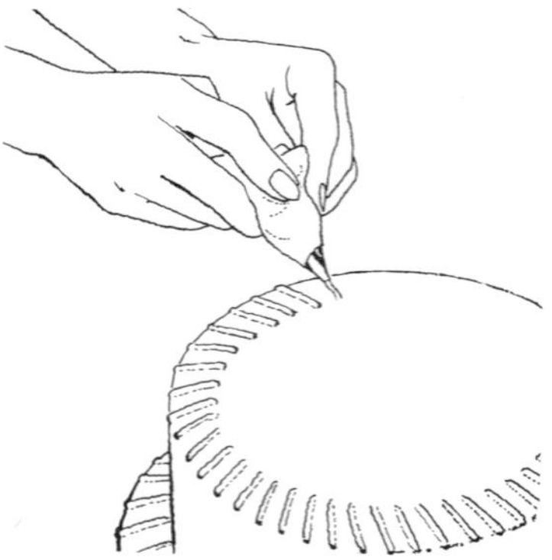

Using a Piping Bag: Place a little icing in the bag and fold the top over once or twice. Hold the bag so that the thumbs can give even pressure. Don't have the nozzle touching the cake but hold it a little above the surface and let the icing fall in a straight line, or as desired. (See Christmas Cake)

Piping Whipped Cream: Use a fabric bag with a large nozzle; hold it in one hand and squeeze with an even pressure; keep the bag and nozzle upright to get rosettes of good shape. (See Grape Gâteau)

you see a cheap buy in a dented can, this is safe, provided there is no sign of rust or seepage from the seams, but use up such cans quickly.

Most canned foods are perfectly sound for periods longer than given in the chart, but excessively long storage may mean that flavour and texture are not so good.

Don't store dog and cat cereals, biscuits, etc. in the larder — any infestation that might be present could spread rapidly to other commodities. (If this should happen, all affected foodstuff must be destroyed and the container washed, sterilised and well dried before re-use.)

### LARDER AND FOOD-CUPBOARD STORAGE TIMES

*Notes*: Times refer to unopened packets, jars or cans. Perishables such as fish, meat, poultry, milk, cream, should be stored for only about 1 day, covered as for refrigerator storage.

| *Food* | *Keeping qualities, time* | *Storage comments* |
|---|---|---|
| Flour, white | Up to 6 months | Once opened, transfer |
| Wheatmeal | Up to 3 months | to container with |
| Wholemeal | Up to 1 month | close-fitting lid |

| *Food* | *Keeping qualities, time* | *Storage comments* |
|---|---|---|
| Baking powder, bicarbonate of soda, cream of tartar | 2–3 months | Dry storage essential; if opened, put in container with close-fitting lid |
| Dried yeast | Up to 6 months | As above |
| Cornflour, custard powder | Good keeping qualities | As above |
| Pasta | As above | As above |
| Rice, all types | As above | As above |
| Sugar, loaf, caster, granulated | As above | Cool, dry storage; if opened, transfer as above |
| Sugar, icing, brown | Limited life—tends to absorb moisture | Buy in small quantities, as required |
| Tea | Limited life—loses flavour if stored long | Buy in small quantities; store in airtight container in dry, cool place |
| Instant and ground coffee in sealed can or jar | Up to 1 year | Cool, dry storage; once opened, re-seal securely; use quickly |
| Coffee beans, loose ground coffee | Very limited life; use immediately | Buy as required; use airtight container |
| Instant low-fat skimmed milk | 3 months | Cool, dry storage is vital; once opened, re-seal securely; use fairly quickly |
| Breakfast cereals | Limited life | Buy in small quantities. Cool, dry place |
| Dehydrated foods | Up to 1 year | Cool, dry place. If opened, fold packet down tightly and use within a week |
| Herbs, spices, seasonings | 6 months | Cool, dry storage, in airtight container. Keep from light. Buy in small quantities |
| Nuts, ground almonds, desiccated coconut | Limited life—depends on freshness when bought. Fat content goes rancid if kept too long | Lidded container |
| Dried fruits | 2–3 months | Cool, dry storage |
| Jams, etc. | Good keeping quality | Dry, cool, dark storage |

| *Food* | *Keeping qualities, time* | *Storage comments* |
|---|---|---|
| Honey, clear or thick | As above | Dry, cool storage. After about 1 year, appearance may alter, but honey is still fit to eat |
| Golden syrup, treacle | As above | As above |
| Condensed milk | 4–6 months | Safe even after some years, but caramelises and thickens. Once opened, harmless crust forms; cover can with foil lid and use within 1 month |
| Evaporated milk | 6–8 months | Safe even after some years, but darkens, thickens and loses flavour. Once opened, treat as fresh milk |
| Canned fruit | 12 months | Cool, dry place |
| Canned vegetables | 2 years | Cool, dry place |
| Canned fish in oil | Up to 5 years | Cool, dry place |
| Canned fish in tomato sauce | Up to 1 year | Cool, dry place |
| Canned meat | Up to 5 years | Cool, dry place |
| Canned ham | 6 months | As above. Cans holding 1 kilo or more should be kept in refrigerator |
| Pickles, sauces | Reasonably good keeping qualities | Cool, dry, dark place |
| Chutneys | Limited life | As above |
| Vinegars | Good keeping qualities—at least up to 2 years | Cool, dry, dark place; strong light affects flavoured vinegar and produces a non-bacterial cloudiness. Re-seal after use; never return unused vinegar to bottle |
| Oils (olive, corn) | Up to 18 months | Cool, dry place |

**Storage in a Home Freezer**

All foods may be frozen, but some more successfully than others; some which freeze perfectly are not in fact worth doing because they are available all the year round. Some can be stored for longer than others—after the optimum period there is still no risk to health, but flavour and quality will deteriorate.

Freeze only those items which *you* use in quantity and which will save time, e.g., given a glut of tomatoes at low prices, you can make a well-flavoured sauce and pack it in the amounts you would use with Spaghetti Bolognese; freeze parsley (sprigs or chopped) when it's at its best in the garden; make bulk meat casseroles in packs to give the right number of servings; freeze vegetables when in season; freeze meat or chicken stocks to use as a basis for soup; have some sliced bread ready for emergencies.

For best results, food to be frozen must be correctly packed or wrapped in moisture- and vapour-proof materials. Experiment with a selection of *thick* polythene bags, plastic boxes, waxed cartons, plastic sheeting or other packaging saved from manufacturers' packs, including plastic ice-cream boxes and yogurt cartons.

The basic principles and technique of home freezing are

Barley Sugar 1 (see Barley Sugar recipe): Pour out on to a greased heat-resisting surface and neaten the edges a little with a palette knife

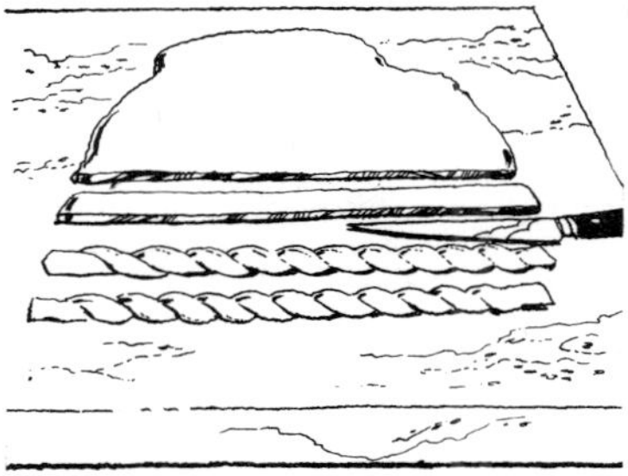

Barley Sugar 2: When cool but not set, cut into strips with a greased knife and twist each strip as evenly as possible. Leave to set

explained in the chapter 'The Science of Food Care'. See also the books for reference given there.

GUIDE TO STORAGE TIMES IN A HOME FREEZER

| | *Food* | *Time* |
|---|---|---|
| Vegetables, Fruit | | Up to 1 year; use up before new season's supply arrives |
| Meat, uncooked: | Beef, Lamb | 12 months |
| | Pork, Veal | 9 months |
| | Mince | 2 months |
| | Tripe, Offal | 2 months |
| | Sausages, cured vacuum-packed bacon | 6 weeks |
| | Vacuum-packed smoked bacon | 1 month |
| Meat, cooked: | Casseroles, Stews, Curries | 2 months |
| Poultry, uncooked: | Chicken, Turkey | 12 months |
| | Duck | 6 months |
| | Giblets | 3 months |
| Game, after hanging | | 6 months |
| Fish (freeze within 24 hrs. of catching): | White fish | 6–12 months |
| | Oily (Salmon, Trout, etc.) | 4 months |
| Dairy produce: | Eggs without shell | 10 months |
| | Butter, unsalted | 6 months |
| | Butter, salted | 3 months |
| | Cream (40% butterfat and over) | 12 months |
| | Soft cheese | 8 months |
| | Hard cheese | 3 months |
| Prepared foods: | Baked bread | 1 month |
| | Baked cakes | 6 months |
| | Baked pastry | 6 months |
| | Uncooked pastry | 3 months |
| | Soups, sauces, stocks | 3 months |
| | Ice cream | 3 months |

CHAPTER 7

# THE FOOD ON THE TABLE

Whether it's sausages and mash, fish and chips or a classic *haute cuisine* dish, a meal should please the senses; that is, it should look, smell and above all taste good.

The presentation of everyday meals is just as important as for party occasions, although the décor and table setting will be simpler. For family meals, the serving is often done in the kitchen, but even so, the food on the plate should be arranged with care, to give instant eye appeal. Attractive presentation will also help your family to accept unfamiliar food.

## Before you Begin Cooking

Presentation really starts at the stage when the food is being bought. It pays to take trouble when selecting it—to ensure, for instance, that fish and meat are correctly trimmed and cut, that vegetables are of the size and shape you need. Try to picture the finished result even while you're in the shop. And this doesn't mean spending a lot of money—good materials don't necessarily have to be expensive, and a little know-how and creative ability go a long way in achieving tempting results.

*Choice of Serving Dishes*: Oven-to-table ware, if you are lucky enough to possess it, is modern and versatile, overcoming the problem of keeping food really hot until you put it on the plate. Casserole cookery is particularly suited to this ware; just remember, when buying such dishes, that they should fit in with the colour of your basic dinner service. Remember, too, that this ware retains heat, so you'll need to use a well-insulated stand or a thick mat on the table.

Copper, which has an elegant and professional air, can often go from cooker to table; it is very practical for food that requires under-the-grill glazing and browning.

The size of dish is important; it should not be so small that it will be over-full—you will find it embarrassingly difficult to serve the first portions, or to carve, say, a large turkey set on a small platter. On the other hand, food can look lost and unappetising if in too large a dish; remember also that food may shrink on cooking and thus need a smaller dish than you imagined.

The serving dish should act as a foil to the food; colours are very much a matter of personal taste, but in general, black, white, and clear, rich hues are all trendy and modern; brown country-style ware is a better choice for hearty food than elegant silver; but that same silver is delightful for such classic dishes as *Canard à l'Orange* and for shimmering aspics and jellies. (Don't by the way put silver in the oven to heat, but instead rinse it in hot water.) A salad may be nonchalantly tossed in rustic wood. A glass dish looks attractive for fruit salads and trifle. For individual servings of starter cocktails, light desserts and so on, you can make full use of any glasses that normally you might only drink from. Tumblers, goblets, rummers, brandy balloons, classic stemmed wineglasses, all are potential winners for presenting food prettily—practical, too, for it's much easier to eat fruit salad, compote or ice cream from a goblet than to chase it round on a flat plate. Simple foods like creamed rice and tapioca develop new appetite appeal when served Condé-style in individual glasses.

**Garnish and Decoration**

Garnishes for savoury dishes and decorations for sweet ones should both be used with discretion, to tempt the appetite and in a few cases to indicate the nature of the dish—what's below a masking sauce, for example. The garnish should be edible, reflect the ingredients and have a right to be there—it should never be just an inedible extra. Generally speaking, it is incorrect to disguise a dish by too much garnish, and silly to add so much that service is slowed up and the food itself chilled. A well-chosen garnish, however, can add texture and flavour, and supply colour and contrast, too—think of crisp, golden buttered crumbs on a macaroni cheese, maître d'hôtel or savoury butter on a plain grilled cod cutlet, touches of the green leaves attached to chunky sprigs of cauliflower, glowing-red tomato sauce with stuffed marrow. The most versatile and useful garnish of all, probably, is parsley; used as sprigs, or freshly chopped, it gives a lift to many a dish at most times of the year.

It's wise from a practical and economic point of view to use a garnish which can be made from part of the main ingredients. Try keeping back a couple of slices from a lemon when the juice or rind goes into the dish; retain a few peas or a ring of green pepper if these are main ingredients. If you are buying mushrooms or watercress for garnish, use a few slices of mushroom caps one day, or a few sprigs of the water-cress, and put the remainder into a soup or salad the next day. A garnish may sometimes be an integral part of the actual dish—for instance, neat groupings of beautifully prepared vegetables round an entree, game chips with pheasant, piped duchesse potatoes with a dish cooked au gratin style.

One last word—respect the classic dishes whose garnish is traditional and often implied by their very name, and don't add new-fangled extras. Here are a few examples:

*Bonne Femme*: with lardons of diced bacon, button onions, mushrooms and potatoes.
*Bourguignonne*: with button mushrooms and onions and with red wine sauce; used with beef.
*Florentine*: with spinach in any form, sometimes with Mornay sauce.

---

Lemon Butterflies: Cut thin slices of lemon and divide each into half. Take one half and divide the rind and membrane at mid-point, but without cutting right through to the centre; open out to give the winged effect. Use to garnish fish

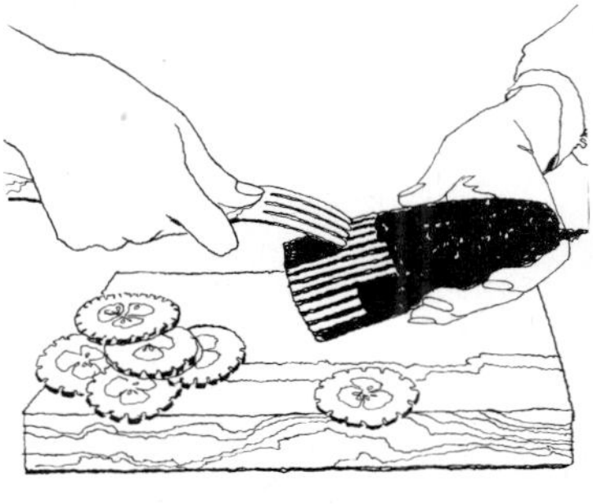

Deckled or Ridged Cucumber: Take piece of washed cucumber and score with the prongs of a fork. When the cucumber is sliced, each piece will have a crinkled or deckled edge. Use in green salads, etc.

*Lyonnaise*: with onions as a garnish; the sauce of the same name is flavoured with onion, tomato and meat glaze.
*Meunière*: fried in butter and served with a *noisette* butter sharpened with lemon juice poured over the food.
*Portugaise*: with rich red tomato sauce.
*St. Germain*: garnished with peas.

When it comes to the decoration of sweet dishes, play down any added finishes for hot puddings—just a light dusting of fine sugar or a sauce is probably sufficient. Cold desserts offer more scope, but even so, avoid unnecessary adornment, and use your commonsense. Suppose the choice is whirls of piped whipped cream—keep these on the bold side, for they will look better, and in any case to pipe whipped cream through a narrow aperture will ruin it. Any decoration likely to weep or melt must be added at the very last minute. And when you are at a loss for a finish to a whip, a fruit fool or a similar sweet, it's amazing how often such simple items as grated chocolate, crushed brandy snaps and toasted almonds can come to the rescue.

### Presentation and Serving

The simplest of food, if nicely presented, will often win the sincerest praises. Take salads: it's a waste of time to spend hours stylising a mixed salad into a precise geometrical design, since, if the ingredients are just naturally arranged, or lightly tossed in dressing and served with a dusting of scissor-snipped chives, they look so appetising.

Dish the food up neatly and quickly (leave yourself sufficient kitchen space for the job) and serve it directly.

Here are some hints and reminders:

Never go to the oven with a *damp* cloth—the steam that rises can scald you.

To remove any little brown rivulets on the sides of a casserole use a damp cloth with a dab of salt.

Always taste such dishes as soups and stews and if necessary adjust the seasoning; but remember, unless you know people's tastes, it's safer to under-season rather than to use too much salt and pepper.

Skim off any fat layer from soups, stews and casseroles, drawing a piece of absorbent paper across the surface.

Make a point of serving hot foods hot and cold foods chilled, though there are some exceptions: pastry flans, etc., are best at room temperature, not chilled, and foods that hold the heat, like mincemeat, treacle tart and apple and toffee sauces, should be warm rather than hot.

Aim at having food piled up in a dish rather than flat: it's easier to handle and looks more tempting. When you are arranging a cold platter, you can give height to the sliced meats with a frame of crumpled kitchen foil; the meats in their turn can be folded over or twisted to give yet more height.

To coat fish, chicken portions, etc., with sauce, use the broad side of the spoon for pouring, giving just a film; serve the rest of the sauce separately, for by no means everyone enjoys sauce in quantity. Talking of sauces, a little spooned into the dish before you arrange, say, cutlets, helps prevent their slipping about.

If foods need re-heating, it's often better to heat them separately, rather than all together—then a sauce, for instance, can safely be stirred with no danger of breaking up tender fish, chicken or similar ingredients.

**Setting the Table**

A sit-down meal may be either formal or informal; for the latter, follow the standard procedure as a general guide.

*Linen*: Neat, crisp table linen or a polished table surface with mats both look attractive. Large paper napkins (white,

Table laid for Formal Meal: If preferred, the side plate and small knife may be put in place from the beginning of the meal, instead of being set out later, when required for cheese

or in a colour to match the décor) may be used to save money and laundering time. Place the napkin to the left of the forks.

*Cutlery*: This should march evenly from the outside towards the plate, in the order of use. The knife blades should face the plate, and all cutlery should be placed with the handle tip 1.5 cm from the edge of the table. Whether the dessert-spoon and fork are placed at the top of the plate or on either side is a question of space and personal choice; on some occasions the spoon for the dessert is brought in with the dessert itself at the moment of serving. The small knife is set either to the right of the cover or on the side plate. Serving cutlery should ideally be placed near the dish.

The minimum width for the place setting is 55 cm, and 65 cm is even better; the service plates should be positioned about 2.5 cm from the edge of the table; table mats a little further in (unless very large).

*Plates*: The service (or cover) plate is a large one, used more frequently on the Continent than here, but becoming more usual in this country for formal occasions; it remains on the table during the starter and soup courses and is removed just before the main-course plates are set out. The bread and butter plate or side plate, with the small knife on it, is placed just beyond the forks; it can also take the folded napkin. Sometimes, at a very formal meal, the side plate and knife are not set until the cheese course is served.

*Glasses*: A single glass is placed above or immediately to the right of the cover plate. Wineglasses are always on the right of the water glass. If several glasses are being used, place them in the order in which they will be required, the first on the extreme right.

*Bread*: Arrange this in a basket, ready cut up, or set it out on the side plate; for formal occasions, include Melba toast, crusty bread, rolls and crispbread. A breadboard usually stands on a side table.

*Table Decoration*: This should be simple and tasteful, to tone with the table and the room décor; its shape should not prevent guests seeing each other across the table; tall, narrow candles, however, are quite permissible, since they do not obscure the view. Flowers look fresh and attractive, but on certain occasions an arrangement of fruit can be effective, while around Christmas time fir and holly give a seasonable touch. Consider the lighting, the china and the colour of the linen in relation to each other and with an eye to the food. Lighting is very important—it must not be too dim, or too harsh and flat.

### Service

For family meals, the first course, such as fruit juice, hors d'oeuvre or soup, is usually on the table when people seat themselves, though you may like in summer to serve a simple first course such as a cold soup or fruit juice on the patio.

When you are ready for the main course, meat and vegetables are served by the head of the family or the mother on to the plates and passed along to the left; alternatively, they may be served from the kitchen, or vegetables may be passed separately for people to help themselves.

At a formal dinner the host and hostess usually sit at either end of the table; a woman guest of honour sits at the host's right and a male guest of honour at the hostess' right. Other guests are placed alternately round the table. The woman guest of honour is served first, the service continuing towards the right. Food is presented to each guest from his left, and empty plates are removed from his right side. The table is cleared before the sweet course.

*Order of Courses*: See 'The Art of Meal Planning', but remember that you are free to vary the accepted order to some extent. Worth trying is the Continental procedure of serving vegetables as a separate course to follow the meat, or to serve cheese *before* the sweet course, since cheese is a palate-cleanser, and after a rich main course can make one more appreciative of a delicate sweet to follow.

*Coffee*: At a formal dinner coffee is served from a tray after the diners have left the table, small demi-tasse cups being used; the cup handle when presented should be to the guest's right, the spoon perpendicular to the handle. Informally, coffee is sometimes served at the table.

### 'How do I Serve it?'

Some of the most delicious things are difficult to eat tidily, but you can at least present guests with the right equipment, or prepare the food as helpfully as possible. Here's a brief check list of such foods:

*Artichokes, Globe*: Although the outer leaves are eaten in the fingers, a small knife and fork are needed for the 'choke', (see sketch below). Have individual small plates or bowls for discarded leaves; finger bowls are a help. (For preparation, see p. 23.)

*Asparagus*: If served as a separate course, asparagus is eaten in the fingers, each spear being dipped in melted butter or dressing, which is poured on the side of the plate. It helps if, when you cook the asparagus, you leave on part of the firm stalk to serve as a 'handle'. Lay a small knife and fork to be used to retrieve any of the tips which may break off. Finger bowls are a help.

*Avocado Pears*: Serve on a small plate, with a teaspoon. It's in order to use your other hand to steady the pear.

*Corn on the Cob*: It is easier to eat this vegetable if special holders are provided to spear into each end of the cob, instead of having to grasp it in the fingers. In any case a small knife and fork should also be laid, the knife to spread butter and the fork to eat the last bits.

*Melon*: For easier eating, pre-cut the melon flesh into bite-sized pieces and arrange these back on the skin. Provide a fruit knife and fork, which is also the best equipment if you have not pre-cut the melon. For the little Charentais and

To eat Globe Artichokes: Dip the base of each leaf in melted butter or a dressing and suck off the soft part

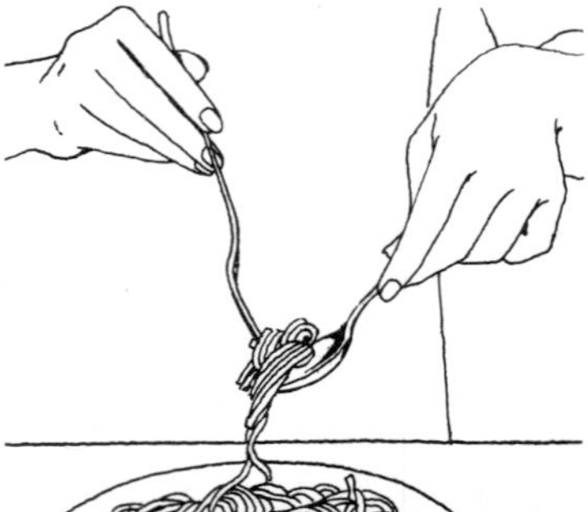

The Continental way of eating spaghetti, with the fork rotated against the bowl of the spoon

Ogen melons, which are served whole or cut in halves, provide a teaspoon.

*Chicken in a Basket*: Fingers only are used, so have plenty of thick paper napkins, and finger bowls if possible (or offer disposable plastic gloves, Corner House fashion).

*Pasta*: Lay a spoon, fork and knife, and serve the pasta in a soup plate. The skilful will twist the strands round the fork in the bowl of the spoon (see sketch opposite), others will use the knife and fork, then the spoon to pick up the difficult bits. It doesn't matter which.

*Lobster*: It's probably more sensible to serve lobster as a salad or in some other way in which the flesh is taken out of the shell. If you serve lobster halves, crack the claws and provide a fish knife and fork.

*Mediterranean Prawns*: Most people find it much easier to pull the shell off the prawns in the fingers and then eat the flesh with the aid of a small fish fork, but lay both fish knife and fork, to meet all preferences.

*Mussels (Moules Marinière)*: These are best eaten from a bowl or soup plate, with a fork to get the mussel from the shell (while this is held in the fingers) and a spoon for the liquor. A discard plate for the shells is essential, and finger bowls are helpful.

*Oysters*: A small fork is all that is needed.

*Prawn or Lobster Cocktail*: Put a teaspoon on the plate which holds the fish cocktail.

*Bouillabaisse*: Serve this thick peasant fish soup with crusty bread, a spoon and a fork to facilitate breaking up the larger pieces of fish. Alternatively, you can pour off the liquor and serve it in bowls, then present the fish to be eaten with a fish knife and fork and bread.

*French Onion Soup*: A soup spoon usually suffices.

## Chilled Cucumber Soup

1 small onion
750 ml white stock
1 large cucumber
A sprig of mint
1 level tbsp. (15 ml) cornflour
2–3 tbsp. (30–45 ml) single cream
Salt and pepper
Green colouring
Cucumber garnish (or mint)

*Serves 4–6*

1. Peel and slice the onion and simmer with the stock for 15 minutes.
2. Cut off some slices of the cucumber for garnish. Peel and finely slice the rest and add to the pan, with the mint.
3. Sieve the soup or purée it in an electric blender, return it to the pan and reheat.
4. Blend the cornflour with a little cold water to a smooth cream. Stir in a little of the hot soup, return this mixture to the pan and bring to the boil, stirring until the soup thickens. Cook for a further 2–3 minutes.

5. Stir in the cream, adjust the seasoning and re-heat without boiling.
6. Tint with green colouring, pour into a large bowl, cover and chill.
7. Serve garnished with the cucumber slices (or with mint, if preferred).

## Melon and Grape Cocktail

A medium-sized melon — about 1½ kilo
200 g black grapes
2–3 tbsp. (30–45 ml) oil
Salt and pepper
1 tbsp. (15 ml) lemon juice
Chopped parsley to garnish

*Serves 6*

1. Cut the melon in half lengthwise and remove the seeds.
2. Using a parisienne cutter, scoop out balls of melon flesh; leave to stand in a basin with the melon juice (p. 52).
3. Halve and de-seed the grapes and add to the melon (p. 52).
4. Add the oil to the salt and pepper in a bowl, and when well blended, whisk in the lemon juice with a fork.
5. Just before serving, combine the fruit with the dressing and pile the mixture into stemmed glasses.
6. Garnish with chopped parsley.

## Prawn Cocktail

150 g peeled prawns (fresh or frozen)
½ a lettuce
Salt and pepper
2 tbsp. (30 ml) mayonnaise
2 tbsp. (30 ml) tomato ketchup
2 tbsp. (30 ml) single cream
A squeeze of lemon juice or a dash of Worcestershire sauce
Cucumber slices or lemon wedges to garnish

*Serves 4*

1. Prepare the prawns if necessary.
2. Shred the lettuce; line some small glasses with it.
3. Mix the remaining ingredients together to make a dressing.
4. Combine the prawns and dressing, pile into the lined glasses and garnish with cucumber or lemon.

## Liver Pâté

1 large onion
150 g streaky bacon
2 cloves of garlic
200 g lamb's liver
50 g butter
200 g chicken livers
A piece of lemon peel
2 bay leaves
A pinch of dried basil
Salt and black pepper
1 level tbsp. (15 ml) tomato paste
6 tbsp. (90 ml) chicken stock

*Serves 6*

1. Heat the oven to 177°C (mark 4, 350°F).
2. Peel and slice the onion; rind the bacon and chop it finely.
3. Skin the garlic and crush well. Wash and cut up the liver.
4. Melt the butter and sauté the onion for 3 minutes. Add the bacon and sauté for 5 minutes. Add all the remaining ingredients, cover and simmer for $\frac{3}{4}$ hr.
5. Drain off and retain the liquor. Remove the bay leaves and lemon peel.
6. Put the pâté mixture through the mincer.
7. Mix with the liquor and put the mixture into a greased tin measuring 8 × 3$\frac{1}{2}$ ins. (20 × 8.75 cm).
8. Bake for 50–60 mins.
9. Cool and chill; serve with hot toast.

## Kipper Pâté

A 7-oz. (approx. 200-g) bag of frozen kipper fillets
$\frac{1}{2}$ a clove of garlic
125 g butter
Juice of $\frac{1}{2}$ a lemon
Yolk of 1 hard-boiled egg
Toast triangles and watercress to garnish

*Serves 6–8*

1. Immerse the bag of frozen kipper fillets in boiling water for 1 min.
2. Take the fillets from the bag, and remove any skin.
3. Skin and chop the garlic; soften the butter. Pound the fish with the garlic, butter, lemon juice and egg yolk.
4. Turn the mixture out into a soufflé dish or 6–8 ramekin dishes, and chill. Serve with toast triangles and sprigs of watercress.

## Fish en Cocotte

2 eggs
A $6\frac{1}{2}$-oz. (185-g) can of herrings in tomato sauce
50 g butter
50 g fresh breadcrumbs
Lemon and parsley

*Serves 4*

1. Heat the oven to 177°C (mark 4, 350°F), and put the eggs on to hard-boil for 12 mins.
2. Flake the contents of the can of herrings and divide between 4 ramekin or cocotte dishes.
3. Shell the hot eggs under cold water and slice them. Arrange on top of the herrings in the sauce.
4. Melt the butter in a small frying pan and fry the crumbs until golden.
5. Put 1 tbsp. (approx. 15–20 ml) of the crumb mixture on top of each ramekin.
6. Bake for 15 mins. Garnish with thick lemon slices and a little parsley.

## Spicy Hot Grapefruit

2 grapefruit
2 tbsp. (30 ml) brown sugar
1½ tsp. (7.5 ml) ground cinnamon

*Serves 4*

1. Prepare the grapefruit by cutting each in half, vandyke fashion (p. 49), and loosening the flesh from the outer skin.
2. Cut between the segments, loosen completely and pile the flesh in the halved skins.
3. Mix the sugar and cinnamon together and sprinkle some over each grapefruit half.
4. 'Flash' the grapefruit under a hot grill, until the sugar caramelises. Serve immediately.

## Cheesy Tomatoes en Croûte

4 medium-sized firm tomatoes
100 g Cheddar cheese
100 g shortcrust pastry
Beaten egg

*Serves 4*

1. Set the oven to 204°C (mark 6, 400°F).
2. Skin the tomatoes and cut a slice from the top of each, then scoop out the seeds. Grate the cheese.

3. Fill the tomato shells with cheese and replace the slice.
4. Reserve a little pastry for decoration. Divide the pastry into 4 equal portions.
5. Knead lightly and roll into rounds, each large enough to wrap round a tomato.
6. Brush the pastry rounds evenly with beaten egg and lightly dust with flour.
7. Place the tomatoes cut side down on the pastry rounds and draw up the pastry to enclose them. Crimp the edges firmly together.
8. Place sealed side down on a baking sheet. Brush with more egg and decorate with pastry leaves.
9. Chill in a cool place for ½ hr. Heat oven and bake tomatoes for 15 mins.
10. Reduce the heat to 177°C (mark 4, 350°F) and continue to cook for a further 5 mins. Serve warm.

## French Onion Soup

| | |
|---|---|
| 200 g medium-sized onions | Salt and pepper |
| 40 g butter | A bay leaf |
| 1½ level tbsp. (22.5 ml) flour | Slices of French bread |
| 750 ml brown stock | Grated cheese to garnish |

*Serves 4–6*

1. Peel and slice the onions.
2. Melt the butter in a pan and fry the onions for 10–15 mins., till browned. Stir in the flour, mixing well.
3. Pour in the stock gradually, season and add the bay leaf. Bring to the boil and simmer in a covered pan for 30 mins.
4. Remove the bay leaf.
5. Put a slice of bread into each individual soup bowl, pour on some soup and top with grated cheese.
6. Alternatively, put all the soup in a casserole, float the slices of bread on it, cover with grated cheese and put under the grill or in a hot oven until the cheese is melted and bubbling.

## Avocado Pear

An avocado pear
A little lemon juice (optional)
Salt and pepper
¼ level tsp. (1.25 ml) dry mustard
¼ level tsp. (1.25 ml) sugar
1 tbsp. (15 ml) vinegar
2 tbsp. (30 ml) oil
Slices of tomato and cucumber to garnish

*Serves 2*

1. Cut the pear open with a stainless steel knife, making a deep cut through the flesh up to the stone and encircling the fruit.
2. Separate the halves by gently twisting them in opposite directions; discard the stone.
3. If the pear is not to be served at once, sprinkle it with lemon juice or cover closely with waxed paper to prevent the flesh from discolouring.
4. Make a vinaigrette dressing; put the salt, pepper, mustard and sugar in a screw-topped jar, add the vinegar and oil, screw the lid well down on the jar and shake vigorously until the dressing forms an emulsion.
5. Just before serving the avocado, fill the hollow with the vinaigrette dressing and garnish with slices of tomato and cucumber.

## Corn on the Cob

4 corn cobs
Melted butter
Salt and freshly ground pepper

*Serves 4*

1. Choose cobs which are plump and of a pale golden yellow colour, and cook while really fresh.
2. Remove the outside leaves and silky threads, put the cobs into boiling unsalted water (salt toughens corn) and cook for 12–20 mins., depending on size.
3. Drain well, and serve with melted butter, salt and freshly ground pepper.
4. To make it easier to eat corn on the cob, insert at each end a special 2-pronged fork, and hold by these.

## Salad Dip Platter

1 clove of garlic
A 5-fl. oz. (140-g) carton of fat-free yogurt
200 g cottage cheese
Salt and pepper
A lettuce
A bunch of radishes
6 new carrots
2 red-skinned eating apples
A little lemon juice
½ a cucumber
A bunch of spring onions
Cheese biscuits

*Serves 6–8*

1. Peel and crush or chop the garlic.
2. Mix the yogurt and cheese together, then beat or blend until the mixture is smooth. Add the garlic and season to taste. Leave for at least 1 hr. before serving.
3. Wash the lettuce and place in a polythene bag in the refrigerator to crisp up. Make radish flowers and stand these in cold water.
4. Scrape and slice the carrots; slice the apples, without peeling, and dip in lemon juice; slice the cucumber.
5. Trim and wash the spring onions.
6. Put the bowl of cheese dip in the centre of a platter. Put some cheese biscuits at two points on the dish. Line the rest of the dish with lettuce, and arrange the salad vegetables on it as seen in picture.

# FISH

## Stuffed Rolled Plaice

1 plaice
1 egg
25 g cheese, grated
1 tsp. (5 ml) chopped parsley
40 g fresh white breadcrumbs
1 rasher of streaky bacon
25 g butter, melted
Salt and pepper
Breadcrumbs for top
Parsley or lemon sauce
Parsley and butter balls to garnish

*Serves 2*

1. Fillet and skin the plaice.
2. Heat the oven to 177°C (mark 4, 350°F).
3. Hard-boil the egg for 12 mins.; shell and chop it.
4. Mix the egg with the cheese, parsley and breadcrumbs.
5. Rind, chop and sauté the bacon and drain thoroughly; add to the egg mixture, with butter and seasoning.
6. Spread this mixture over the skinned side of the fillets and roll up, starting from tail end; secure if necessary with wooden cocktail sticks.
7. Put in a buttered ovenproof dish, sprinkle with remaining crumbs and bake in centre of oven for 20 mins., till the fish is tender and the crumbs crisp.

8. Make the sauce, using the stock from the fish.
9. Garnish the fish with parsley and balls of butter.

## Sole Meunière

2 small soles, skinned
Seasoned flour
75 g butter
Juice of 1 lemon
1 tbsp. (15 ml) chopped parsley
Lemon slices to garnish

*Serves* 2

1. Cut off the fins and wipe the fish. Coat with flour.
2. Heat 50 g of the butter in the frying pan, put the fish in, upper side first, and fry gently for 5 mins., until brown.
3. Turn the soles over carefully and continue frying for a further 5 mins., or until tender and golden. Drain on paper and place on a hot serving dish.
4. Heat the fat gently until lightly browning. Add the lemon juice and parsley and immediately pour the mixture over the fish.
5. Garnish with lemon wedges or butterflies (p. 111).

## Tuna au Gratin

125 ml white coating sauce
125 g Cheddar cheese, grated
2 tbsp. (30 ml) dried onion flakes
3 tbsp. (45 ml) chopped parsley
A 7-oz. (200-g) can of tuna
A 6-oz. (170-g) can of pimientos, chopped
Salt and pepper
A baked pastry case, 9 inches × $1\frac{1}{2}$ inches deep (22.5 × 4 cm)

*Serves* 6

1. Heat the oven to 218°C (mark 7, 425°F).
2. Make the sauce, using the roux method. Add 75 g of the cheese, the onion flakes, parsley, drained tuna and pimiento to the sauce; season well.
3. Pour the mixture into the pastry case.
4. Sprinkle with the remaining cheese and bake for 10–15 mins.
5. Serve with a tossed green salad and jacket potatoes.

## Mackerel with Gooseberry Sauce

400 g small gooseberries
4 mackerel
4 rashers of bacon, rinded
Salt and freshly ground pepper
25 g margarine
1 tbsp. (15 ml) lemon juice
25 g sugar
125 ml water
1 level tsp. (5 ml) dried fennel
Lemon and fennel to garnish

*Serves 4*

1. Top and tail the gooseberries.
2. Heat the oven to 177°C (mark 4, 350°F).
3. Prepare the mackerel: remove the fins and head; slit down the underside and remove the 'innards'; wash and dry.
4. Chop the bacon and sauté for a few mins.; drain, then place in a bowl.
5. Add half the gooseberries to the bacon and season the mixture. Stuff the fish with this filling.
6. Melt the margarine in a pan and brush the fish over with it.
7. Place the fish in a piece of buttered aluminium foil, sprinkle with salt and pepper and a little lemon juice and completely cover with the foil.

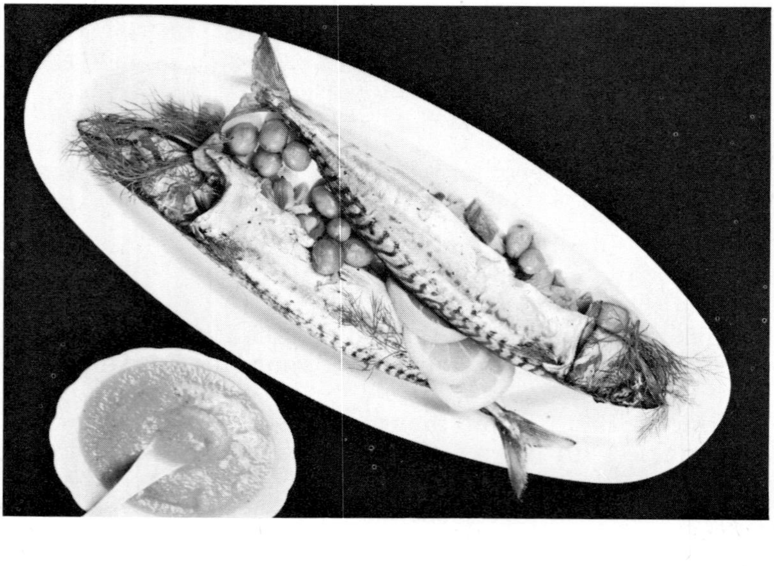

8. Bake for 25 mins.
9. Dissolve the sugar in the water and simmer the rest of the gooseberries in this liquid for 5 mins.
10. Sieve or put through the blender. Stir in the fennel and return the sauce to the pan to heat through.
11. Place the fish on a platter and garnish with lemon and fennel; serve the gooseberry sauce separately. A few cooked gooseberries can be reserved for garnishing.

## Russian Fish Pie

225 g white fish, e.g. cod, haddock
25 g butter
25 g flour
125 ml milk and liquid from fish
2 tbsp. (30 ml) chopped parsley
Salt and pepper
1 hard-boiled egg, chopped
150 g bought flaky pastry
Beaten egg to glaze

*Serves 4*

1. Heat the oven to 232°C (mark 8, 450°F).
2. Wash the fish in cold water and remove the skin, using the back of a knife. Poach gently in salted water for 15 mins., retaining 125 ml of the cooking liquid to make the sauce. Flake the fish when cooked.
3. Melt the butter, stir in the flour and cook for 2–3 mins. Remove the pan from the heat and gradually stir in the fish liquid, with the milk.
4. Bring to the boil and continue to stir until the sauce thickens.
5. Mix half the sauce with the flaked fish, salt, pepper, parsley and chopped egg.
6. Roll out the pastry thinly into a fairly large square and place on a baking tray.
7. Put the filling in the centre in a square, brush the edges of the pastry with beaten egg and draw them up to the middle, to form an envelope shape.
8. Press the edges well together and flake and scallop them.
9. Brush the pie with beaten egg and bake towards the top of the oven for about 30 mins., until golden. Serve with the remaining parsley sauce.

## Flaky Fish Roll

300 g haddock or other white fish fillets
A little butter and milk to cook fish
Salt and pepper
200 g flaky pastry
4 lean bacon rashers, rinded and chopped
100 g mushrooms, sliced
Beaten egg to glaze
Lemon wedges and parsley to garnish

*Serves 4–6*

1. Heat the oven to 218°C (mark 7, 425°F).
2. Wash and wipe the fish, put on a greased plate, dot with butter and add 1 tbsp. (15 ml) milk and a little seasoning. Cover with another plate, place over a pan of boiling water and steam for 15 mins.
3. Roll out the pastry on a lightly floured board to give an oblong about 45 cm × 35 cm.
4. Drain, skin and flake the fish. Fry the bacon and drain on paper. Sauté the mushrooms in the bacon fat.
5. Spread the fish, bacon and cooled mushrooms over the pastry. Roll up tightly, sealing with beaten egg.
6. Place on a large baking sheet, brush lightly with egg and bake for 30 mins.
7. Serve cut in slices, with lemon wedges and parsley.

## Salmon Shells

2 eggs
250 ml binding sauce
A 7-oz. (approx. 200-g) can of salmon
A little chopped parsley
Salt and freshly ground pepper
200 g shortcrust pastry

*Serves 4*

1. Heat the oven to 204°C (mark 6, 400°F).
2. Put the eggs on to hard-boil for 12 mins. Grease 4 deep natural scallop shells.
3. Make the sauce and add the flaked salmon, the sliced eggs and the parsley; adjust the seasoning.
4. Divide the pastry into 4; using three-quarters of each piece, roll out and line the shells. Divide the filling between them. Roll out the remaining quarter-portions of pastry for the lids; brush with water and put, damp side down, over the fish mixture.

Salmon Shells

5. Seal the edges and trim off any excess pastry. Use the trimmings to make pastry leaves for decoration (p. 31).
6. Bake for 20–25 mins., until golden-brown.

## Cheese and Salmon Quiche

½ a medium-sized onion
100 g Cheddar cheese
100 g shortcrust pastry
1 egg
125 ml milk
Salt and pepper
A 3¾-oz. (approx. 100-g) can salmon, drained and flaked
Parsley sprigs for garnish

*Serves 4*

1. Heat the oven to 204°C (mark 6, 400°F).
2. Peel and grate the onion. Grate the cheese.
3. Roll pastry out thinly and line 4 individual 4-in. (10-cm) flan rings, or one 8-in. (20-cm) ring.
4. Whisk together the egg, milk, salt and pepper, then add the onion and cheese and mix well.
5. Divide the flaked salmon between the pastry cases and spoon the cheese custard over.
6. Bake in centre of oven for 15 mins. Reduce the heat to 177°C (mark 4, 350°F) and cook for a further 25 mins., until the quiches are golden-brown and set.
7. Remove the flan rings, and serve the quiches hot or cold, garnish with sprigs of parsley.

## Prawn and Egg Kedgeree

2 eggs
100 g long-grain rice
Salt and pepper
25 g butter
100 g peeled prawns
½ a lemon
Chopped parsley and lemon twists to garnish

*Serves 3–4*

1. Hard-boil the eggs for 12 mins.
2. Boil rice in boiling salted water for 12–15 mins.
3. Melt the butter in a saucepan; add prawns, 1 tbsp. (15 ml) lemon juice and seasoning; cook for a few mins.
4. Remove eggs from pan, pour cold water over, then crack the shells; slice the eggs and add to the prawns.
5. Drain the rice, then rinse with hot water; add to the prawn mixture, mix well and re-season if necessary.
6. Pile the kedgeree in a hot dish, sprinkle with chopped parsley and add the lemon twists. Serve with a salad.

## Soused Herrings

4 large or 6–8 small herrings, cleaned and boned
Salt and pepper
1 small onion
6 peppercorns
1–2 bay leaves
A few parsley stalks
125 ml malt vinegar
125 ml water

*Serves 4*

1. Heat the oven to 177°C (mark 4, 350°F).
2. Trim off the heads, tails and fins of the herrings, sprinkle the fish with salt and pepper and roll up from the head end.
3. Peel the onion and slice finely.
4. Pack the herrings into a fairly shallow ovenproof dish and add the onion, peppercorns and herbs.
5. Pour in the vinegar and enough water to almost cover the fish.
6. Cover with greaseproof paper or foil and bake in centre of oven for about ¾ hr., or until tender.
7. Leave to cool in the cooking liquid. Serve as an appetiser, or with salads.

## Salmon and Rice Moulds

200 g long-grain rice
A 7-oz. (approx. 200-g) can of salmon
2 tbsp. (30 ml) lemon juice
4 tbsp. (60 ml) oil
1 banana
1 small piece of cucumber
Lemon twists and parsley to garnish

*Serves 4*

1. Boil the rice in boiling salted water for 10–15 mins., until tender.
2. Drain thoroughly and pour boiling water through it to separate the grains; leave to cool.
3. Drain and flake the salmon.
4. Beat the lemon juice and oil well together.
5. Slice and chop the banana, and toss in the lemon dressing; slice the cucumber.
6. Lightly oil the inside of 4 teacups and place a slice of cucumber in the base of each.
7. Combine the rice, salmon and bananas and press a small portion of mixture firmly into each cup. Chill well.
8. Turn out; garnish each with a lemon twist and parsley.

## Fish Jalousie

A $3\frac{3}{4}$-oz. (approx. 100-g) can of brisling in oil
200 g bought puff pastry
Beaten egg to glaze

*Serves 6–8*

1. Heat the oven to 232°C (mark 8, 450°F).
2. Mash the contents of the can of brisling.
3. Roll out the pastry to an oblong 32 × 27 cm.
4. Cut in half crosswise and place one half on a baking tray.
5. Spread the mashed brisling over the pastry on the baking tray, to within 1 cm of the edges.
6. Brush the edges of the pastry with beaten egg, cover with the other half of the pastry and seal the edges. Slash across at intervals of 2.5 cm.
7. Bake for 20 mins., then cool on a wire rack.
8. Cut into fingers before serving.

## Haddock and Sweet Pepper Sauté

300 g thick haddock fillet
Seasoned flour
2 rashers of streaky bacon
25 g butter
$\frac{1}{2}$ a red pepper, de-seeded and chopped
$\frac{1}{2}$ a pkt. of instant potato (approx. 75 g)
A knob of butter
Milk
25 g Cheddar cheese, grated
2 tbsp. (30 ml) single cream (optional)

*Serves 2*

1. Skin the fish, cut into largish pieces and dredge with seasoned flour.
2. Scissor-snip the bacon into small pieces.
3. Lightly fry the bacon and add the butter; when melted, add the fish; turn it occasionally to brown both sides, but avoid breaking it up.
4. Blanch the chopped red pepper in water for a few mins., then drain. Add to the fish and heat through.
5. Make up the potato as directed, using butter and milk to give a piping consistency.
6. Beat the cheese into the potato. When it is melted, pipe

the potato round 2 large, deep scallop shells. Brown under a hot grill.

7. Pile fish mixture in the centre. Spoon half the cream over each, and brown again under a hot grill.

## Individual Tuna Pizza

200 g bought puff pastry
1 onion
25 g butter
A 7-oz. (approx. 200-g) can of tuna
A 7-oz. (approx. 200-g) can of tomatoes
50 g cheese, grated
Gherkin fans and black olives for garnish

*Serves 4*

1. Heat the oven to 232°C (mark 8, 450°F).
2. Roll out the pastry into a piece about 25 cm square.
3. Using a pastry wheel, cut into 4, to give 12.5-cm squares. Place each piece in a shallow 4-in. (9-cm) square or round Yorkshire pudding tin.
4. Peel the onion and chop finely. Melt the butter and sauté the onion until clear.
5. Mix the onion with the drained tuna and pile onto the pastry. Top with tomato and sprinkle with the cheese.
6. Bake for 10–15 mins., till well risen and golden-brown. Serve garnished with gherkin fans and olives.

## Cheese Soufflé

| | |
|---|---|
| 25 g butter | 3 eggs, separated |
| 25 g flour | 75 g cheese, grated |
| 1 level tsp. (5 ml) dry mustard | A pinch of dried thyme |
| 125 ml milk | Salt and pepper |

*Serves 4–6*

1. Heat the oven to 177°C (mark 4, 350°F).
2. Grease a 2-pint (approx. 1-litre) soufflé dish.
3. Melt the butter in a saucepan and stir in the flour and mustard; cook slowly for 2–3 mins.
4. Gradually stir in the milk and beat until smooth.
5. Cook for a further 3–4 mins. Beat the egg yolks into the sauce, and stir in the cheese and thyme.
6. Season with salt and pepper. Fold in the stiffly whisked egg whites until evenly distributed.
7. Turn mixture into the dish and bake for 45 mins., until well risen and golden-brown. Serve at once.

## Eggs à la Mornay

| | |
|---|---|
| 4 eggs | Salt and pepper |
| 25 g butter | 50 g cheese, grated |
| 25 g flour | Butter for topping |
| 250 ml milk plus 2 tbsp. (30 ml) | Chopped parsley for garnish |

*Serves 4*

1. Put the eggs on to hard-boil for 12 mins.
2. Melt the butter, stir in the flour and cook the roux for 2–3 mins. Remove from the heat.
3. Stir in the milk, boil and continue to stir until the mixture is thick; adjust the seasoning.
4. Add most of the cheese, saving a little for garnishing.
5. Slice the eggs, using an egg slicer; lay them in an au gratin dish, reserving 4–5 slices for garnishing.
6. Pour sauce over eggs, sprinkle with remaining cheese, dot with butter and pop the dish under the grill.
7. Garnish with the egg slices and parsley.

## Curried Cheese Eggs

| | |
|---|---|
| 4 eggs | Salt and pepper |
| 25 g butter | Milk if necessary |
| 50 g cheese, grated | Chopped chives or paprika pepper for garnish |
| ½ level tsp. (2.5 ml) curry powder | |

*Serves 4*

1. Hard-boil the eggs, then cool in running cold water.
2. Shell the eggs, cut each in half lengthwise and scoop out the yolks.
3. Cream the butter until soft, and mix in the cheese, egg yolks and curry powder.
4. Season with salt and pepper, and add a little milk, if necessary, to give a piping consistency.
5. Place the mixture in a piping bag fitted with a ½-in. (1 cm) vegetable nozzle, and pipe it into the egg whites.
6. Garnish with chopped chives or paprika. Serve with a tossed salad.

## Cheese and Bacon Quiche

100 g shortcrust pastry
165 ml milk
2 eggs, beaten
Salt and freshly ground pepper
A pinch of grated nutmeg
100 g streaky bacon
150 g Cheddar cheese
Garnish

*Serves 6*

1. Heat the oven to 204°C (mark 6, 400°F).
2. Roll out the pastry to line an 8-in. (20-cm) flan case, placed on a baking sheet.
3. Bake blind for 15 mins. (p. 41).
4. Stir the milk into the beaten eggs and season with salt, pepper and nutmeg.
5. Rind the bacon and cut into strips; grate the cheese. Put the bacon and cheese over the surface of the pastry, then pour the egg mixture over.
6. Bake for 15 mins., then reduce the oven temperature to 177°C (mark 4, 350°F) and continue to cook for about 30 mins., until the quiche is just set.
7. Garnish—for example, with sliced tomato—and serve hot, or cold with a tossed green salad.

## Cheese and Leek Pie

250 g shortcrust pastry
450 g leeks
40 g margarine
40 g flour
250 ml leek stock
100 g Cheddar cheese, grated
Salt and pepper

*Serves 4–6*

1. Heat the oven to 204°C (mark 6, 400°F).
2. Use half the pastry to line the base of a 9-in. (22-cm) ovenproof plate.
3. Wash and slice the leeks, blanch in boiling salted water for 5 mins. and drain, retaining the liquor.
4. Melt the margarine, stir in the flour and cook for a few mins. Gradually add 250 ml of the leek stock. Stir the grated cheese into the sauce and season well.
5. Arrange the drained leeks over the pastry and coat with the sauce. Brush the pastry rim with water.
6. Roll out the remaining pastry to make a lid; place it over filling. Seal the edges and knock up.
7. Bake for 45 mins., until the pastry is golden-brown.

## Baked Cheese Celery

2 heads of celery
80 g butter
40 g flour
375 ml celery liquid
40 g browned breadcrumbs
75 g cheese, grated
Butter to top

*Serves 4*

1. Wash the celery, cut into 8-cm lengths and boil in salted water till tender; drain, reserving liquid.
2. Melt half the butter in a pan, stir in the flour and cook for 30 secs.
3. Withdraw pan from heat, stir in the liquid, bring to the boil, stirring, and cook for 3 mins. Season well.
4. In a frying pan melt the remaining butter and fry the breadcrumbs until light brown. In a pie dish arrange alternate layers of celery, sauce, cheese and breadcrumbs, ending with cheese and buttered breadcrumbs.
5. Dot with butter and bake in the oven at 218°C (mark 7, 425°F) for 15 mins.
6. Serve hot, with stuffed tomatoes.

## Pizza

200 g plain flour
Salt and pepper
1 level tsp. (5 ml) fresh yeast or
½ level tsp. (2.5 ml) dried yeast
½ level tsp. (2.5 ml) sugar
125 ml water
5 g lard
Oil
100 g Cheddar cheese, grated
A 14-oz. (approx. 400-g) can of tomatoes
1 level tsp. (5 ml) dried oregano
A 2-oz. (approx. 55-g) can of anchovy fillets
25 g black olives

*Serves 4–6*

Pizza is an Italian dish made from yeast dough, which is rolled into a flat round and covered with tomato, grated cheese, anchovies or other additions such as sautéed mushrooms and strips of thinly sliced ham (raw or cooked) or bacon. The Italians use Mozzarella cheese for their basic Pizza, but this is not available everywhere in England; however, Bel Paese or Gruyère makes a very good substitute, while Cheddar cheese, which is cheaper and even easier to obtain, is quite acceptable.

1. Sift the flour and ½ level tsp. (2.5 ml) salt.
2. Blend the fresh yeast in the water (or, if using dried yeast, dissolve ½ level tsp. sugar in 125 ml water and sprinkle the dried yeast on top; leave until frothy, which takes about 10 mins.).
3. Rub the lard into the flour and bind together with the yeast liquid. Work to a firm dough, until it will leave the bowl clean.
4. Turn the dough on to a lightly floured board and knead by pulling it up and pressing it down until it feels smooth and elastic.
5. Put the dough inside a lightly oiled polythene bag, tie lightly (or put in a pan or plastic storage jar with a lid) and leave to rise until it doubles in size and springs back when pressed with a floured finger. The rising times vary as follows:

   45–60 mins. in a warm place
   2 hrs. at room temperature

Pizza

12 hrs. in a cold room or larder
24 hours in a refrigerator (refrigerated dough should be allowed to return to room temperature before it is shaped)

6. Heat the oven to 232°C (mark 8, 450°F).
7. Turn the risen dough out onto a board. Flatten it with the knuckles or a rolling pin into a long strip. Brush it with oil and roll up like a Swiss roll. Repeat 3 times in all.
8. Roll out the dough to fit an $8\frac{1}{2}$-in. (21-cm) plain flan ring placed on an oiled baking sheet.
9. Brush the dough with oil and cover with alternate layers of grated cheese, tomato and seasonings plus oregano; finish with a layer of cheese.
10. Decorate with a lattice of anchovy fillets. Stone and halve the olives and complete the decoration with these (see picture).
11. Bake for 20–30 mins. on the top shelf of the oven.
12. Garnish with parsley or watercress and serve hot.

## Cheese and Ham Pancakes

100 g plain flour
Salt and pepper
1 egg
200 ml milk
200 g mature Cheddar cheese
8 thin slices of ham
½ level tsp. (2.5 ml) mixed dried herbs
25 g butter
Lard for frying

*Serves 4*

1. Sift together the flour and a pinch of salt.
2. Make a well in the centre, pour in the lightly beaten egg and gradually add half the milk, beating all the time.
3. Beat well, then stir in the remaining milk.
4. Grate the cheese, chop the ham, and mix with the herbs and seasoning.
5. Melt the butter in a frying pan and sauté the chopped ham and the seasonings for a few mins. Add the grated cheese and cook for a few mins. Keep this filling warm.
6. Grease a frying pan lightly with lard. Pour in enough batter to cover the base of the pan thinly, and cook quickly. When the surface is dull, toss the pancake. Repeat with the remaining batter.

7. Put the pancakes into a cool oven (lowest setting) to keep warm.
8. Fold each pancake into 4; divide the ham filling into equal portions and fill each pancake. 'Flash' them under the grill.
9. Serve with grilled tomatoes (these may be vandyked as seen in the picture). Garnish with parsley.

## Cheese Fondue

300 g Cheddar or other well-flavoured cheese
1 clove of garlic
40 g butter
2 tbsp. (30 ml) flour
250 ml medium-sweet cider
A loaf of French bread
Salt and pepper
$\frac{1}{4}$ level tsp. (1.25 ml) grated nutmeg

*Serves 4*

*Note*: Fondue is easier to serve if you have a hot-plate, heated by nightlights or electricity, to keep it warm.

1. Grate the cheese.
2. Peel and halve the garlic clove and rub it round the inside of a flameproof casserole.
3. Melt the butter in the dish over a low heat, stir in the flour and cook for a few secs.
4. Measure the cider, pour it slowly into the flour mixture, stir and bring to the boil, stirring all the time; allow to simmer for 2 mins.
5. Stir the grated cheese into the sauce and heat gently until it melts.
6. Cut the bread into bite-sized pieces.
7. Season the fondue with salt, pepper and nutmeg and mix well. Light the nightlights or switch on the electricity in the heater.
8. Transfer the fondue to the hot-plate. It's now ready for you to dip in your pieces of bread, speared on forks. Stir the mixture occasionally if it thickens.

## Cheese and Potato Cakes

450 g potatoes
25 g butter
150 g cheese, grated
1 tbsp. (15 ml) chopped chives (or grated onion)
Salt and pepper
2 level tbsp (30 ml) flour, if necessary
Beaten egg and dry breadcrumbs

*Serves 4*

1. Heat the oven to 190°C (mark 5, 375°F).
2. Peel the potatoes and boil in salted water until cooked. Drain thoroughly and mash well.
3. Mix the potatoes with the butter, cheese and chives. Add salt and pepper and beat until smooth, adding a little flour if necessary to give a firm texture.
4. Turn the mixture onto a floured board and form into a roll. Cut into 2.5 cm slices and shape into round cakes. Coat with beaten egg and breadcrumbs (p. 88).
5. Place on a baking sheet and bake near the top of the oven for 20 mins.
6. Serve with grilled bacon and tomatoes.

## Quick Curried Eggs

100 g long-grain rice
4 eggs
1 medium-sized onion
1 cooking apple
A little lemon juice to cover apple
25 g dripping or lard
1–2 tbsp. (15–30 ml) curry powder
1 tsp. (5 ml) marmalade
1 tbsp. (15 ml) sultanas
Salt and pepper
1 tsp. (5 ml) lemon juice
375 ml chicken stock

*Serves 4*

1. Boil the rice in salted water for 10 mins., until soft. Put the eggs on to hard-boil for 12 mins.
2. Peel the onion and slice thinly; peel, core and roughly chop the apple and leave it in the lemon juice, to avoid discoloration.
3. Meanwhile heat the fat in a frying pan; add the onion and fry until soft.
4. Stir in the remaining flavourings and stock, cover, and cook for 15 mins.

5. Shell eggs, arrange on rice and pour the sauce over.
6. As accompaniments, serve: a small can of pineapple pieces, drained; 2 bananas, sliced and tossed in lemon juice; 2 tomatoes, sliced; sultanas; shredded coconut.

## Cheese and Tomato Bars

100 g cheese
200 g tomatoes
Salt and pepper
½ level tsp. (2.5 ml) dried basil
200 g flaky pastry

*Serves 6*

1. Heat the oven to 218°C (mark 7, 425°F).
2. Grate the cheese; peel and slice the tomatoes, and mix both with the cheese. Add the seasoning and basil.
3. Divide the pastry in half and roll out into 2 oblongs about 30 cm by 10 cm. Slash one piece at intervals, using kitchen scissors.
4. Spread the tomato and cheese mixture over the plain piece of pastry, leaving 1 cm clear all the way round.
5. Damp the pastry edges with water, cover with the remaining slashed piece of pastry, and bake for 15–20 mins.
6. When the pastry is cold, cut into bars 2–3 cm wide.

## Egg Mayonnaise

4 eggs
A few lettuce leaves
Chopped parsley or paprika to garnish

*For the Mayonnaise*

1 egg yolk
½ level tsp. (2.5 ml) dry mustard
¼ level tsp. (1.25 ml) pepper
½ level tsp. (2.5 ml) salt
½ level tsp. (2.5 ml) sugar
125 ml oil
1 tbsp. (15 ml) vinegar

*Serves 4*

1. Put the 4 eggs on to hard-boil for 12 mins.
2. Shell the eggs and cut them lengthwise into halves or quarters.
3. Put the egg yolk into a basin with the seasonings and sugar; mix thoroughly. Add the oil drop by drop, stirring briskly with a whisk or wooden spoon, until the sauce is thick and smooth. When all the oil is added, add the vinegar gradually and mix thoroughly.
4. Wash and drain the lettuce and put on a shallow dish. Place the eggs on the lettuce, cut side down.
5. Coat the eggs with the mayonnaise and garnish with parsley or paprika.

## Cheese and Apple Salad

200 g spinach
4 medium-sized red eating apples
Lemon juice for apples
200 g Cheddar cheese
Salt and pepper
2 tbsp. (30 ml) oil
4 tbsp. lemon juice

*Serves 4–6*

1. Wash the spinach and apples.
2. Cut the unpeeled apples into largish dice, and leave these standing in lemon juice until required.
3. Chop the cheese into large dice.
4. Make a dressing by shaking the salt, pepper, oil and lemon juice in a screw-top jar till well mixed.

Cheese and Apple Salad

5. Drain the apples, and toss them and the cheese in the dressing. Arrange the mixture on a bed of spinach.

## Egg, Ham and Rice Salad

150 g long-grain rice
200 g ham
1 level tsp. (5 ml) dried onion flakes
2 level tsp. (10 ml) dried pepper flakes
2 tbsp. (30 ml) corn oil
1 tbsp. (15 ml) vinegar
1 tbsp (15 ml) lemon juice
Salt and pepper
2 hard-boiled eggs, chopped

*Serves 4*

1. Boil the rice in the usual way; allow to cool.
2. Cut the ham into slices, then into long strips.
3. Soak the onion and pepper flakes in cold water to soften; drain them.
4. Make a dressing with the oil, vinegar, lemon juice and seasoning.
5. Lightly mix all the ingredients, and pile the salad on a serving dish.

# MEAT

## Latticed Meat Roll

1 clove of garlic (optional)
200 g sausage-meat
200 g lean minced meat
2 tbsp. (30 ml) tomato paste
1 tsp. (5 ml) mixed herbs
Salt and freshly ground pepper
1 small egg, beaten
300 g bought puff pastry
Beaten egg to glaze

*Serves 4*

1. Heat the oven to 218°C (mark 7, 425°F).
2. Peel and crush the clove of garlic (if used).
3. Blend together the sausage-meat, minced meat, tomato paste, herbs, garlic, salt and pepper; bind with beaten egg.
4. Roll out the pastry into a 20-cm square. Shape the meat into a roll 20 cm long and place down the centre of pastry.
5. Make diagonal cuts 2.5 cm apart along the uncovered pastry at each side, to within 1 cm of the meat.

6. Brush pastry strips with egg and plait over meat.
7. Brush outside of pastry with egg; put on baking sheet.
8. Bake for 15 mins. Reduce heat to 177°C (mark 4, 350°F) and bake for about 45 mins. longer.
9. Serve hot, cut in slices, with sautéed mushrooms and asparagus or *haricots verts*, or serve cold with salad.

## Beef Cobbler

450 g chuck steak
2 onions
2 sticks of celery
3 carrots
½ a swede
40 g lard or 2 tbsp. (30 ml) oil
2 level tbsp. (30 ml) flour
250 ml beef stock
Salt and pepper

*Cobbler Topping*

200 g self-raising flour
A pinch of salt
50 g margarine
125 ml milk

*Serves 4*

1. Heat the oven to 163°C (mark 3, 325°F).
2. Cut the meat into 2.5 cm cubes.
3. Peel and chop the onions, chop the celery, scrape and slice the carrots and peel and dice the swede.
4. Heat the fat or oil and fry the onion until golden-brown; remove and place in a casserole.
5. Fry the celery, carrots and swede, drain and place in the casserole.
6. Fry the meat until brown—about 5 mins. Transfer to the casserole.
7. Add the flour to the fat remaining in the pan, stir well and add the stock gradually; bring to the boil, season and add to the casserole. Cover and cook in the centre of the oven for 1½–2 hours.
8. Make the cobbler topping by the usual scone method. Roll out the dough mixture 1 cm thick. Using a 2-in. (5-cm) cutter, cut 8 scone shapes and arrange on top of the casserole.
9. Turn up the oven to 232°C (mark 8, 450°F) and bake for a further 10–15 mins.

## Lancashire Hot-pot

8 middle neck chops
40 g margarine
200 g onions, peeled and sliced
4 medium-sized carrots, scraped and sliced
$1\frac{1}{2}$ tbsp. (22.5 ml) flour
250 ml stock
2 lamb's kidneys
Salt and pepper
450 g potatoes, peeled and sliced
Oil for brushing potatoes

*Serves 4*

1. Heat the oven to 163°C (mark 3, 325°F).
2. Remove any excess fat from the chops.
3. Melt the fat in a large pan and gently fry the chops for 2 mins. Remove, drain and place in a casserole.
4. Fry the onions and carrots for a few mins. Add the flour and cook for 1 min.
5. Pour the stock on and stir until boiling. Pour over meat.
6. Wash, skin and dice the kidneys and add, with seasoning.
7. Arrange the slices of potato on the top of the other ingredients, brush lightly with oil.
8. Cover and cook for 2 hrs., until the meat and potatoes are tender. For the last 20 mins. of the cooking time, remove the lid to allow the potatoes to brown.

## Meat Roly-poly

200 g suetcrust pastry
2 rashers of streaky bacon
1 onion
300 g minced beef
Salt
Freshly ground pepper
$\frac{1}{2}$–1 tsp. (2.5–5 ml) mixed herbs
1 tbsp. (15 ml) water

*Serves 4–6*

1. Prepare a steamer.
2. Make the pastry, roll it out to an oblong and damp the edges.
3. Rind and chop the bacon. Peel and chop the onion.
4. Add the bacon and onion to the minced beef, season well and add the herbs. Bind together with water.
5. Spread the filling on the pastry and roll it up, keeping the edges neat.

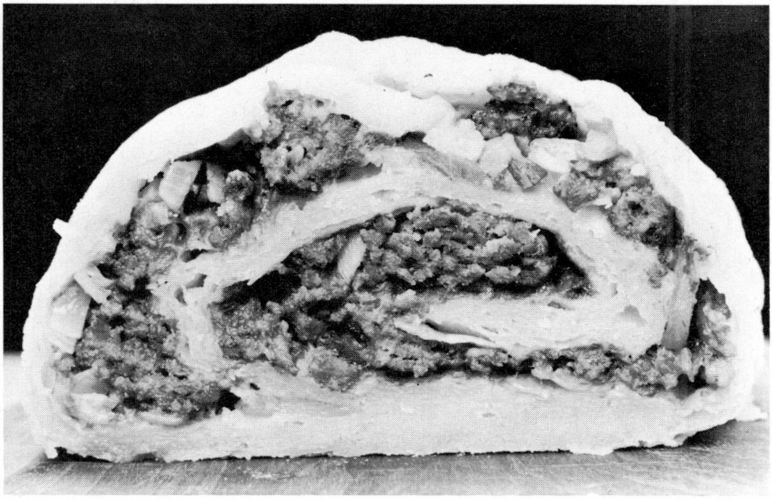

Meat Roly-Poly

6. Roll the pastry in a greased covering paper, foil or cloth; secure the ends by twisting or tying with string.
7. Steam the roll for $2\frac{1}{2}$–3 hrs.

## Chilli Con Carne

675 g flank or chuck steak
1 large onion
1 small green pepper
A 29-oz. (approx. 820-g) can of tomatoes
1 bay leaf
A pinch of cayenne
1–2 level tsp. (5–10 ml) mild chilli powder
2 level tsp. (10 ml) salt
A pinch of paprika pepper
A 15-oz. (approx. 425-g) can red kidney beans

*Serves 4–6*

1. Mince the beef, peel and slice the onion, de-seed and slice the pepper.
2. Brown the meat in a pan without extra fat. Add the onion and pepper and cook for a further 10 mins.
3. Add all the other ingredients, except the beans. Cover and simmer for 2 hrs.
4. Add the drained beans and heat through. Remove the bay leaf. Serve in shallow bowls, accompanied by a tossed green salad.

## Country Pasties

200 g shortcrust pastry
50 g kidney or liver
100 g potato
1 onion
150 g minced meat
2–3 tbsp. (30–45 ml) beef stock
Salt and pepper
Beaten egg or milk to glaze

*Serves 4*

1. Heat the oven to 204°C (mark 6, 400°F).
2. Make the pastry and divide into 4 portions. Roll each piece into a 20-cm round.
3. Wash the liver or kidney in warm water, remove any skin, tubes, etc., and chop into small pieces.
4. Peel and dice the potato; skin and chop the onion. Add both to the minced meat.
5. Mix the ingredients for the filling together and add seasoning to taste and the stock.
6. Pile a quarter of the mixture onto each round of pastry, damp the edges and join together along the top of the pasties, pressing the edges firmly. Flute the edges with the thumb and forefinger.
7. Brush the pasties with beaten egg or milk.

8. Bake for 20 mins. and then turn the oven down to 163°C (mark 3, 325°F) for the remaining ½ hr., to cook the meat through.

VARIATIONS

A variety of different fillings can be used in these Pasties—for instance, lean pork or mutton could be substituted for the minced beef in this recipe.

Sweet pasties may also be made, with a filling of fruit (take care however that it is not too juicy).

## Beef Olives

50 g bacon
½ a lemon
8 thin slices of topside
50 g shredded suet
100 g fresh white breadcrumbs
2 level tsp. (10 ml) chopped parsley
¼ level tsp. (1 ml) mixed herbs
Salt and pepper
½ beaten egg to bind
25 g fat or 3 tbsp. (45 ml) oil
2 level tbsp. (30 ml) flour
375 ml stock

*Serves 4*

1. Heat the oven to 177°C (mark 4, 350°F).
2. Rind and chop the bacon. Grate the lemon rind.
3. Trim the beef slices.
4. Mix the suet, bacon, breadcrumbs, parsley, mixed herbs, lemon rind, salt and pepper. Bind together with the beaten egg.
5. Spread each slice of meat with the stuffing, roll up and secure with fine string.
6. Heat the fat or oil in a frying pan and brown the beef olives lightly; remove and place in a casserole.
7. Add the flour to the juices in the frying pan, brown well, gradually add the stock and bring to the boil. Season to taste and pour over the olives.
8. Add the onion slices, cover and cook in the centre of the oven for ½ hr.
9. Serve with a tossed green salad.

## Gammon Rashers with Pineapple

4 gammon rashers, 1 cm thick
200 g soft brown sugar
An $8\frac{1}{2}$-oz. (240-g) can of pineapple rings (4 rings)
Parsley to garnish

*Serves 4*

1. If you think the gammon is likely to be salt, leave it to soak in cold water for 1 hr. prior to cooking. Pat it dry.
2. Trim the rind from the gammon rashers and snip the fat at intervals.
3. Mix together the brown sugar and pineapple juice.
4. Lay the gammon on the grill rack and coat evenly with some of the sugar mixture.
5. Cook under a medium grill for 15 mins., basting every 5 mins. with the pan drippings.
6. Turn the gammon, coat with the remaining sugar mixture and cook for a further 15 mins.
7. Cut the pineapple rings in half, place 2 of the halves on each rasher, baste and cook for a further 5 mins.
8. Serve hot, garnished with parsley and the pineapple.

## Baked Gammon

A 2-kilo piece of hock
Demerara sugar to coat the joint
A 15-oz. (425-g) can of apricots

*Serves 4–6*

1. Set the oven to 177°C (mark 4, 350°F).
2. Weigh the bacon and calculate the cooking time, allowing 20–25 mins. per 450 g plus 20 mins. over. Soak for 1 hr.
3. Boil for half the cooking time, skin side down, then drain and wrap in foil.
4. Heat oven; bake gammon in centre until ½ hour before the end of the cooking time.
5. Raise the oven heat to 218°C (mark 7, 425°F).
6. Undo the foil and cut the rind from the bacon; press Demerara sugar over the surface of the joint.
7. Drain the juice from the can of apricots and pour about 125 ml of it over the joint, basting well.
8. Finish the cooking, basting joint every 10 mins. Serve garnished with the apricots.

## Liver Casserole

450 g lamb's liver
2 level tbsp. (30 ml) seasoned flour
6 rashers of bacon
4 onions
50 g fat or oil
A 14-oz. (400-g) can of tomatoes
1 tbsp. (15 ml) Worcestershire sauce

*Serves 4*

1. Heat the oven to 177°C (mark 4, 350°F).
2. Wash the liver and remove any skin or tubes. Cut it into even-sized pieces and coat with seasoned flour. Rind and chop the bacon and peel and slice the onions.
3. Fry the liver, bacon and onions in the hot fat or oil until just brown, then put in a casserole and add the tomatoes and Worcestershire sauce.
4. Cook in the centre of the oven for 45 mins., or until the liver is tender.

## Beef Balls en Casserole

1 large onion
1 clove of garlic (optional)
4 tbsp. (60 ml) corn oil
450 g lean minced beef
50 g fresh white breadcrumbs
2 tsp. (10 ml) Worcestershire sauce
Salt
Freshly ground pepper
1 egg
25 g flour
450 g carrots
450 g potatoes
A 14-oz. (approx. 400-g) can of tomatoes
½ tsp. (2.5 ml) dried sage
1 bay leaf
500 ml beef stock, made with a stock cube
Chopped parsley to garnish

*Serves 4*

1. Heat the oven to 177°C (mark 4, 350°F).
2. Peel and chop the onion. Peel the clove of garlic (if used) and crush or chop finely (p. 9).
3. Heat 2 tbsp. oil in a frying pan and fry the onion until golden-brown.
4. Fry the garlic for a few mins.; drain both and place in a 3-litre casserole.
5. Meanwhile mix together the minced beef, breadcrumbs, Worcestershire sauce, salt, pepper and egg. Work together, then form into 16 balls.

6. Toss the balls in flour. Heat the remaining oil in a frying pan and fry the meat balls until light golden-brown. Add to the casserole.
7. Peel and slice the carrots; peel the potatoes and dice into $2\frac{1}{2}$-cm cubes. Add to the casserole, with the tomatoes, sage, bay leaf and stock. Season well.
8. Cover and cook in the oven for $1\frac{1}{2}$ hrs.
9. Serve sprinkled with chopped parsley.

## Casseroled Kidneys

450 g lamb's kidneys
4 rashers back bacon
3 small onions
600 g old potatoes
25 g lard
15 g seasoned flour
Salt and pepper
165 ml stock
Beaten egg or melted butter
Chopped parsley for garnish

*Serves 4*

1. Heat the oven to 177°C (mark 4, 350°F).
2. Clean the kidneys, halve, then remove the cores and skin. Place in cold water, bring to the boil and throw away the water. Repeat twice more.
3. Rind and chop the bacon and peel and slice the onions. Peel the potatoes and cook in boiling salted water until tender; drain and mash well.
4. Melt the lard in a pan and fry the onions until a light golden-brown. Stir in the flour and place the mixture in a casserole.
5. Arrange the kidneys on top of the onions and season with salt and pepper. Top with the pieces of bacon and pour the stock over.
6. Cover the casserole and cook in the oven for 30 mins. until the kidney is tender. Turn the oven up to 204°C (mark 6, 400°F).
7. Line a heatproof dish with creamed potato, brush with egg or butter and brown in the oven.
8. To serve, place the kidney mixture in the potato-lined dish and sprinkle with chopped parsley.

## Raised Veal and Ham Pies

1 egg
300 g pie veal
100 g cooked ham
1 tbsp. (15 ml) chopped parsley
Grated rind and juice of 1 lemon
Salt
Freshly ground pepper
A little stock or water
300 g hot-water crust pastry
Beaten egg to glaze
1½ level tsp. (7.5 ml) aspic jelly crystals
125 ml water

*Makes 4*

1. Hard-boil the egg.
2. Dice the veal and chop the ham; add the parsley, lemon rind, lemon juice, seasoning and chopped hard-boiled egg, with a little stock or water.
3. Grease a double strip of greaseproof paper 5 cm deep and long enough to go loosely round a 1-lb. (450-g) jam jar. Cut 3 more pieces.
4. Divide the pastry into 4 pieces and cut off one quarter from each piece for a lid; keep the pastry warm and covered until used.
5. Knead one of the larger pieces and roll out to a round 1.75 cm thick.
6. Press the pastry round a jam jar to cover the bottom and three-quarters of the sides. Avoid stretching the pastry and take care to keep it the same thickness all over; to keep the lower edge flat and even after the pastry is set and cool, slip the case off directly on to a baking tray.
7. Re-shape the case if necessary. Repeat with the other 3 larger pieces of pastry. (See p. 21.)
8. Heat the oven to 218°C (mark 7, 425°F).
9. Pack some filling carefully into each case.
10. Place a greaseproof paper strip round the outside of each pie, drawing the pastry into a good shape, and clip paper in position, leaving 1 cm pastry above the paper.
11. Roll out the remaining small pieces of pastry for lids. Brush each with beaten egg and press onto the upper edge of a pie, crimping the edge between finger and thumb. 'Knock up' the edges with the blade of a knife.
12. Brush the tops of the pies with egg. Any leftover pastry may be made into leaves or tassels—see pp. 31 and 35.
13. Make a hole in each pie top to let out the steam.

Raised Veal and Ham Pies

14. Bake the pies for 45 mins., then reduce the heat to 177°C (mark 4, 350°F) and take out the pies.
15. Remove the bands of paper from the pies, glaze the sides with egg and bake for a further 20–25 mins., to crisp the sides.
16. Make up a jelly stock by dissolving the aspic jelly crystals in boiling water and stirring thoroughly.
17. Pour the jelly stock into the pies through the holes in the tops, when the pies are cool. Serve cold.

*Note*: For a more elaborate-looking raised pie, you can use a special metal mould. These are available in various sizes, but are all made in two parts, joined by a hinge, so that they can easily be removed when the pie is cooked.

VARIATIONS

Use 450 g pie pork, with parsley and seasoning, as an alternative filling.

A raised game pie can be made, using sausage-meat, lean ham, lean chuck steak and the meat of 1 cooked pheasant or 2 pigeons.

## Kebabs

200–250 g long-grain rice
8 small tomatoes
8 rashers of streaky bacon
8 button mushrooms
4 large gherkins
200 g chipolata sausages
Melted butter

*Serves 4*

1. Cook the rice as described under Liver Stroganoff, p. 170.
2. Halve the tomatoes; rind the bacon and roll up tightly, wipe the mushrooms; slice the gherkins.
3. Thread 8 skewers alternately with sausages, tomato, bacon rolls, whole mushrooms and gherkins.
4. Brush with melted butter and cook the kebabs under a low grill for 10–15 mins., turning about 3 times.
5. Serve on the rice, with the following sauce:

## Lemon Barbecue Sauce

1 clove of garlic
50 g butter
4 level tbsp. (60 ml) flour
2 level tbsp. (30 ml) sugar
A pinch of salt
Freshly ground pepper
½ level tsp. (2.5 ml) dried thyme
¼ tsp. (0.5 ml) Tabasco sauce
Grated rind of 1 lemon
4 tbsp. (40 ml) lemon juice
125 ml chicken stock

*Makes 250 ml*

1. Skin and chop the garlic; heat the butter in a saucepan. Add the garlic and sauté for a few mins.
2. Stir in the flour and cook for a few mins.
3. Stir in the remaining ingredients.
4. Cover and simmer for 15 mins. Serve hot.

## Crown Roast of Lamb

2 pieces of best end of lamb, each with 8 cutlets (from opposite sides of animal, if possible), chopped, not chined, and sliced between bones to about half-way
75 g fresh white breadcrumbs
90 g butter
225 g onions
225 g apples
1 clove of garlic
2 level tsp. (10 ml) curry powder
50 g sultanas
75 g long-grain rice, boiled
Salt and pepper

*Serves 8*

1. Heat the oven to 177°C (mark 4, 350°F).
2. Scrape ends of bones clean. Trim meat neatly and bend the two pieces round backwards, fat side innermost, to form a crown; secure them with skewers and string. Put the joint on kitchen foil in a roasting tin.
3. Pack central cavity with foil to keep shape. Twist buttered paper or foil round each bone tip to stop burning.
4. Roast in centre of oven; allow 25–30 mins. per 450 g.
5. At half-time, remove foil from cavity and fill with rice stuffing; return joint to oven to finish cooking.
6. Put joint on serving dish, remove papers or foil and replace by cutlet frills. Garnish with baby mushrooms and watercress; serve with gravy and red-currant jelly.

*To make Stuffing*

1. Brown the crumbs in 50 g butter; transfer to a plate.
2. Peel and chop onions; peel, core and finely chop apples; crush the garlic clove.
3. Fry onion in remaining butter till soft; add apple, garlic, curry powder and sultanas; fry for a few mins.
4. Add rice and crumbs, stir together and season well.

## Roast Stuffed Breast of Lamb

450 g breast of lamb
Salt
Freshly ground pepper
Lemon juice
Flour to coat joint
15 g dripping

*Stuffing*

10 g dripping
½ an onion
150 g sausage-meat
2 tsp. (10 ml) chopped parsley
3 tbsp. (45 ml) fresh white breadcrumbs

*Serves 2–3*

1. Heat the oven to 177°C (mark 4, 350°F).
2. Wipe the breast of lamb and sprinkle the inside with salt, pepper and lemon juice.
3. Now make the stuffing: melt the dripping in a pan; peel and chop the onion and combine with the sausage-meat, parsley, breadcrumbs and dripping.
4. Work the ingredients together and spread over the meat.
5. Roll up loosely and tie in several places with string. Weigh the joint.

6. Season the flour and rub into the surface of the lamb. Melt the dripping in a roasting tin and put in the meat.
7. Roast in the centre of the oven for 30–35 mins. per 450 g, plus 35 mins. Baste once or twice.
8. Either serve hot, with gravy, or allow to become cold, slice and arrange on a serving dish and serve with salad.

## Navarin of Lamb

900 g (2½ lb.) best end of neck or scrag end of neck
10–15 g fat or 2 tbsp. (30 ml) oil
1 tsp. (5 ml) sugar
2 tbsp. (30 ml) flour
4 onions
1–2 turnips
4 carrots
8 even-sized potatoes
375 ml stock or water
2 tbsp. (30 ml) tomato paste
Salt and pepper
A bouquet garni (p. 15)
Chopped parsley for garnishing

*Serves 4*

This is a traditional dish of French origin.

1. Trim the meat and cut into serving portions. Fry lightly on all sides in the fat or oil.
2. Stir in the sugar, heat until it browns lightly, then add the flour, stirring until this cooks and browns.
3. Peel and quarter the onions and turnips; peel and slice the carrots; peel the potatoes.
4. Remove the pan from the heat, stir in the stock gradually, then bring to the boil and add the tomato paste, seasonings and bouquet garni. Add the onions, carrots and turnips and continue cooking for another ½ hr.
5. Finally, add the potatoes and continue cooking for 25 mins., until tender.
6. Garnish with chopped parsley.

## Pork Chops in Orange-pepper Sauce

4 pork loin chops
Salt and pepper
25 g sugar
½ a green pepper
2 oranges
25 g butter
1 clove of garlic
25 g cornflour
½ level tsp. (2.5 ml) dried rosemary
250 ml water
3 tbsp. (45 ml) lemon juice
3 tbsp. (45 ml) orange juice

*Serves 4*

1. Trim the chops and season both sides with salt, pepper and 1 tbsp. sugar.
2. De-seed and slice the green pepper.
3. Peel one of the oranges, taking care to remove the pith, and cut the flesh into segments.
4. Melt the butter in a frying pan, add the garlic and brown the chops well on both sides. Place the chops to one side and discard the garlic.
5. Add the rest of the sugar, the cornflour and the rosemary to the dripping. Stir well and gradually add the water. Cook, stirring, until glossy.

6. Add the fruit juices and green pepper. Return chops to the pan and place the orange segments in the pan. Cover with a lid, plate or foil.
7. Simmer over a low heat for 40 mins., until the chops are tender, basting occasionally. Uncover for the last 10 mins.
8. Serve garnished with the remaining orange, divided into segments (pp. 48–49).

## Moussaka

1 aubergine
Flour
4–6 tbsp. (60–90 ml) oil
2 medium-sized onions, peeled and thinly sliced
4 firm tomatoes, peeled and thickly sliced
450 g minced beef
125 ml well-seasoned stock
125 ml tomato paste
2 large eggs
125 ml single cream
Salt and freshly ground pepper

*Serves 4*

*Note*: Moussaka is a savoury dish eaten in various Balkan and Near-Eastern countries. There are many variations, but it generally contains meat and aubergines, as in this typical recipe.

1. Heat the oven to 177°C (mark 4, 350°F).
2. Slice the aubergine and dust with flour.
3. Heat the oil in a frying pan and fry the sliced aubergine; when it is beginning to colour, drain, then arrange around a shallow ovenproof casserole.
4. Peel and slice the onions and tomatoes.
5. Add 1 tbsp. (15 ml) of the oil to the pan, re-heat and fry the onions and meat until lightly browned. Place on top of the aubergines.
6. Fry the tomatoes in 1 tbsp. oil and add to the dish: pour in the stock and tomato paste.
7. Bake, uncovered, for 45 mins.
8. Beat together the eggs and cream, season well and pour over the contents in the casserole.
9. Return casserole to oven and continue to cook for a further 15–20 mins, until sauce is set and golden.

## Curry

- 450 g stewing steak
- 2 large onions
- 3 large carrots
- 1 cooking apple
- 2 tomatoes
- 50 g fat
- 1 level tbsp. (15 ml) curry powder
- 25 g flour
- 250 ml stock or water
- Salt and pepper
- 1 tbsp. (15 ml) chutney
- 50 g sultanas
- A squeeze of lemon juice
- Baked rice and accompaniments

*Serves 4*

The savoury dishes we know as curries are of Eastern origin. In the East they are very highly flavoured with a mixture of spices. Here, we mostly use a prepared curry powder, and sometimes also a curry paste, to flavour the dish. Connoisseurs of Eastern cookery, however, prefer to use the fresh spices. Onion and lemon juice are nearly always included among the ingredients.

Almost any meat or poultry may be curried—lamb chops, lean veal or pork, minced meat, chicken and so on—and fish, eggs and vegetables also make good curries. The main ingredients in a curry should be so prepared that the dish may be eaten with a spoon.

1. Heat the oven to 177°C (mark 4, 350°F).
2. Trim the meat and cut into 2.5-cm cubes.
3. Skin and chop the onions. Scrape the carrots and cut into dice. Peel and dice the apple and leave to stand in lemon juice and water to prevent discoloration. Skin and chop the tomatoes.
4. Melt the fat in a frying pan and fry the meat until brown. Drain well, and put into a casserole.
5. Fry the onion and apple in the remaining fat and add to the meat.
6. Fry the curry powder, add the flour and cook together for 2–3 mins. Add the stock gradually and bring to the boil. Add the seasoning and remaining ingredients and cook for 2–3 mins.
7. Pour the sauce over the meat. Cover the casserole and cook gently in the centre of the oven for about 1½ hrs., until the meat is fork-tender.

Curry

8. Adjust the seasoning as required and serve the curry with boiled rice (see p. 170) and with side dishes chosen from the selection given below.

ACCOMPANIMENTS FOR CURRY

The side dishes served with a curry are often known as *sambols*. Some can be bought ready to eat, others need preparation. They are usually served in small dishes. Here are a few examples:

*Bananas*—Peel and slice thinly. Sprinkle with lemon juice to prevent browning.

*Tomatoes*—Slice thinly; sprinkle with chopped herbs or leave plain.

*Mango chutney*

*Coconut*—desiccated or long shred.

*Melon*—cut into cubes and remove the seeds.

*Green pepper*—slice, removing the pips and pith. Blanch for 2 mins., drain.

*Pappadums*—thin wafer-like biscuits, that can be bought in tins. To cook, fry one at a time in a little hot fat until crisp, holding it down with a spoon as it swells. Heat for 1–2 mins. under a hot grill.

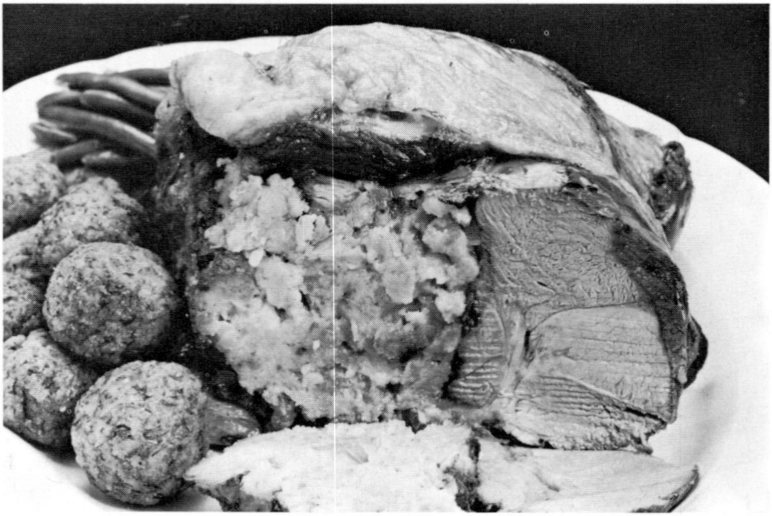

## Colonial Goose

A 2-kilo leg of lamb (boned by the butcher)
1 onion
1 clove of garlic (optional)
200 g sausage-meat
100 g fresh white breadcrumbs
Salt and pepper
1 tbsp. (15 ml) chopped parsley
1 egg, beaten

### *Forcemeat Balls*

100 g lean veal
75 g lean bacon
1 onion
1 large mushroom
50 g butter
Salt and pepper
75 g fresh white breadcrumbs
1 level tsp. (5 ml) chopped parsley
1 egg, beaten

1. Heat the oven to 177°C (mark 4, 350°F).
2. Wipe and weigh the leg of lamb.
3. Peel and finely chop the onion and the clove of garlic (if used). Mix the sausage-meat, breadcrumbs, onion, garlic, salt, pepper and parsley, and bind with the egg.
4. Fill the cavity in the meat left by the bone, and truss firmly. Place in a roasting tin with some water and cook, allowing 25–30 mins. per 450 g.
5. Mince the veal and bacon for the forcemeat balls and beat them well together in a bowl.

6. Peel and finely chop the onion. Wipe and chop the mushrooms.
7. Melt half the butter in a saucepan and fry the onion until soft but not coloured. Add to the meat, together with the seasoning, breadcrumbs, mushroom, parsley and beaten egg. Mix well together.
8. Divide the mixture into 6–8 portions and shape into rounds.
9. Melt the remaining butter in a frying pan. Toss the forcemeat balls lightly in it, transfer to an ovenproof dish and bake for 35–40 mins.
10. Serve the forcemeat balls with the lamb.

## Hamburgers with Barbecue Sauce

½ an onion
450 g lean minced beef
1 level tsp. (5 ml) dried mixed herbs
Salt and pepper
Melted butter or oil
4 slices of tomato and watercress to garnish

*For the Sauce*

1 small onion, grated
10–15 g margarine
2 tbsp. (30 ml) tomato ketchup
1 tbsp. (15 ml) vinegar
1 tsp. (5 ml) Worcestershire sauce
½ level tsp. (2.5 ml) salt
A pinch of pepper
4 tbsp. (60 ml) water

*Serves 4*

1. Peel and finely chop the onion.
2. Mix the minced beef, onion, herbs, salt and pepper.
3. Shape lightly into 6–8 round flat cakes. Brush sparingly with melted butter or oil and grill for 4–6 mins., turning once.
4. For the sauce, mix all the listed ingredients in a small pan and simmer for 10 mins.
5. Pour the sauce over the cooked hamburgers, and garnish with watercress and tomatoes.

## Liver Stroganoff

450 g lamb's liver, sliced thickly
3 tbsp. (45 ml) seasoned flour
100 g onion
100 g button mushrooms,
75 g butter
125 ml stock
Salt and pepper
4 tbsp. (60 ml) soured cream
Snipped parsley for garnish

*Serves 4*

1. Cut the liver into strips with a sharp knife; toss in the flour.
2. Peel and slice the onion. Wipe and slice the mushrooms.
3. Melt 40 g butter and sauté the liver until just cooked through—about 7–10 mins.; put aside.
4. To the pan juices add the rest of the butter, re-heat and sauté the onion for 5 mins.
5. Add the mushrooms, stir and cook for a further min.
6. Add the stock and bring to the boil. Adjust the seasoning.
7. Stir in the soured cream and re-heat without boiling. Garnish with snipped parsley.
8. Serve with savoury rice and an apple and celery salad.

*To Boil Rice*

1. Wash 1 cupful long-grain rice (this will serve 3–4 people). Place in a saucepan with 2 cupfuls water and 1 level tsp. (5 ml) salt.
2. Bring quickly to the boil, stir well and cover with a tight-fitting lid. Reduce the heat and simmer for 14–15 mins.
3. Remove from the heat, and before serving separate the grains by forking gently. The rice will not need draining, as the water will have been absorbed.

*Savoury Rice*: Flavour with sautéed mushrooms, chopped green pepper or chopped parsley, or add a can of corn kernels or peas.

## Lasagne

1 medium-sized onion
1 tbsp. (15 ml) oil
200 g minced beef
2 level tbsp. (30 ml) tomato paste
A 7-oz. (200-g) can of tomatoes
½ a bay leaf
Salt and pepper
150–200 g natural lasagne or lasagne verdi
250 ml coating cheese sauce
25 g Parmesan cheese

*Serves 4*

1. Heat the oven to 177°C (mark 4, 350°F).
2. Peel and finely chop the onion. Melt the oil in a pan.
3. Fry the onion in the oil until it is beginning to colour.
4. Add the beef and fry until evenly browned.
5. Add the tomato paste, canned tomatoes and bay leaf. Stir well and season to taste.
6. Bring to the boil, reduce the heat, cover and simmer for 20 mins. Remove the bay leaf.
7. Cook the lasagne according to the directions on the packet; drain well. Make up the cheese sauce, using the roux method.
8. Grease an oblong ovenproof dish about 5 cm deep.
9. Arrange a single layer of lasagne on the base, then layer the meat sauce, lasagne and cheese sauce until all are used up. Sprinkle with grated Parmesan cheese.
10. Bake for 30 mins. Garnish with parsley.

## Spaghetti Alla Paesana

2 onions
200 g back bacon rashers
A 14-oz. (400-g) can of tomatoes
100 g button mushrooms
½ a green pepper
50 g butter
1 level tbsp. (15 ml) tomato paste
½ a chicken stock cube
1 level tsp. (5 ml) dried basil
1 level tbsp. (15 ml) cornflour
300 g spaghetti
Salt and butter for spaghetti

*Serves 4–6*

1. Peel and chop the onions. Rind and mince the bacon. Sieve the tomatoes. Wipe and slice the mushrooms. Seed and chop the pepper.
2. Melt 25 g of the butter in a saucepan and sauté the onions until clear. Add the bacon and cook for 5 mins.
3. Add the sieved tomatoes, tomato paste, stock cube and basil.
4. Blend the cornflour to a smooth paste with a little water and stir into the bacon mixture. Bring to the boil and simmer for 10 mins.
5. Melt the remaining butter and sauté the mushrooms and green pepper slices; add to the bacon mixture.

6. Cook the spaghetti in boiling salted water until tender, drain, add a knob of butter, toss, and pile onto a hot dish.
7. Pour the bacon mixture on top and serve at once.

*Note*: Pasta constitutes the staple food of much of Italy, supplying carbohydrate, protein, some vitamins and a certain amount of minerals. Most pasta recipes come from Italy.

All pasta dishes are best eaten immediately they are cooked, as pasta does not re-heat well, but becomes tough and leathery.

## Osso Bucco

900 g shin of veal (ask the butcher to saw it into 4 slices about 5 cm thick)
Salt and pepper
1 medium-sized onion
2 carrots
2 stalks of celery
1 clove of garlic
1 lemon
300 g tomatoes
50 g butter
1½ level tbsp. (22.5 ml) flour
250 ml chicken stock or dry white wine
A pinch of dried rosemary
2 level tbsp. (30 ml) chopped parsley

*Serves 4*

1. Heat the oven to 177°C (mark 4, 350°F).
2. Season the veal with salt and pepper.
3. Peel and slice the onion and carrots; chop the celery; peel and crush or finely chop the garlic; grate the lemon rind coarsely; skin and quarter the tomatoes.
4. Melt the butter in a large pan. Brown the veal, then put it aside. Add a little more butter before frying the onion, carrots and celery until just beginning to brown. Add the crushed garlic.
5. Return the meat to the pan, add the flour and cook for a few mins., then add the stock or wine. Cover and cook gently for 1 hr.
6. Transfer to a large casserole and add the tomatoes and rosemary.
7. Cover the casserole, place in the oven and cook for 1 hr., until the meat is tender.
8. Sprinkle with parsley and lemon rind before serving.

## Ham Bouchées

200 g bought puff pastry
Beaten egg
150 g ham
250 ml thick white coating sauce
Parsley to garnish

*Makes 8*

1. Heat the oven to 218°C (mark 7, 425°F).
2. Roll out the pastry 1 cm thick.
3. Using a 2-in. (5-cm) plain cutter, cut out 16 rounds and place on a wet baking tray.
4. Cut through the centre of 8 rounds with a 1-in. (2.5-cm) plain cutter.
5. Glaze around the edges of each complete round with egg and press the outer cut rounds on top of the complete rounds. Glaze the bouchées and the lid pieces with the remaining egg.
6. Bake at the top of the oven for 10–15 mins.
7. Make the filling: chop the ham and add to the sauce.
8. Remove the bouchées from the oven. Press down the centres, or remove with a pointed knife.
9. Pour the sauce into the bouchée cases and add the lids.
10. Serve hot or cold, garnished with parsley sprigs.

## Sausages en Croûte

300 g bought puff pastry
4 rashers of back bacon, rinded
100 g onions, peeled
200 g pork sausages
1 egg, lightly beaten

*Serves 4*

1. Heat the oven to 218°C (mark 7, 425°F).
2. Roll out the pastry to form four 20-cm squares.
3. Chop the bacon and cook in a frying pan until the fat runs. Peel the onions and chop finely.
4. Sauté the onion until soft but not coloured.
5. Place 2 sausages in the centre of each pastry square.
6. Divide the bacon mixture between the squares.
7. Wrap the pastry round tightly, sealing with egg.
8. Brush each parcel with egg and decorate as desired.
9. Bake for 10 mins., then reduce heat to 177°C (mark 4, 350°F) and cook a further 30–35 mins.
10. Cover lightly with foil if browning too rapidly. Serve with a green vegetable and tomato sauce.

## Tomato Sauce

1 clove of garlic
2 tbsp. (30 ml) oil
A 14-oz. (400-g) can of tomatoes
A $2\frac{1}{4}$-oz. (approx. 60-g) can of tomato paste
$\frac{1}{2}$ level tsp. (2.5 ml) dried basil
1 level tsp. (5 ml) sugar
1 level tsp. (5 ml) salt
Freshly ground pepper

*Makes 400 ml*

1. Peel and slice the garlic.
2. Heat the oil in a saucepan, add the garlic and sauté for 5 mins., then remove from the pan.
3. Add the contents of the can of tomatoes and the can of tomato puree, with the basil, sugar, salt and pepper.
4. Cover the pan and simmer (don't boil) for 30 mins. to 1 hr. —the longer the better. Stir occasionally.
5. Adjust the seasoning and serve with meat, fish, stuffed marrow, cheese dishes, etc.

## Poulet en Cocotte

100 g sausage-meat
40 g fresh white breadcrumbs
1 chicken liver
½ an onion
½ level tsp. (2.5 ml) dried sage or 1 level tsp. (5 ml) fresh sage
Salt
Freshly ground pepper
A 2-kilo oven-ready chicken
75 g butter
150 g lean back bacon, in one slice
¾ kilo potatoes
½ kilo small new carrots
½ kilo courgettes (optional)
Fresh sage for garnish

*Serves 6*

1. Heat the oven to 177°C (mark 4, 350°F).
2. Mix the sausage-meat and breadcrumbs.
3. Wash the chicken liver, remove the skin and chop finely. Peel the onion and chop finely; add to the sausage-meat, with the sage. Season, and work well together.

4. Prepare the chicken by removing the giblets and wiping the inside with a clean damp cloth.
5. Stuff the bird at the neck end, plump up, and secure with a skewer. Truss as for roasting, and season well.
6. Melt the butter in a large frying pan and brown the chicken all over. Transfer to a large casserole.
7. Rind the bacon and cut into 2-cm cubes; add to the casserole. Cover, and cook in the oven for 15 mins.
8. Meanwhile peel the potatoes and cut into 2.5-cm cubes. Scrape the carrots and slice the courgettes (if used).
9. Remove casserole from oven and baste chicken. Surround it with the vegetables, turning them in the fat; season.
10. Cook for 1½ hrs. longer, till everything is tender.
11. Garnish with a sprig of sage. Paper frills may be placed on the chicken legs (see picture).
12. Carve the chicken on a large plate. Serve the vegetables and juice straight from the casserole.

## Chicken Salad

A 1½-kilo oven-ready chicken, roasted
200 g long-grain rice
Salt and pepper
French dressing—2 tbsp. (30 ml) oil, 1 tbsp. (15 ml) vinegar, salt, pepper
½ a lettuce
3 bananas
3 oranges
125 ml mayonnaise
Chopped parsley and toasted flaked almonds for garnish

*Serves 4–6*

1. When the chicken is cold, carve into slices, then into strips. Keep in a cool place.
2. Cook the rice in the usual way, drain and cool.
3. Make up the French dressing. Line a dish with lettuce.
4. Peel and slice the bananas and toss in the dressing. Grate the orange rind and add to the mayonnaise.
5. Peel the oranges free of pith and divide into segments. Add any orange juice to the mayonnaise; season well.
6. Fold dark chicken meat and half the banana and orange into the rice, with some mayonnaise; pile in the dish.
7. Arrange the chicken breast on the rice and add the remaining fruit round the edge. Coat the chicken breast with mayonnaise. Garnish with parsley and almonds.

## Sweet 'n Sour Chicken

4 chicken joints
Salt and pepper
2 green peppers
250 ml chicken stock
2 level tbsp. (30 ml) cornflour
125 ml vinegar
2 tsp. (10 ml) soy sauce
3–4 level tbsp. (45–60 ml) light brown sugar
An 11-oz. (approx. 310-g) can of pineapple pieces
3 large tomatoes, skinned

*Serves 4*

1. Heat the oven to 177°C (mark 4, 350°F).
2. Trim the chicken joints, season and grill till golden-brown. Transfer to a casserole.
3. Seed the green peppers and slice thinly. Simmer in the chicken stock for 5 mins., then drain.
4. In a saucepan blend the cornflour with a little water; add the vinegar, soy sauce and sugar, and stir in the strained chicken stock. Cook the mixture until thickened, stirring all the time.
5. Add the contents of the can of pineapple and the quartered tomatoes, and pour the mixture over the chicken joints.

Cover the casserole with foil and cook at the centre of the oven for 30 mins.

6. Serve the chicken and sauce in a border of boiled rice.

## Coq au Vin

- 100 g streaky bacon rashers, rinded
- 4 small onions
- 100 g button mushrooms
- 25 g butter
- 4 chicken joints
- A bay leaf
- A few parsley sprigs
- A pinch of thyme
- Salt and pepper
- 250 ml dry red wine (or 125 ml wine and 125 ml stock)
- Beurre manié (20 g flour and 20 g butter—see p. 15)

*Serves 4*

1. Heat the oven to 177°C (mark 4, 350°F).
2. Cut the bacon into cubes; peel and chop the onions; de-stalk the mushrooms.
3. Melt the butter and fry the bacon and onions until beginning to colour. Drain and keep on one side.
4. Fry the chicken in the re-heated fat in the pan until lightly browned.
5. Place the chicken in the casserole with the juices; add the onion and bacon mixture, whole mushrooms, herbs and seasoning. Pour the wine (or wine and stock) over.
6. Cover and cook in the oven for 1–1¼ hrs., until the chicken is tender. Take it out and keep hot.
7. Strain off the liquor from the casserole into a saucepan. Skim off any fat, discard the bay leaf and sprigs of parsley.
8. Cream together the butter and flour for the Beurre Manié and whisk into the liquor a little at a time over a low heat.
9. Cook gently for 5 mins. Adjust the seasoning and strain over the chicken. Return the dish to the oven for 15 mins. before serving.

## Roast Chicken

1. For 4 people, choose an oven-ready bird weighing about 1¾–2 kilos.
2. If the bird is frozen, thaw it out completely, then remove the bag of giblets.
3. Heat the oven to 190°C (mark 5, 375°F).
4. Wash the inside of the bird and stuff at the neck end before folding flap over. If no stuffing is used, put an onion, thick lemon wedge or knob of butter inside body.
5. Brush the chicken with melted butter or margarine or with oil, and sprinkle with salt and pepper.
6. Put in a shallow roasting tin; a few strips of streaky bacon may be laid over the breast to keep it moist.
7. Bake in centre of oven, basting occasionally; allow 20 mins. per 450 g plus 20 mins. Put greaseproof paper over breast if it becomes too brown.
8. Meanwhile stew the giblets for stock.
9. Serve the chicken with roast potatoes and a green vegetable, or with a tossed green salad. Bacon rolls, forcemeat balls, chipolata sausages, bread sauce and thin gravy are the usual accompaniments.

*Bacon Rolls*: Roll streaky bacon rashers (p. 21), thread on a skewer and grill until crisp—3–5 mins.

*Thin Gravy*: Pour off all but 1 tbsp. (15 ml) fat from the tin. Sprinkle in 4 level tsp. (20 ml) flour and stir in 250 ml giblet stock. Bring to the boil, stirring, season and add a touch of gravy browning to improve the colour.

## Bread Sauce

1 medium-sized onion, peeled
2 cloves
375 ml milk
Salt
A few peppercorns
½ a small bay leaf
20 g butter
75 g fresh white crumbs

*Serves 4–5*

1. Stick onion with cloves, put in a pan with milk, salt, peppercorns and bay leaf; bring almost to boiling point and leave to infuse in a warm place for 20 mins.

2. Add strained milk to butter and breadcrumbs, mix well and cook slowly for 15 mins.; remove the onion.
3. Serve with roast chicken, turkey or pheasant.

## Creamed Chicken Casserole

300 g cooked chicken
100 g mushrooms
½ a red pepper
½ a green pepper
75 g butter
2 level tbsp. (30 ml) flour
125 ml chicken stock
(made from ½ a cube)
125 ml single cream
Salt and pepper

*Serves 4*

1. Heat the oven to 177°C (mark 4, 350°F).
2. Dice the chicken; wipe and slice the mushrooms; seed and chop the peppers.
3. Melt 50 g of the butter and sauté the sliced mushrooms and peppers. Add to the chicken.
4. Melt remaining butter in a pan, stir in flour and cook slowly for 2–3 mins. Gradually add stock, stirring continuously. Cook for a few minutes, blend in the cream and pour over the chicken. Adjust seasoning.
5. Turn the mixture into a casserole, cover and bake for 30 mins. Serve hot.

## Roast Duck

2-kilo oven-ready duckling
Salt and freshly ground pepper
50 g bacon
1 onion
2 sticks of celery
2 medium-sized cooking apples
25 g butter
75 g fresh white breadcrumbs
2 tbsp. (30 ml) chopped parsley
25–50 g margarine
15 g flour
250 ml giblet stock
Orange to garnish

*Serves 4*

1. Heat the oven to 190°C (mark 5, 375°F).
2. Wipe the duck. (If frozen, thaw, and remove the giblets.)
3. To make stock for the gravy, place the giblets in a pan, cover with water and stew gently for $\frac{3}{4}$–1 hr.
4. Sprinkle the duck well inside and out with salt and pepper.
5. For the stuffing, rind and chop the bacon, skin and chop the onion, scrub and chop the celery, peel and core the cooking apples.
6. Fry the bacon in the butter for 2–3 mins., until golden-brown, and remove from the pan with a slotted spoon. Fry the onion and celery for 5 mins. and remove from the pan. Fry the apples for 2–3 mins. until soft. Mix all these ingredients together with the breadcrumbs and parsley.

7. Stuff the duck at the tail end.
8. Melt the margarine and brush the duck over with it. Place in a roasting tin and cook, allowing 20 mins. per 450 g.
9. When the duck is cooked, remove it from roasting tin and keep warm on a hot plate in the oven (reduced to 163°C (mark 3, 325°F)).
10. Skim off the excess fat into a bowl. Add the flour to the juices in the pan, mix to a paste and cook for a minute.
11. Remove from the heat and pour on the giblet stock, stirring all the time.
12. Stir until boiling and simmer for 2 mins.
13. Garnish the duck with orange rind and slices of orange. Serve with broccoli and boiled potatoes (or other vegetables, as preferred).

## Duck with Cherries

2 duck portions
½ level tsp. (2.5 ml) salt
15 g butter
2 tsp. (10 ml) corn oil
An 8-oz. (225-g) can of stoned cherries
1½ level tsp. (7.5 ml) cornflour
1 tbsp. (15 ml) giblet stock
Watercress
New potatoes

*Serves 2*

1. Sprinkle the duckling joints with salt.
2. Heat the butter with the oil in a large saucepan and brown the duckling joints on all sides.
3. Remove from pan, drain off the fat and wipe pan clean.
4. Replace the duckling joints in the pan in a single layer. Pour the juice from the cherries over, bring to the boil, cover and simmer for 40 mins., until tender.
5. Lift the joints from the pan, drain well and keep warm on a serving dish.
6. Skim the fat from the pan juices. Blend the cornflour with the stock and stir into the juices. Bring to the boil, add the cherries and heat through. Check the seasoning.
7. Pour the sauce over the duckling joints.
8. Garnish with watercress and minted new potatoes.

## Turkey Julienne

450 g cooked roast turkey meat
40 g butter
40 g flour
250 ml rich turkey stock
250 ml milk
Grated rind of ½ a lemon
2 tbsp. (30 ml) lemon juice
A pinch of dried rosemary
Salt and pepper
25 g cheese, grated
25 g flaked almonds, toasted
Chopped parsley and a lemon twist to garnish

*Serves 4*

1. Heat the oven to 177°C (mark 4, 350°F).
2. Cut the carved turkey into long strips and place in an oven-proof dish.
3. Melt the butter, stir in the flour and cook for a few mins. Slowly add the stock and milk, beating well.
4. Bring to boil, stirring; cook gently for 2–3 mins.
5. Add the lemon rind and juice, rosemary and seasoning and pour over chicken. Sprinkle with the cheese and nuts.
6. Cover and place in the oven for 40 mins.
7. Serve in a border of boiled rice, garnished with chopped parsley and a lemon twist.

## Pigeon Casserole

2–3 pigeons
50 g bacon
2 carrots
1 onion
50 g margarine
3 level tbsp. (45 ml) flour
500 ml chicken stock
1 tbsp. (15 ml) tomato paste
Salt and pepper

*Serves 2–3*

1. Heat the oven to 177°C (mark 4, 350°F).
2. Rind and chop the bacon; peel and slice the carrots; peel and chop the onion.
3. Heat the fat in a frying pan and fry the pigeons for 5 mins., till golden-brown; transfer to a casserole.
4. Fry the bacon, carrots and onion in the remaining fat for about 5 mins., till golden-brown.
5. Transfer the vegetables to the casserole.
6. Stir the flour into the remaining fat in the pan and cook for 2–3 mins.

7. Remove pan from heat and gradually stir in stock. Bring to the boil, continue to stir until the mixture thickens and add the tomato paste and seasoning.
8. Pour the sauce over the pigeon joints, cover, and cook in centre of oven for $\frac{3}{4}$–1 hr., or until the pigeon is tender. Serve with creamed potatoes.

*Note*: If frozen pigeons are used, thaw them overnight.

## Rabbit Casserole

| | |
|---|---|
| 4 rabbit joints | 450 g potatoes |
| 25 g seasoned flour | A little parsley |
| 2–3 onions | Stock or water |

*Serves 4*

1. Heat the oven to 163°C (mark 3, 325°F).
2. Wash the rabbit joints, dry and toss in the flour.
3. Skin and slice the onions; cut the peeled potatoes into chips 5 cm long. Chop the parsley.
4. Place a layer of onion in a casserole. Put the rabbit on top, sprinkle liberally with chopped parsley and cover with onion and potato.
5. Add the liquid, nearly covering the rabbit, put on the lid and bake for 2–2$\frac{1}{2}$ hrs. Remove the lid a short time before serving, to brown the potatoes.

## Baked Stuffed Marrow

1 medium-sized vegetable marrow
100 g savoury tomato rice
50 g bacon
25 g butter
400 g minced beef
100 g cheese, grated
1 egg
Salt and freshly ground pepper

*Serves 6*

1. Heat the oven to 177°C (mark 4, 350°F).
2. Wash the marrow, cut a slice from one end and scoop out the seeds, using the handle end of a spoon.
3. Cook the savoury rice as directed on the packet.
4. Rind and chop the bacon and fry lightly in a pan. Add the butter and minced beef and 'seal' the meat quickly.
5. Remove the meat from the pan and drain. Add the grated cheese and bind with the egg. Season.
6. Push the stuffing into the marrow cavity, wrap the marrow loosely in buttered foil and place in a roasting tin. Bake for $\frac{3}{4}$–1 hr.
7. Serve the marrow sliced, with a tomato sauce.

## Stuffed Mushrooms

4 large fresh mushrooms
15 g butter
20 g fresh breadcrumbs
2 level tbsp. (30 ml) chopped parsley
Salt and pepper
A pinch of onion powder
A pinch of garlic powder
Grated rind of $\frac{1}{4}$ of a lemon
$\frac{1}{2}$ tsp. (2.5 ml) lemon juice
50 g cheese, grated
Parsley to garnish

*Serves 2*

1. Heat the oven to 163°C (mark 3, 325°F).
2. Remove the stems from the mushrooms and chop finely.
3. Melt butter and sauté the mushroom stalks for a few mins. Add all the remaining ingredients, mixing well.
4. Fill the mushroom caps with the mixture, place on a baking tray and bake for 15–20 mins. Garnish.

## Courgettes with Tomatoes

225 g courgettes
Salt
225 g tomatoes
1 clove of garlic (optional)
40 g cheese
50 g butter
2 tsp. (10 ml) chopped parsley
Pepper
$\frac{1}{2}$ level tsp. (2.5 ml) sugar
15 g fresh breadcrumbs

*Serves 2–3*

1. Heat the oven to 177°C (mark 4, 350°F).
2. Cut the courgettes into 5-cm slices, sprinkle with salt and allow to drain for about 1 hr.; dry well.
3. Meanwhile peel and chop the tomatoes and peel and crush or chop the garlic (if used). Grate cheese.
4. Melt 25 g of the butter in a frying pan and put in the courgettes. Cook gently until soft and slightly transparent, then place in an ovenproof dish.
5. Melt remaining butter and cook the tomatoes, garlic, parsley, pepper and sugar till a thickish purée forms.
6. Re-season, if necessary, and pour over courgettes.
7. Sprinkle with the cheese. Melt the remaining 10 g butter and lightly fry the breadcrumbs. Top the dish with the crumbs and bake for 20–25 mins.

## Belgian Pie

450 g potatoes
½ an egg
Salt and pepper
Beaten egg to glaze
250 ml cheese sauce
An 8-oz. (approx. 225-g) pkt. of frozen mixed vegetables

*Serves 6*

1. Heat the oven to 177°C (mark 4, 350°F).
2. Peel the potatoes, cook and mash; beat in the egg, salt and pepper. Using a ½-inch (1-cm) star vegetable nozzle, pipe a 20-cm potato nest onto a greased baking sheet. Pipe strips at intervals down the sides.
3. Brush the potato nest with a little egg and bake for 30 mins., till golden-brown. Transfer to a dish.
4. Make the cheese sauce, using the roux method.
5. Cook the vegetables as directed on the packet, drain and add to the sauce, with salt and pepper to taste.
6. Pour the mixture into the potato nest; serve at once.

## Stuffed Jacket Potatoes

6 large even-sized potatoes

CURRIED EGG FILLING

2 eggs
50 g onion
50 g cooking apple
25 g butter
½ level tsp. (2.5 ml) curry powder
Salt and pepper

BACON FILLING

25 g onion
75 g bacon rashers
100 g Lancashire cheese
25 g butter
1 tbsp. (15 ml) milk
½ level tsp. (2.5 ml) dried marjoram
Salt and pepper

*Serves 6*

1. Heat the oven to 204°C (mark 6, 400°F).
2. Wash, scrub and dry the potatoes. Prick with a fork, place on baking sheets and bake for about 1 hr.
3. Fill as described below and keep warm in a low oven.

CURRIED EGG FILLING

1. Put the eggs on to hard-boil; peel and chop the onion; peel and dice the apple.
2. Sieve one of the hard-boiled eggs.
3. Melt the butter in a pan and fry the onion until soft but not coloured. Add the apple and curry powder and fry for a further 5 mins. Add the sieved egg.
4. Cut a lid from 3 of the potatoes, scoop out the centre part and add to the curry mixture. Season well and replace inside the potato shells.
5. Garnish with the remaining hard-boiled egg, sliced.

BACON FILLING

1. Peel and chop the onion; rind and chop the bacon; grate the cheese.
2. Melt the butter, fry the onion until soft and put it aside. Add the bacon to the pan and fry until crisp.
3. Scoop out the remaining 3 potatoes as above. Cream with the milk, add the onion, bacon and marjoram and season the mixture well.
4. Re-fill the potato cases. Top with grated cheese and keep hot. Brown under a hot grill before serving.

## Tuna-filled Tomatoes

4 large tomatoes
$\frac{1}{2}$ an onion
50 g button mushrooms
A 4-oz. (approx. 112-g) can of tuna fish
25 g butter
1 tbsp. (15 ml) chopped parsley
25 g breadcrumbs
4 tbsp. (60 ml) pulp from tomatoes
Parsley to decorate

*Serves 4*

1. Heat the oven to 177°C (mark 4, 350°F).
2. Remove the top from each tomato and retain.
3. Scoop out the soft core in the centre and the seeds, retaining this pulp.
4. Place the tomatoes on a greased baking sheet.
5. Peel and chop onion; wipe mushrooms and slice thinly.
6. Drain and flake the tuna. Melt the butter in a frying pan, add the onion and cook until soft. Add the mushrooms and cook for a few mins.
7. Add the tuna, parsley, breadcrumbs and scooped-out tomato flesh to the pan and mix well together.
8. Divide the filling between the tomatoes and replace the tops. Cover with foil and bake for 20 mins.
9. Garnish with sprigs of parsley.

## Ratatouille

2 onions
1 green pepper
1 aubergine
½ marrow or 5 courgettes
6 tomatoes
2 tbsp. (30 ml) oil
Salt and pepper
Chopped parsley

*Serves 4*

1. Heat the oven to 177°C (mark 4, 350°F).
2. Peel and slice the onions; seed and thinly slice the pepper; dice the aubergine; peel and dice the marrow or slice the courgettes; skin and chop the tomatoes.
3. Heat half the oil, add the onions and pepper and fry for 2–3 mins. Drain, and transfer to a casserole.
4. Add the remaining oil, aubergine and marrow or courgettes; mix well, then add the tomatoes and seasoning.
5. Put into the casserole with the other ingredients, cover and bake for 30 mins. Garnish with parsley.

## Tossed Green Salad

1 clove of garlic
1 lettuce
½ a cucumber
2 spring onions
Pinch of salt
Pinch of pepper
Pinch of dry mustard
Pinch of sugar
1 tbsp. (15 ml) vinegar
2 tbsp. (30 ml) oil

*Serves 3–4*

1. Peel the clove of garlic and rub a large salad bowl with it.
2. Wash the lettuce well; slice the cucumber (if you wish, ridge it first—p. 111), chop the spring onions.
3. Make French dressing by combining the salt, pepper, mustard, sugar, vinegar and oil in a screw-topped jar and shaking vigorously just before using.
4. Pile the greens into the prepared salad bowl and toss them lightly with the dressing, using a set of salad servers, until they are well coated. Serve immediately.

## Pineapple and Pepper Salad

A 15-oz. (approx. 425-g) can of pineapple pieces
1 green pepper
¼ of a cucumber
½ a lettuce
50 g sultanas
4 tbsp. (60 ml) French dressing

*Serves 3–4*

1. Drain the pineapple; blanch, de-seed and finely chop the pepper; wipe and dice the cucumber; chop the lettuce.
2. Mix all the salad ingredients together.
3. Add 2 tbsp. (30 ml) of the pineapple juice to the dressing, pour over the salad and toss well.

## Cole Slaw

½ a hard white cabbage
A small piece of onion
4 tbsp. (60 ml) salad cream
1 level tbsp. (15 ml) sugar
Salt and pepper
1 tbsp. (15 ml) chopped parsley
A few drops of vinegar

*Serves 4–6*

1. Wash and finely shred the cabbage; peel the onion and chop finely. Mix the cabbage and onion in a large bowl.
2. Mix the salad cream with the sugar, salt, pepper and parsley and enough vinegar (or lemon juice) to sharpen.
3. Toss the cabbage and onion in the dressing until lightly coated, adding more salad cream if necessary.

## Winter Salad

2 red eating apples
4 sticks of celery
1 medium-sized cooked beetroot
½ a small onion
Salad cream to bind
A few chopped walnuts to garnish

*Serves 4*

1. Core and roughly chop the apples, without peeling; scrub and chop the celery; peel and dice the beetroot; peel and finely chop the onion.
2. Combine these ingredients and bind with salad cream.
3. Pile into a dish and sprinkle with the walnuts.

## Jellied Salad Mould

A 5-oz. (approx. 140-g) lime or lemon jelly tablet
125 ml vinegar
1 leek
$\frac{1}{4}$ of a cucumber
1 stick of celery
1 red-skinned eating apple
Lemon juice

*Serves 4–6*

1. Dissolve the jelly tablet in 125 ml boiling water. Make up to 375 ml with cold water, and add the vinegar.
2. Leave the mixture in the refrigerator to cool until it is of the consistency of unbeaten egg white.
3. Wash the leek, remove the green part of the leaves, slice the white part into rings and blanch for 5 mins. in boiling salted water, then drain.
4. Slice the cucumber and the celery.
5. Dice the apple into large pieces, without peeling, but discarding the core, and leave it to stand in lemon juice to prevent discoloration.
6. Rinse out a 1-pint (570-ml) jelly mould with cold water.
7. When the jelly is just on the point of setting, fold in the vegetables, and pour into the wetted mould.
8. Leave the jelly to set until firm; un-mould, and serve as an accompaniment to a cold meat platter.

## Lemon Soufflé

3 eggs, separated
75 g caster sugar
Grated rind and juice of 2 lemons
2 level tsp. (10 ml) gelatine
2 tbsp. (30 ml) water
65 ml double cream, whipped
Finely chopped almonds
A lemon twist
Imitation double cream, whipped

*Serves 4–6*

1. Firmly tie a band of non-stick parchment paper or oiled greaseproof paper round a 5-ins. (12.5-cm) soufflé dish, letting it extend at least 5 cm above the rim of the dish; fasten securely with paperclips (p. 37).
2. Whisk together the egg yolks, sugar, lemon rind and juice over a pan of hot water, until thick and creamy. Remove from the heat and continue whisking until cool.
3. Dissolve the gelatine in the water, i.e., put the measured amount of water in a cup, sprinkle the measured gelatine

over it, stand the cup in a little hot water in a saucepan and heat until completely dissolved. Allow to cool slightly, then pour in a thin stream into the egg mixture. Stir thoroughly.

4. Whisk the cream until it just holds its shape, then stir into the lemon mixture.
5. When the mixture is almost setting, fold in the stiffly beaten egg whites, combining thoroughly.
6. Pour the mixture into the prepared soufflé dish and chill.
7. When the soufflé is completely set, remove the band of paper by using a palette knife with a wetted blade. Decorate the soufflé sides with chopped almonds, and pipe whirls of whipped imitation cream on top, adding a twist of lemon.

## Charlotte Russe

½ a 5-oz. tablet (i.e. 70 g) of yellow or red jelly
Some glacé cherries and angelica to decorate
1 pkt. of sponge fingers
250 ml double cream
125 ml cold custard (made with 3 level tsp. (15 ml) custard powder, 10 g sugar and 125 ml milk)
2 level tsp. (10 ml) gelatine
3 tbsp. (45 ml) water

*Serves 4*

1. Make up the jelly and set a quarter of it in the bottom of a 6-in. (approx. 15-cm) round cake tin.
2. When it is set, decorate with pieces of cherry and angelica arranged in the shape of a flower. Carefully cover with more jelly and allow to set.
3. Trim the sponge fingers, then brush the edges with liquid jelly. Line the sides of the mould with the sponge fingers, pressing them closely together.
4. Whip up the cream and combine this with the cold custard.
5. Dissolve the gelatine in the water over a pan of hot water. Add to the cream and custard, when the mixture is on the point of setting, pour it into the centre of the mould.
6. Trim off the surplus from the top of the sponge fingers.
7. When the cream is set, dip the bottom of the mould in hot water and invert it onto a serving dish to turn out the Charlotte Russe.

## Crème Caramel

### *For the Caramel*

140 g caster sugar
Water to dissolve

### *For the Custard*

3 eggs
15 g caster sugar
Vanilla essence
500 ml milk

*Serves 4*

1. Heat the oven to 163°C (mark 3, 325°F).
2. Dissolve the sugar for the caramel in 2 tbsp. (30 ml) water over a low heat, without boiling. When it is dissolved, bring to the boil and heat until it is a good brown colour.
3. To the pan of caramel add 2 tbsp. (30 ml) warm water and work it round until the caramel is of flowing consistency.
4. Pour the caramel into a 1-pint (approx. 500-ml) ring mould, or a 5-in. (12.5-cm) soufflé dish.
5. Beat the eggs together with the sugar. Add vanilla essence to taste. Bring the milk almost to the boil and pour onto the eggs, stirring.
6. Strain the mixture into the dish and stand this in a tin with water to a depth of about 2.5 cm. Cover the mould or dish with a plate or paper.
7. Bake just below the centre of the oven for $1\frac{1}{4}$ hrs., until the custard is set. Leave until cold.
8. Turn the Crème Caramel out onto a large plate.

## Marshmallow Desserts

1 level tbsp. (15 ml) gelatine
125 ml cold water
125 ml boiling water
150 g sugar
1 egg, separated
1 tsp. (5 ml) vanilla essence

*Number of servings depends on the way the mixture is used—see opposite.*

1. Sprinkle the gelatine over the cold water and leave to swell.
2. Add the boiling water, and stir to dissolve.

Marshmallow Desserts

3. Pour the mixture into a mixing bowl and add the sugar and the egg white. Beat with an egg beater, until thick and fluffy.
4. Quickly add the egg yolk and the vanilla essence. Beat, pour into glasses and leave to set.
5. Serve chilled, with fruit.

VARIATIONS (*see picture*)

1. Pour the mixture into a Swiss roll tin; when set, cut into squares and roll these in crushed cornflakes. Serve in individual glasses, layered with sliced fruit.
2. Half-fill an individual glass with fruit jelly and chopped fruit. Place the glass in the refrigerator in a tilted position and leave to set. When the jelly is firm, fill up the glass with marshmallow mixture, and again leave to set.
3. Set a 5-cm layer of fruit jelly in the base of an individual glass. Add a layer of marshmallow. Top with jelly and a whirl of cream.

## Lemon Fluff

3 eggs, separated
125 g caster sugar
Juice of 3 lemons and grated rind of 2
3 tbsp. (45 ml) water
2 level tsp. (10 ml) gelatine
Whipped cream and brandy snaps to decorate

*Serves 4–6*

1. Using a rotary whisk, cream together the egg yolks and sugar until pale and thick.
2. Gradually whisk in the juice of the lemons.
3. Put the water in a small bowl or cup, sprinkle the gelatine over, place the bowl in a pan with a little water and heat until the gelatine dissolves.
4. Whisk the gelatine into the egg yolk mixture, then add the grated lemon rind.
5. When the mixture is showing signs of just beginning to set, quickly but evenly fold in the stiffly beaten egg whites.
6. Divide the mixture between 4–6 individual glasses. Chill in the refrigerator.
7. Serve decorated with whipped cream and small whole brandy snaps (or crushed brandy snaps).

## Orange Velvet

3 eggs, separated
50 g caster sugar
Juice and grated rind of 1 orange
2 level tsp. (10 ml) gelatine
4 tbsp. (60 ml) water

*Serves 6–7*

1. Beat the egg yolks and sugar until light and fluffy.
2. Beat in the orange rind and juice.
3. Dissolve the gelatine in the water in the usual way and add to the orange mixture.
4. Whisk the egg whites stiffly and fold into the mixture.
5. Pour into tall individual glasses and leave to set.

## Orange Sorbet

200 g caster sugar
500 ml water
Thinly pared rind and squeezed-out juice of 3 oranges
2 egg whites
4 oranges to make cases for service
Sprigs of mint (optional)

*Serves 4*

1. Dissolve the sugar in the water over a low heat; add the pared orange rind and boil gently for 10 mins.
2. Leave to cool. Add the orange juice and strain the mixture into an ice-cube tray.
3. Place in the freezing compartment of the refrigerator and half-freeze.
4. Turn the mixture into a bowl. Stiffly whisk the egg whites and fold into the mixture. Replace the sorbet in the tray and re-freeze.
5. Scoop out the flesh of the oranges and replace it in the base of each orange-case, with scoops of sorbet. Alternatively, serve the portions of sorbet in stemmed glasses, each decorated with a sprig of mint.

## Meringue Pineapples

4 medium-sized cooking apples
15 g sultanas
2 tbsp. (30 ml) apricot jam
3 egg whites
150 g caster sugar
A few currants
Angelica

*Serves 4*

1. Heat the oven to 135°C (mark 1, 275°F).
2. Peel and core the apples.
3. Poach the apples in a pan of boiling water for 2 mins.; place in a shallow ovenproof dish.
4. Put some sultanas in the hole of each apple, pushing them down well to make a base.
5. Fill up the holes with apricot jam.
6. Use the egg whites and sugar to make a meringue. Pipe all round each apple, starting at the base and using a $\frac{1}{2}$-in. (approx. 1-cm) star vegetable nozzle.
7. Put a currant on the point of each meringue star.
8. Cut pieces of angelica to represent pineapple stalks and insert into the top of the apples.
9. Bake for 45–50 mins.

## Lemon Sponge

10 g gelatine
250 ml water
50 g sugar
Grated rind and juice of 2 lemons
2 egg whites

*Serves 4–6*

1. Dissolve the gelatine in the water, add the sugar and infuse the lemon rind in the water over a low heat. Cover and leave for $\frac{1}{4}$ hr.
2. Strain the mixture and leave until quite cold and beginning to thicken.
3. Add the strained lemon juice and the whisked egg whites.
4. Whisk all together till quite stiff. Either set the jelly in a $1\frac{1}{2}$-pint (approx. 750-ml) ring mould, or pour it into 4–6 individual glasses and leave to set.

## Pavlova Cake

3 egg whites
150 g caster sugar
$\frac{1}{2}$ tsp. (2.5 ml) vanilla essence
2 level tsp. (10 ml) cornflour
1 tsp. (5 ml) vinegar
250 ml double cream
200 g fresh cherries (or a small can of cherries, well-drained)

*Serves 8*

1. Heat the oven to 121°C (mark $\frac{1}{2}$, 250°F).
2. Draw a 17-cm circle on non-stick parchment paper and place the paper on a baking sheet.
3. Beat the egg whites till very stiff, then beat in the sugar, half at a time.
4. Beat in the vanilla essence, cornflour and vinegar.
5. Pile this meringue mixture over the round.
6. Bake in the centre of the oven for 1 hr., until firm.
7. Leave to cool, then remove the paper.
8. Place the case on a flat plate, top side down. Whip the cream and pile it over the Pavlova. Either decorate with fresh cherries, or arrange the drained fruit on top.

## French Fruit Flan

*Pâte Sucrée*

150 g plain flour
A pinch of salt
75 g butter
40 g caster sugar
1 small egg, beaten

*Filling*

An 11-oz. (310-g) can of sliced peaches
4 glacé cherries
$1\frac{1}{2}$ level tsp. (7.5 ml) arrowroot
125 ml fruit juice

*Serves 6*

1. Sift the flour and salt onto a working surface.
2. Make a well in the centre; add the butter (cut in pieces) and the sugar.
3. Cream the butter and sugar together with the fingertips.
4. Add the egg and gradually work in the flour, still using the fingertips.
5. Put the pastry into the refrigerator, wrapped in polythene, for at least 1 hr. to let it relax.

6. Heat the oven to 190°C (mark 5, 375°F).
7. Roll out the pâte sucrée and line an 8½-in. (21.5 cm) loose-bottomed flan ring.
8. Bake blind (see p. 41) for 15 mins. Cool on a wire rack.
9. Drain the can of fruit and arrange the peach slices in the flan case. Decorate with the cherries.
10. To make a glaze, blend the arrowroot with a little of the fruit juice to a smooth paste; heat the remainder of the fruit juice and pour this onto the blended arrowroot.
11. Return the mixture to the pan and heat through until boiling, stirring continuously. Simmer for a few mins.
12. Glaze the fruit in the flan case and leave to set.

*Note*: Other canned or suitable soft fruits may be used as a flan filling.

## Mocha Mousse

A 5-oz. (140-g) pkt. of pineapple jelly
3 tsp. (15 ml) coffee essence
100 g chocolate
1 tbsp. (15 ml) water
2 eggs, separated
Chocolate leaves for decoration (see p. 65)

*Serves 6*

1. Prepare the jelly as directed on the packet. To half of the liquid jelly add the coffee essence, and chill until half-set.
2. Melt the broken chocolate with the water in a basin over hot water.
3. When it is melted, cool, then beat in the egg yolks.
4. Add to the remaining liquid jelly and chill as for the coffee jelly.
5. Stiffly whisk 1 egg white and fold it through the coffee jelly. Half-fill 6 stemmed glasses and leave to set.
6. Stiffly whisk the second egg white and fold through the chocolate jelly. Spoon this mixture over the coffee jelly.
7. When set, decorate with chocolate leaves.

## Profiteroles

### *Choux Pastry*

25 g margarine
125 ml water
75 g plain flour
2 standard eggs
125 ml double cream

### *Chocolate Sauce*

75 g plain chocolate
1 tbsp. (15 ml) milk
10 g butter

*Makes 12*

1. Heat the oven to 218°C (mark 7, 425°F).
2. Heat the margarine and water gently until the fat has melted; bring to the boil, then remove from the heat and add the sifted flour all at once.
3. Beat until the mixture forms a smooth, shiny ball and leaves the sides of the pan.
4. Add the eggs separately, beating well after each addition, until the mixture is light and the egg incorporated. Cover and chill.
5. Using a plain ½-in. (1-cm) vegetable nozzle, pipe 12 small bun shapes well apart on greased baking sheets. Bake just

above the oven centre for 20 mins., until well risen, puffed and crisp.

6. Cool on a wire rack. Split, and fill with whipped cream.
7. Make the chocolate sauce by melting the chocolate with the milk in a basin over a pan of hot water and adding the butter when the chocolate has melted; stir well.
8. Pile the profiteroles on a plate in a pyramid shape and pour the chocolate sauce over (or serve it separately, if you prefer).

## Lemon Meringue Pie

100 g shortcrust pastry
3 level tsp. (15 ml) cornflour
125 ml water
Juice and grated rind of 2 lemons
50–75 g sugar
2 eggs, separated
75 g caster sugar
Glacé cherries and angelica to decorate

*Serves 6*

1. Heat the oven to 204°C (mark 6, 400°F).
2. Roll out the pastry and line a 7-in. (17.5-cm) flan ring or a deep pie plate. Trim the edges and bake blind towards the top of the oven for 15 mins. Remove the paper and baking beans and return the case to the oven for a further 5 mins.
3. Reduce the oven temperature to 177°C (mark 4, 350°F).
4. Blend the cornflour with the water in a saucepan, add the lemon juice and grated rind and bring slowly to the boil, stirring until the mixture thickens, then add the sugar.
5. Remove from the heat, cool the mixture slightly and add the egg yolks. Beat well and pour into the pastry case.
6. Whisk the egg whites stiffly, whisk in half the caster sugar and fold in the rest. Pile this meringue mixture on top of the lemon filling and bake in the centre of the oven for about 20 mins., or until the meringue is crisp and lightly browned.
7. Before serving, decorate with chopped glacé cherries and angelica.

## Mincemeat Tranche

250 g shortcrust pastry
1 large cooking apple
400 g mincemeat
Icing sugar to decorate

*Serves 8*

1. Heat the oven to 204°C (mark 6, 400°F).
2. Roll the shortcrust pastry out into a rectangle measuring 40 × 16.5 cm.
3. Line a tranche frame measuring 14 × 4½ ins. (35 × 12 cm).
4. Trim the edges of the pastry, using a rolling pin. From the trimmings cut 8 strips 1 cm wide, using a pastry wheel (p. 31).
5. Peel, core and slice the apple and place the slices in the base of the tranche. Cover with the mincemeat, spreading it evenly.
6. Place the pastry strips across the tranche in a criss-cross fashion.
7. Bake for 20–25 mins., until the pastry is cooked.
8. Remove the tranche frame and transfer the pastry to a long serving dish, using a fish slice or a palette knife.
9. Dust sifted icing sugar over the pastry strips.
10. Serve hot or cold, with whipped cream.

## Jam Tartlets

*(See picture on page 240)*

100 g shortcrust pastry
12 tbsp. (180 ml) jam or curd

*Makes about 12*

1. Heat the oven to 204°C (mark 6, 400°F).
2. Roll out the pastry thinly. Using a 2½-in. (3.75 cm) fluted pastry cutter, cut about a dozen rounds.
3. Put into greased patty tins and place 1 tbsp. of filling in each pastry case.
4. Bake for 15 mins.

## Rhubarb Cream Cheese Pie

400 g rhubarb
A little water
Grated rind of ½ a lemon
2 tbsp. (30 ml) cornflour
1 tbsp. (15 ml) rhubarb juice
75 g sugar
A shortcrust flan case, cooked in a 7-in. (17.5-cm) case
150 g soft cream cheese
1 egg, beaten
125 ml soured cream
50 g walnuts, chopped

*Serves 6*

1. Heat the oven to 177°C (mark 4, 350°F).
2. Wash the rhubarb and cut into even-sized pieces; stew the fruit gently in a little water for a few mins.
3. Drain thoroughly, retaining a little of the juice. Add the grated lemon rind to the cooked fruit.
4. Blend the cornflour with a little rhubarb juice. Heat the fruit and 50 g of the sugar in a pan, add the blended cornflour and cook, stirring all the time, until thick.
5. Pour the mixture into the flan case.
6. Beat the cream cheese, egg and remaining sugar together and gently spoon over the rhubarb. Bake in the centre of the oven for 30 mins.
7. Allow to cool, then cover the pie with the soured cream and decorate with chopped walnuts.

## Cheese Cake

150 g digestive biscuits
25 g caster sugar for case
75 g butter
200 g enriched curd cheese
25 g caster sugar for filling
1 egg, beaten
125 ml soured cream
Grated rind of 1 lemon
Lemon twists for decoration

*Serves 6–8*

1. Heat the oven to 177°C (mark 4, 350°F).
2. Crush the biscuits with a rolling pin and put into a bowl, with the sugar.
3. Melt the butter and pour onto the crumb mixture; mix well with a fork.
4. Oil a 9-in. (22-cm) shallow ovenproof dish or a 9-in. (22-cm) loose-bottomed fluted flan case. Press the crumb mixture against the sides and base.
5. Bake for 10 mins. and leave to cool.
6. Cream the cheese with the sugar until soft, beat in the egg a little at a time and finally the soured cream and the grated lemon rind.
7. Pour the mixture into the biscuit crust and bake for about 30 mins. until set. Cool.
8. Remove the ring (if a flan case was used). Decorate the cake with lemon twists and serve cut in wedges.

## Spicy Apple Pie

1½ kilos cooking apples
½ an orange
1 level tsp. (5 ml) ground cinnamon
150 g bought puff pastry
25 g sultanas
Beaten egg to glaze

*Serves 4–6*

1. Heat the oven to 218°C (mark 7, 425°F).
2. Peel and core the apples, slice thickly and leave in water to prevent discoloration. Grate the orange rind.
3. Roll out the pastry into an oblong. Cut off a strip to go round the rim of a 1½-pint (approx. 750-ml) dish and put in position.
4. Put the drained apples, orange rind, cinnamon and sultanas in the pie dish.

Spicy Apple Pie

5. Place the pastry on top of the fruit, trim the edges and seal well to the strip of pastry.
6. 'Knock up' and flute the edges (p. 29); glaze with egg.
7. Bake for 20 mins., turn heat down to 177°C (mark 4, 350°F), and bake for a further 25 mins., to cook through.

## Jamaican Crunch Pie

150 g gingernuts
50 g butter
125 ml double cream
A small can of sweetened condensed milk
6 tbsp. (90 ml) lemon juice
Grated rind of 1 lemon
3 slices of lemon for decoration

*Serves 6*

1. Crush the gingernuts with a rolling pin and place in a bowl. Melt the butter and add to the crushed biscuits.
2. Use the gingernut mixture to line a 7½-in. (19-cm) pie plate or flan ring placed on a flat plate. Work the crumbs up with the back of a metal spoon to form a shell; the edge should appear just above the plate rim.
3. Lightly whip the cream and fold in the condensed milk, lemon juice and rind. Whisk for 3 mins. longer; pour into the biscuit case and leave to thicken.
4. Chill and, before serving, decorate with lemon twists.

## Christmas Pudding

75 g plain flour
$\frac{1}{2}$ level tsp. (2.5 ml) mixed spice
$\frac{1}{2}$ level tsp. (2.5 ml) grated nutmeg
40 g fresh white breadcrumbs
50 g shredded suet
50 g stoned raisins
100 g currants, cleaned
100 g sultanas, cleaned
50 g apple, peeled, cored and chopped
40 g Demerara sugar
Grated rind of 1 lemon
Grated rind of 1 orange
2 eggs, beaten
Just under 125 ml brown ale

*Serves 4*

1. Prepare a steamer or fill a large saucepan with water and heat until boiling.
2. Grease a 1-pint (approx. 500-ml) pudding basin.
3. Sift together the flour, mixed spice and nutmeg.
4. Add the breadcrumbs, suet, dried fruit, apple, sugar and lemon and orange rind. Mix well.
5. Gradually stir in the beaten eggs and the ale and mix thoroughly. If liked, leave overnight.
6. Turn the mixture into the prepared basin and cover with greased paper and kitchen foil or a pudding cloth.
7. Place in a pan with water half-way up the side, or place in a steamer; reduce heat and steam or boil for 8 hrs. (A piece of lemon placed in the water during the boiling helps to prevent the pan from discolouring.)
8. Remove the kitchen foil or pudding cloth and replace with more foil or greaseproof paper for storage, but don't remove the greaseproof paper directly in contact with the pudding, since this is sterilised.
9. When the pudding is required, re-boil for 3 hrs.
10. Traditionally, Christmas pudding is accompanied by a brandy-flavoured white sauce or by Brandy Butter (see below), and caster sugar is handed separately.

*Brandy Butter*: Cream 50 g unsalted butter with 50 g caster sugar and flavour with 2 tsp. (10 ml) brandy. Put in a cool place until wanted, and serve piled up in a small dish, with a sprinkling of grated nutmeg on top.

*Rum Butter* is made in the same way.

## Fruity Steamed Pudding

200 g mixed dried fruit (apples, apricots, etc.)
3 tbsp. (45 ml) apricot jam
100 g butter
100 g sugar
2 eggs
100 g self-raising flour

*Serves 4–6*

1. Soak the fruit for 1 hr. in sufficient water to cover.
2. Prepare a steamer. Oil a $1\frac{1}{2}$-pint (approx. 750-ml) pudding basin and put the jam in the base. Arrange the fruit round the base of the basin and halfway up the sides, fixing those on the side with a little jam.
3. Cream the butter and sugar together until light and fluffy. Beat in the eggs one at a time. Sift the flour and fold into the mixture.
4. Spoon half the mixture into the pudding basin, taking care not to shift the fruit around the sides of the bowl.
5. Chop the remainder of the fruit and place evenly over the flour mixture.
6. Add the rest of the flour mixture and level the surface. Cover with greaseproof paper and aluminium foil, or secure with a pudding cloth, and steam for $1\frac{1}{2}$ hrs.

# BAKED GOODS

## FAMILY AND PARTY CAKES, BISCUITS, YEAST COOKERY

*Note*: For cakes likely to be eaten up at one meal, we give the approximate number of servings, but we omit this for the 'cut and come again' cakes, like Gingerbread

---

### Grape Gâteau

100 g margarine
100 g caster sugar
2 eggs
100 g self-raising flour
200 g black grapes
125 ml double cream
A few flaked almonds
7 tbsp. (105 ml) apricot jam

*Serves 6*

1. Heat the oven to 177°C (mark 4, 350°F). Line an 8-in. (20-cm) cake tin.
2. Cream the fat and sugar together until light and fluffy. Beat in the eggs one at a time.
3. Sift the flour and lightly beat into the mixture.
4. Spoon the mixture into the cake tin and bake for about 45 mins. Cool the cake on a wire rack.
5. Meanwhile, wash grapes, halve, and discard seeds.

6. Whip the cream stiffly. Toast the almonds.
7. When the cake is cold, coat the sides with cream, reserving some for the top; roll it in the almonds.
8. Warm 3 tbsp. jam and brush top of cake with it.
9. Arrange the grapes in circles on top of the cake.
10. Boil remaining jam with 1 tbsp. water and glaze the fruit. Alternatively, use arrowroot glaze (see French Fruit Flan), blending the arrowroot with 125 ml lemon juice and water and 1 level tsp. (5 ml) caster sugar.
11. Pipe on the remaining cream in whirls (p. 104).

## Battenburg Cake

150 g butter or margarine
150 g caster sugar
3 eggs
150 g self-raising flour
15 g cocoa
Milk if necessary
Raspberry jam
200 g bought almond paste
Caster sugar

*Serves 8*

1. Heat the oven to 190°C (mark 5, 375°F).
2. Use a Swiss roll tin measuring $11\frac{1}{2} \times 7\frac{1}{2}$ ins. (27.5 × 19 cm). Line it, and divide it lengthwise with a greaseproof paper 'wall'.
3. Make up a Victoria sandwich cake mixture using the butter, sugar, eggs and flour. Put half the mixture into one side of the tin.
4. Add the cocoa to the other half, with a little more milk if necessary, and put into second side of tin.
5. Bake for 45–50 mins. just above the centre of the oven, until well-risen and firm to the touch.
6. Cool the cakes, trim to equal size and cut each in half. Spread the sides of the strips with sieved warmed jam and stick together, alternating the colours and pressing the pieces well together.
7. Coat the whole outside of the cake with jam. Roll out the almond paste thinly on a board dusted with caster sugar, forming an oblong 20 × 25 cm.
8. Wrap paste round cake; seal join well and trim edges.
9. Crimp along the top outer edges to make a decorative border, and score the surface with a sharp knife in a criss-cross pattern.

## Mandarin Cream Gâteau

3 large eggs
75 g caster sugar
75 g plain flour
3 tbsp. (45 ml) oil
5 tbsp. (60 ml) apricot jam
1–2 11-oz. (310-g) cans of mandarin oranges
250 ml double or synthetic cream
Angelica and a glacé cherry to decorate

*Serves 6*

1. Heat the oven to 190°C (mark 5, 375°F).
2. Grease and line base of two 6-in. (15.2-cm) sandwich tins.
3. Put the eggs and sugar in a large bowl over a pan of hot (not boiling) water and whisk until thick and creamy. (The mixture should be stiff enough to retain the impression of the whisk for a few seconds.)
4. Sift the flour over the whisked eggs and fold in lightly and quickly, alternately with the oil.
5. Pour the mixture into the tins and bake towards the top of the oven until golden-brown and firm to the touch – about 20–25 mins. Cool on a wire rack.
6. Heat the apricot jam slowly in a saucepan until runny.
7. Brush the top surface of one cake with the warmed jam.
8. Drain the mandarins and arrange the segments in groups round the cake. Chop any surplus fairly small.

9. Place the bottom cake on a serving plate. Lightly whip the cream and spread most of it over the bottom cake. Top with any remaining mandarins.
10. Carefully lift the other cake onto the base. Fill the holes round the side with piped cream, using a ½-in. (1-cm) star vegetable nozzle.
11. Decorate with angelica leaves and the glacé cherry.

## Genoese Sponge

3 eggs
100 g caster sugar
75 g plain flour, sifted
3 tbsp. (45 ml) oil

*Serves 6*

1. Heat the oven to 190°C (mark 5, 375°F).
2. Grease and line base of two 6-in. (15-cm) sandwich tins.
3. Put the eggs and sugar in a large bowl, stand this over a pan of hot water and whisk until light and creamy—the mixture should be stiff enough to retain an impression of the whisk for a few seconds.
4. Remove from the heat and whisk until cool.
5. Lightly fold in the flour alternately with the oil.
6. Pour the mixture into the tins and bake towards the top of the oven until golden-brown and firm to the touch. When cold, sandwich together with jam and decorate either with butter icing or with American Frosting (see below).

## American Frosting

200 g granulated sugar
4 tbsp. (60 ml) water
1 egg white

*Sufficient to coat top and sides of a sponge as above*

1. Gently heat the sugar in the water, stirring until dissolved. Heat *without stirring* to 240°F.
2. Beat the egg white until stiff. Remove the sugar syrup from the heat and, when the bubbles subside, pour it on to the egg white. Beat the mixture continuously.
3. When it thickens and is almost cold, pour it quickly over the cake.

## Creamy Walnut Gâteau

A 6-in. (15-cm) Victoria sandwich cake
6 tbsp. (90 ml) apricot jam
100 g butter or margarine
200 g icing sugar
1 tsp. (5 ml) vanilla essence
1 tbsp. (15 ml) milk
50 g shelled walnuts

*Serves 6–8*

1. Split the cake, trim and fill with jam.
2. Beat the butter or margarine in a bowl until creamy.
3. Sift the sugar and gradually beat in with the essence. Add 1 tbsp. milk to make of a spreading consistency.
4. Place the cake on an icing turntable and coat the entire surface with the icing, using a palette knife.
5. Using an icing comb at an angle of 45° to the cake, draw it round the sides to give the ridged design.
6. Using a ½-in. (1-cm) star vegetable nozzle, pipe 2 ropes of cream on the top of the cake, forming a cross and dividing the surface into 4 sections.
7. Chop the walnuts roughly and sprinkle in each section.

## Apricot Gâteau

A round sponge cake
Apricot jam
1 pkt. sponge fingers
75 g chocolate, melted

*For the Topping*

A 15-oz. (425-g) can of apricots, drained
3–4 tbsp. (60 ml) rum (optional)
2 level tsp. (10 ml) arrowroot
125 ml whipped cream
25 g grated chocolate

*Serves 6*

1. Spread sides and centre of cake with jam. Dip one end of each sponge finger in chocolate and leave to harden.
2. Trim the other end of the fingers; arrange upright round cake, keeping them in place with a piece of tape.
3. Arrange the apricots over the cake. Pour the rum (if used) over the fruit and allow to soak for 2–3 hrs.
4. Glaze with 125 ml fruit juice thickened with arrowroot.
5. Decorate with whipped cream and sprinkle with chocolate. Before serving, replace the tape by a ribbon.

## Strawberry Butterfly

100 g sandwich cake mixture
200 g strawberries, prepared
25 g icing sugar
125 ml double cream

*Serves 6*

1. Heat the oven to 190°C (mark 5, 375°F).
2. Divide the sandwich mixture between two 6-in. (15-cm) sandwich tins, and bake for 20 mins.
3. Slice the strawberries and sprinkle with a little sugar.
4. Whip the cream to piping consistency.
5. Spread half the cream on one of the cakes. Drain the strawberries and arrange on top of the cream, leaving a space about 3.5 cm wide across the centre.
6. Halve the other cake to make 'wings', and place on top of the fruit, with the bases meeting in the empty space.
7. Using a ½-in. (1-cm) star vegetable nozzle, pipe the cream in a rope down the centre where the two wings meet.
8. Sprinkle with the remaining icing sugar.

## Cream Horns

150 g bought flaky pastry
A little caster sugar
7 tsp. (35 ml) jam or fruit
125 ml whipped cream
Icing sugar

*Makes 6–7*

1. Heat the oven to 204°C (mark 6, 400°F).
2. Roll out the pastry thinly into an oblong about 30 cm long. Cut lengthwise into strips 1 cm wide.
3. Moisten one edge of each strip and roll it round a cream horn tin, starting at the pointed end of the tin and overlapping the moistened edge of the pastry very slightly at each turn. Brush pastry with water, sprinkle with sugar.
4. Bake towards top of oven until crisp—10–15 mins.
5. Slip the pastries off the tins, and when they are cold, fill each with a spoonful of jam or fruit, top with whipped cream and dredge with icing sugar.

## Mille-feuilles

A 13-oz. (approx. 370-g) pkt. of puff pastry
5 tbsp. (75 ml) raspberry jam
100 g icing sugar, approx.
1 egg white
250 ml whipping cream or imitation cream (or 125 ml of double and 60 ml single cream)

*Makes 8 portions*

1. Heat the oven to 232°C (mark 8, 450°F).
2. Divide the pastry into 3 equal portions.
3. Roll each piece out to an oblong about 14 × 30 cm.
4. Place on a wetted baking sheet, prick with a fork and allow the pastry to relax for ½ hr.
5. Bake for 15 mins.; cool on a rack and trim edges.
6. Spread pastry base with jam; and top with the second layer of pastry.
7. Beat the icing sugar into the egg white and use to ice the flat side of the third piece of pastry; leave to set.
8. Using a thick, heated skewer, brand the iced top in a trellis pattern.
9. Spread stiffly whipped cream onto the centre of the puff paste layer; top with the iced pastry layer.

## Decorated Fairy Cakes

100 g sandwich cake mixture
100 g butter icing
100 g glacé icing
Decorations, including angelica, chocolate squares and triangles, chocolate dots

*Makes 12–16 cakes*

1. Heat the oven to 190°C (mark 5, 375°F).
2. Spread 12–16 paper cases out on baking trays.
3. Two-thirds fill each case with cake mixture and bake towards the top of the oven for 15–20 mins.
4. Make butter icing (see Creamy Walnut Gâteau).
5. Using a star nozzle, pipe various designs on some cakes.
6. Decorate rest of cakes with glacé icing, and add chocolate triangles, squares and dots, and angelica shapes.

*To make Chocolate Triangles and Squares (see p. 65)*

1. Melt 100 g plain cooking chocolate in a basin over a pan of hot water—don't overheat.
2. Pour the melted chocolate onto a piece of non-stick paper placed on a baking sheet and leave until almost set.
3. Using a sharp knife dipped in hot water, divide the chocolate into squares and triangles. Leave to set in the refrigerator. Use for decorating cakes and desserts.

## Christmas Cake

- 200 g stoned raisins
- 200 g currants
- 200 g sultanas
- 100 g small glacé cherries
- 50 g blanched almonds
- 100 g mixed chopped peel
- 1 lemon
- 200 g plain flour
- ½ level tsp. (2.5 ml) ground cinnamon
- ½ level tsp. (2.5 ml) ground mace
- 200 g butter
- 200 g dark, soft brown sugar
- 4 large eggs, beaten
- 1–2 tbsp. (15–30 ml) brandy or sherry (optional)
- Icing and decoration (see opposite page)

1. Heat the oven to 149°C (marks 1–2, 300°F).
2. Grease and double-line an 8-in. (20-cm) round cake tin. Tie a band of brown paper firmly round outside, or put tin inside a slightly larger one, and omit the paper.
3. Wash fruit (if not pre-washed), spread on baking trays in a single layer and dry in a cool oven for ¾ hr.
4. Chop raisins, cherries, nuts; put all fruit in a large bowl. Grate lemon rind. Sift flour and spices together.
5. Cream the butter and sugar together until light and creamy. Gradually add the beaten eggs.

6. Fold in the flour alternately with the fruit and nuts. Finally, stir in the brandy or sherry, if used.
7. Put mixture into the tin; hollow centre top slightly.
8. Bake below oven centre for about 3¼ hrs. Cool in tin for 10 mins., then cool on a wire rack.
9. To store, wrap in greaseproof paper and kitchen foil.
10. During storage the brandy or sherry may be poured over the cake—prick the surface first with a fine skewer.

### ICING AND SANTA CLAUS DECORATION

A cake of this size takes about 675 g ready-made almond paste, and royal icing made with 900 g icing sugar, 4 egg whites and 2 tsp. (10 ml) glycerine.

1. Put on a layer of almond paste and leave to dry out thoroughly; this takes about a week.
2. Place on a 10-in. (25–cm) silver cake-board. Coat with royal icing.
3. Make the Santa Claus; tint some pliable almond paste pale pink, using a very little powdered colouring.
4. Roll the paste out thinly between layers of waxed paper and stamp out a 2.5-cm round for the head.
5. Using a little more red colouring, tint remainder of the paste deep red. Roll out as before, stamp out a 5-cm round for the body and cut a 2-cm triangle for a hat.
6. Position the pink round so that it slightly overlaps the red one and press lightly together. Place the hat.
7. To shape the arms, cut a curved line about 1.5 cm in from edge at each side, cutting half-way down the body.
8. Cut a short straight line in from outside edge to meet this line; pull arms out from body; leave to dry.
9. Mark a circle 2.5 cm from the cake edge, using a pin. With a No. 2 writing nozzle, pipe royal icing lines round top edge at 5-cm intervals; then repeat in opposite direction to form a lattice. Repeat around the cake-board. (See pp. 103, 104.)
10. When dry, put the Santa and some holly leaves on top, fixing them with a smear of royal icing. Pipe features, etc., using royal icing and a writing nozzle.

## Dundee Cake

100 g currants
100 g stoned raisins
100 g sultanas
100 g candied peel
250 g plain flour
200 g butter or margarine
200 g soft brown sugar
Grated rind of 1 lemon
4 eggs, beaten
A little milk if needed
50 g whole almonds, blanched

1. Heat the oven to 163°C (mark 3, 325°F).
2. Line an 8-in. (20-cm) round cake tin.
3. Prepare the fruit and chop the peel. Sift the flour.
4. Cream the fat, sugar and lemon rind till pale and fluffy.
5. Beat in the eggs and fold in the flour. Add a little milk if necessary to give a dropping consistency.
6. Put into the tin and hollow the centre slightly. Arrange the almonds on top.
7. Bake just below the centre of the oven for $2\frac{1}{2}$–3 hrs. Cover top with brown paper if cake browns too fast.
8. When the cake is firm to the touch, take from the oven. Allow to cool in the tin, and remove when cold.

## Orange Tea Bread

50 g butter
150 g caster sugar
1 egg, beaten
Grated rind and juice of $\frac{1}{2}$ an orange—2 tbsp. (30 ml)
2 tbsp. (30 ml) milk
200 g plain flour
$2\frac{1}{2}$ level tsp. (12.5 ml) baking powder
A pinch of salt

*Serves 6–8*

1. Heat the oven to 190°C (mark 5, 375°F).
2. Use a loaf tin measuring 8 × $4\frac{1}{4}$ × $2\frac{1}{4}$ ins. (20 × 12 × 5 cm). Grease and bottom-line it.
3. Beat the butter, add the sugar and beat again until well mixed; gradually beat in the egg until smooth and creamy. Slowly add the orange rind and juice—don't worry if the mixture curdles.
4. Lightly beat in the milk, alternately with the sifted flour, baking powder and salt.
5. Turn the mixture into the prepared tin. Bake in the centre of the oven for 40–50 mins.

6. Turn the cake out and cool on a wire rack. Slice, and spread with honey and cream cheese spread, or with butter.

## Banana Tea Bread

3 small ripe bananas
1 tbsp. (15 ml) lemon juice
25 g shelled walnuts
2 level tsp. (10 ml) baking powder
200 g plain flour
100 g butter
175 g sugar
2 eggs

*Serves 6–8*

1. Line and grease a loaf tin measuring $8\frac{1}{2} \times 4\frac{1}{4} \times 3$ ins. (approx. $21 \times 11 \times 7.5$ cm).
2. Heat the oven to 190°C (mark 5, 375°F).
3. Mash the bananas with the lemon juice. Chop the walnuts. Sift the baking powder with the flour.
4. Cream the butter and sugar until light and creamy. Beat in the beaten eggs.
5. Stir the mashed bananas into the creamed mixture.
6. Fold in the flour, then stir in the chopped walnuts.
7. Turn the mixture into the tin and bake for 1 hr.
8. When cold, serve in buttered slices.

## Hungarian Chocolate Biscuits

100 g butter
100 g caster sugar
A few drops of vanilla essence
100 g plain flour
1 level tbsp. (15 ml) cocoa
A pinch of salt
25–50 g nibbed or chopped almonds

*Makes about 2 dozen*

1. Heat the oven to 177°C (mark 4, 350°F). Grease a baking sheet.
2. Cream the butter and sugar together until light and creamy; add the essence.
3. Sift the flour, cocoa and salt together and fold into the creamed mixture.
4. Form the dough into small balls, roll these in the nibbed almonds and place them on the baking sheet, a fair distance apart.
5. Flatten the balls with a fork dipped in water and then bake for 10–15 mins.
6. Cool on a wire rack.

## Coconut Biscuits

100 g butter
100 g sugar
1 egg
150 g self-raising flour
100 g desiccated coconut
1 tsp. (5 ml) vanilla essence
12 glacé cherries
12 walnut halves

*Makes about 2 dozen*

1. Heat the oven to 190°C (mark 5, 375°F).
2. Cream the butter and sugar until light and fluffy. Beat in the egg well.
3. Sift the flour and stir it into the mixture, with the desiccated coconut and the vanilla essence, to make a firm dough.
4. Divide the mixture into 24 pieces and roll each piece of dough into a small ball in the hands. Place on a baking sheet, well apart. Press a cherry half or a walnut half into each ball.
5. Bake for 15 mins.
6. Cool on a wire rack.

Whirligigs and Coconut Biscuits

## Whirligigs

75 g butter
75 g caster sugar
150 g plain flour
½ level tsp. (2.5 ml) baking powder
A pinch of salt
1 tsp. (5 ml) vanilla essence
1 tbsp. (15 ml) milk
1 level tbsp. (15 ml) cocoa

*Makes about 14*

1. Heat the oven to 190°C (mark 5, 375°F).
2. Cream the butter and sugar until light and fluffy.
3. Sift the flour with the baking powder and salt and stir into the creamed mixture, with the essence and milk.
4. Divide the mixture in half and blend the cocoa into one half.
5. Roll out each piece a rectangle about 22 × 17 cm.
6. Place the chocolate layer over the plain one and roll up tightly, Swiss roll fashion.
7. Leave in a cool place for 30 mins.
8. Cut into slices about 5 cm thick.
9. Bake for 12–15 mins.
10. Cool on a wire rack.

## Breads and Rolls

400 g strong plain flour
1 level tsp. (5 ml) salt
2 level tsp. (10 ml) fresh yeast *or* 1 level tsp. (5 ml) dried yeast
250 ml water
Egg glaze or milk, if required
Poppy seeds, if required

*Note*: For use of dried yeast, see opposite page.

TIN LOAF

1. Sift the flour and add the salt.
2. Blend the fresh yeast in the water.
3. Add the yeast to the dry ingredients and mix to a dough that will leave the bowl clean.
4. Knead the dough thoroughly on a lightly floured surface. Heat the oven to 232°C (mark 8, 450°F).
5. Shape the dough to half-fill a well-greased 1-lb. (approx. 450-g) loaf tin.
6. Put to rise in a large greased polythene bag, loosely tied, and leave until the dough has doubled its size and springs back when lightly pressed with a floured finger.
7. Remove the polythene bag and bake the loaf on the middle shelf of the oven for 30–35 mins.

DINNER ROLLS (This quantity makes 1 dozen)

1. Make dough as above, put on an unfloured board and flatten it to 1 cm thick. Divide it into 12 pieces and roll each into a round, or make a plait, or shape into a criss-cross roll (see picture).
2. Brush tops with water, milk, or beaten egg mixed with water or milk. Sprinkle a few poppy seeds on top if liked.
3. Cover the rolls with greased polythene and allow to rise to double the original size. Then bake at the top of the oven for 20–25 mins.

CROWN LOAF

1. Divide part of dough into 6 50-g pieces; work each into a smooth ball. Put 5 in a ring in a greased 6-in. (approx. 15-cm) sandwich tin, with sixth in the centre.
2. Brush with egg wash and sprinkle with poppy seeds. Cover and prove as above, then bake for 25 mins.

COTTAGE LOAF

1. Take three-quarters of the dough and shape it into a large round. Shape the remaining dough into a small round and press this down lightly on top of the larger one.
2. Make a hole in centre of rounds, using a finger and pressing almost to bottom; brush with beaten egg and milk.
3. Cover, prove, and bake for 30–35 mins.

USING DRIED YEAST

Dried yeast is available in tins and packets, and may be stored for long periods.

When replacing fresh yeast by dried, use only half the amount stated in the recipe, e.g., use 1 level tsp. (5 ml) dried yeast instead of 2 level tsp. (10 ml) fresh yeast.

To reconstitute dried yeast, take $\frac{1}{2}$ cup (about 125 ml) of the liquid given in the recipe and warm it to blood heat. Pour it into a cup and sprinkle the yeast on top, whisking with a fork. Leave to stand in a warm place for 10–15 mins., or until the surface of the liquid is covered with bubbles and the granules of yeast are dissolved.

If milk is used, it will hasten the process if you first dissolve 1 level tsp. (5 ml) sugar in the milk.

## Croissants

450 g strong plain flour
2 level tsp. (10 ml) salt
25 g lard
25 g fresh yeast or 1 level tbsp. (15 ml) dried
200 ml water, less 2 tbsp. (30 ml)
1 egg, beaten
100–150 g margarine

### *Egg Glaze*

1 egg, beaten
A little water
½ level tsp. (2.5 ml) caster sugar

*Makes 12*

*Note*: The dough needs to be made the day beforehand.

1. Sift the flour and salt into a bowl; rub in lard.
2. Blend the yeast and water and stir in with the egg.
3. Mix to a firm dough, turn on to a lightly floured surface and knead until dough is smooth—10–15 mins. Roll out into a strip measuring about 50 × 15 cm.
4. Divide the margarine into three. Take one portion and put little flakes over top two-thirds of the dough.
5. Fold in three—bring up plain part, then fold top over.
6. Turn the dough so that the fold is on the right. Seal edges by pressing with rolling pin. Roll out again as above, keeping corners square. Repeat with rest of fat.

7. Place the dough in an oiled polythene bag and allow to relax in the refrigerator for 30 mins.
8. Repeat folding and rolling 3 times, without adding extra fat. Put in the oiled bag and refrigerate overnight.
9. Roll the dough into a rectangle 50 × 30 cm. Cover with the oiled bag and leave for 10 mins.
10. Trim edges and divide in half lengthwise. Cut each strip into 6 triangles 15 cm high with a 15-cm base.
11. Mix egg glaze ingredients. Glaze each triangle, roll up loosely from base towards point, then shape into crescents. Place on ungreased baking sheets, well apart.
12. Put in the oiled bag and leave at room temperature for about ½ hr., till light and fluffy. Glaze again.
13. Bake in the centre of the oven at 218°C (mark 7, 425°F) for about 20 mins. Serve warm.

## Fruit Tea Bread

(*see picture on page 231*)

225 g plain flour
1 level tsp. (5 ml) salt
10 g lard
20 g fresh yeast or 2½ level tsp. (12.5 ml) dried
65 ml water
½ tbsp. (7.5 ml) honey, made up to 65 ml with warm milk
50 g seedless raisins
50 g currants
50 g cut mixed peel

*Serves 6–8*

1. Sift the flour, add the salt and rub in the lard.
2. Blend or dissolve the yeast in the usual way; pour into the flour mixture, with the honey and milk.
3. Work to a dough by squeezing with the finger-tips.
4. Turn out onto a lightly floured board and knead until smooth and elastic—about 5 mins.
5. Put dough in a greased polythene bag and tie tightly; leave to rise until it doubles its size and springs back when lightly pressed with a floured finger.
6. Heat the oven to 190°C (mark 5, 375°F).
7. Turn the dough onto a board and work in the fruit. Divide dough in two, flatten each piece and roll up like a Swiss roll to fit a greased 1-lb. (approx. 450-g) loaf tin. Put in a polythene bag and leave till dough reaches top of tin.
8. Bake on the middle shelf of the oven for 30–40 mins.

## Danish Pastries

15 g fresh yeast or $1\frac{1}{2}$ level tsp. (7.5 ml) dried yeast plus $\frac{1}{2}$ level tsp. (2.5 ml) sugar
5 tbsp. (75 ml) warm water
200 g strong plain flour
A pinch of salt
25 g lard
1 level tbsp. (15 ml) caster sugar
1 egg, beaten
125 g butter
Egg glaze
Glacé icing

### *Almond Paste for Crescents*

25 g ground almonds
25 g caster sugar
A little egg white

### *Filling for Pinwheels*

25 g butter
25 g caster sugar
1 level tsp. (5 ml) ground cinnamon
A few currants
A little candied peel, finely chopped

*Makes about 14–16*

1. Blend the fresh yeast with the water, or dissolve the dried yeast and sugar in the water (see pp. 226–227).
2. Sift the flour and salt and rub in the lard. Add the sugar, egg and yeast liquid and mix to a soft dough.
3. Turn it onto a lightly floured board and knead very lightly until smooth. Put in a lightly greased polythene bag and leave in a cool place for 10 mins.
4. Beat butter until soft. Roll out dough to a 25-cm square.
5. Shape all the butter into a rectangle, put in middle and fold up the two unbuttered sides so they just overlap in the middle. Seal the bottom and top.
6. Roll out to an oblong strip about three times as long as it is wide. Fold evenly in three. Put in a polythene bag and leave in a cool place for 10 mins., then roll out for use as required. See opposite.
7. Heat the oven to 218°C (mark 7, 425°F).
8. Cover the shaped and filled pastries with a lightly greased polythene bag and prove in a slightly warm place until puffy—about 20 mins.
9. Bake towards the top of the oven for 12–15 mins.
10. Coat while still hot with glacé icing.

Fruit Tea Bread (p. 229), Doughnuts (p. 232) and Danish Pastries (recipe on these pages)

TO MAKE CRESCENTS

1. Roll out half the basic dough to a round 27 cm across, and cut into wedge-shaped sections.
2. Put a piece of almond paste in the middle of each piece, roll up towards the point and curve into a crescent.
3. Place on a baking sheet about 3 cm apart and brush with egg glaze.

TO MAKE PINWHEELS

1. Roll out the basic dough into an oblong about 30 × 20 cm. Cream the butter, sugar and cinnamon.
2. Spread the dough with the spice mixture and scatter with the fruit and peel. Roll up one strip from the short end to make a fat roll about 10 cm wide.
3. Cut into four 2.5-cm slices. Place cut side down on a baking sheet and brush with egg glaze.

## Doughnuts

(*see picture on page 231*)

*For Batter Mixture*
(*see note below*)

100 g plain flour
1 level tsp. (5 ml) sugar
25 g fresh yeast (or 1 level tbsp. (15 ml) dried yeast)
125 ml warm milk
125 ml less 4 tbsp. (60 ml) warm water

*For Dough Mixture*

50 g butter or margarine
300 g plain flour
1 level tsp. (5 ml) salt
50 g sugar
1 egg, beaten

*For Finishing*

Stiff jam
Fat for deep-frying
A little caster sugar
A little ground cinnamon

*Makes 12–14*

*Note*: A lighter texture is achieved if the yeast and liquid are mixed with part of the flour and allowed to work before being mixed with the bulk of the flour, as here.

1. Blend the batter ingredients together in a large bowl and set aside till the batter froths (20–30 mins.).
2. Rub the butter or margarine into the flour and mix all the dough ingredients into the batter, to give a fairly soft dough that leaves the sides of the bowl clean.
3. Turn the dough onto a lightly floured surface and knead till it is smooth and no longer sticky—about 5 mins.
4. Leave the dough to rise in a lightly greased and loosely tied polythene bag till doubled in size—1–1½ hrs. at room temperature.
5. Turn dough onto a floured surface and flatten with the knuckles, to knock out air bubbles. Knead till firm.
6. Divide dough into 12–14 pieces and shape into buns, using the palm of the hand; don't overwork it. A little oil on the working surface and the palm gives a smooth finish.
7. Cover and leave to rise.
8. Place a little stiff jam in the centre of each ball of risen dough and pinch back into shape.
9. Heat the fat in a deep-fat frying pan to 177°C and fry the doughnuts, a few at a time, for about 4 mins. each.
10. Roll the doughnuts in sugar and cinnamon.

## Irish Soda Bread

225 g plain flour
1 level tsp. (5 ml) bicarbonate of soda
2 level tsp. (10 ml) cream of tartar
1 level tsp. (5 ml) salt
225 g wholemeal flour
25 g margarine
285 ml milk

1. Heat the oven to 204°C (mark 6, 400°F). Grease a 2-lb. (approx. 900-g) loaf tin, if needed (see below).
2. Sift together the plain flour, soda, cream of tartar and salt; add wholemeal flour; rub in margarine.
3. Mix in milk to form a fairly soft dough. Turn it out on to a lightly floured board and knead until smooth.
4. Put into the tin; alternatively, shape dough into 2 rounds, place on a baking sheet and score the tops.
5. Bake for 40–45 mins. (allow 30–35 mins. for rounds). Cool on a rack. Eat the day it is made.

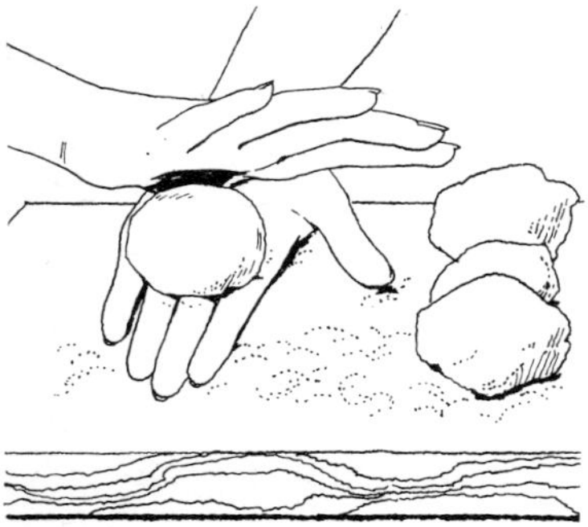

SHAPING BREAD ROLLS 1: Cut the dough into small portions and roll each portion into a ball.
2: (*above right*) Divide a portion of dough into three, roll each small piece into a strip and plait, pressing the ends firmly together

PROVING BREAD ROLLS: Place the shaped but uncooked rolls on a baking sheet and cover with a sheet of polythene before leaving to rise

# PETITS FOURS; COCKTAIL SAVOURIES; CANDIES; PRESERVES

## PETITS FOURS

### Chocolate Cups

125 g Kake Brand plain chocolate-flavoured cake covering
100 g glacé cherries
1 tbsp. (15 ml) rum
1 egg yolk
5 g icing sugar

*Makes about 16*

1. Melt 100 g chocolate in a bowl over hot water.
2. Make up 16 paper petits fours cases, each consisting of 2 layers one inside another. Place on a baking sheet.
3. Spoon some chocolate into each to coat; leave to set.
4. Coat the thin inside edges with more cool chocolate; let excess drip off; upturn cases on baking sheet.
5. Chill the cases, then peel off the outer layers. Gently pull away the inner paper cases.
6. Chop the cherries and marinade in the rum for 1 hr.
7. Melt the remaining 25 g chocolate. When cool, stir in the rum from the cherries, egg yolk and sifted sugar.
8. Put the chopped cherries into the chocolate cases. Pipe with the chocolate cream, using a small star nozzle.

## Mandarin Barquettes

100 g plain flour
A pinch of salt
50 g butter
25 g caster sugar
1 egg yolk
¼ tsp. (1 ml) vanilla essence
An 11-oz. (310-g) can of mandarin oranges
Apricot glaze
5 g pistachio nuts, blanched and halved, or halved glacé cherries, for decoration

*Makes about 1½ dozen*

1. Heat the oven to 177°C (mark 4, 350°F).
2. Sift the flour and salt onto a working surface. Cream the butter and sugar together in a well in the centre of the flour. Add the egg yolk and flavouring.
3. Mix to a soft dough with the heel of the hand. Roll out 5 cm thick between sheets of non-stick paper.
4. Lay some barquette moulds over the pastry and press out the shapes by rolling the rolling pin over the moulds. Re-mould the pastry trimmings and roll out.
5. Slide a knife under each barquette, turn it over and mould the pastry up the sides. Prick with a fork and bake on a baking sheet for about 15 mins.
6. Cool slightly, and carefully remove from the moulds.
7. Drain the fruit; put 3 mandarin segments in each case.
8. Heat 2 tbsp. apricot jam and 1 tbsp. water in a small pan; sieve, and brush over the fruit. Decorate.

## Almond Stars

2 eggs, separated
150 g ground almonds
75 g caster sugar
A few drops of almond essence
Angelica to decorate

*Makes about 2 dozen*

1. Heat the oven to 149°C (mark 2, 300°F).
2. Line 2 baking sheets with non-stick paper.
3. Put the egg whites into a mixing bowl. Whisk them until they are stiff and will just cling to the bowl.
4. Using a tablespoon, fold in almonds, sugar and essence.
5. Using a large star vegetable nozzle, pipe stars, quite close together, on to the lined baking sheets.
6. Decorate each star with a small angelica strip, and bake for 15–20 mins., till just beginning to colour.

## COCKTAIL SAVOURIES

### Savoury Barquettes

100 g plain flour
A pinch of salt
50 g butter or margarine
Cold water
A 200-g pkt. of full-fat soft cream cheese
6 gherkins

*Makes about $1\frac{1}{2}$ dozen*

1. Heat the oven to 204°C (mark 6, 400°F).
2. Make shortcrust pastry with the flour, salt, fat and water. Roll it out. Lay some $3\frac{1}{2}$-in. (approx. 9-cm) barquette tins on a flat surface, about 1.5 cm apart.
3. Wrap the pastry around the rolling pin and position it over the tins.
4. Push the tins together and gently ease the pastry into the tins.
5. Draw the rolling pin over the surface of the tins and mould the pastry into each barquette. Re-roll the pastry trimmings and use again.
6. Prick the base of the cases with a fork and bake on a baking sheet for 15 mins.

7. After 5 mins., remove the tins from the oven and press the pastry firmly down, if it has risen. Return the tins to the oven for the remaining time.
8. When the cases are cooked, remove from tins; cool.
9. Soften the cream cheese with a wooden spoon. Spoon it into a piping bag fitted with a medium-sized star nozzle, and pipe into the pastry cases.
10. Garnish each barquette with a slice of gherkin.

## Bacon and Onion Tartlets

100 g shortcrust pastry
50 g onion, peeled
100 g bacon
15 g butter
1 egg
125 ml milk
Salt and pepper
A pinch of mixed herbs

*Makes 24*

1. Heat the oven to 204°C (mark 6, 400°F).
2. Roll the pastry to 5 cm thick. Use 2-in. bouchée tins $\frac{3}{4}$ in. deep (approx. 5.5 × 2 cm). Lay them on a flat surface with about 1.75 cm between them. Line with pastry, as for Barquettes.
3. Finely chop the onion; rind and finely chop the bacon.
4. Melt butter in a small pan, sauté onion until tender, add bacon and fry for a further 3–4 mins.; cool.
5. Beat the egg and milk, season well and add herbs.
6. Spoon a little bacon and onion into each case, then pour the savoury mixture over. Put on a baking sheet.
7. Bake for 20 mins. Serve hot or cold.

## Tomato Pop-ins

5 slices from a large ready-sliced loaf
75 g liver pâté
5 tomatoes (approx. 300 g), sliced
60 ml thick mayonnaise

*Makes 20*

1. Stamp 20 5-cm rounds out of the bread.
2. Toast on both sides; when cold, spread with pâté.
3. Top each croûte with a tomato slice.
4. Spoon the mayonnaise into a forcing bag with a small vegetable nozzle. Pipe a star on each tomato slice.

## CANDIES

### Walnut Fudge

450 g granulated sugar
55 g butter
140 ml evaporated milk
140 ml fresh milk
25 g walnuts, chopped
Vanilla essence

1. Grease a tin measuring 8 × 6 ins. (20 × 15 cm).
2. Put the sugar, butter and milks in a heavy-based pan; heat gently till the sugar dissolves and the fat melts.
3. Bring to the boil and boil steadily to 115°C (240°F—soft ball stage—stirring occasionally.
4. Remove from heat, put on a cool surface and add nuts and a few drops of essence; beat until the mixture becomes thick and creamy and 'grains'.
5. Quickly pour into tin and mark into squares. Alternatively, leave fudge until cool, shape into balls and roll in chocolate vermicelli—see top left of photo.

## Barley Sugar

½ a lemon
400 g sugar
125 ml water
A pinch of cream of tartar

1. Peel off the lemon rind and cut it into strips.
2. Put sugar and water into a pan, heat gently and, when the sugar dissolves, add lemon rind and cream of tartar.
3. Boil to 115°C (240°F)—soft ball stage. Remove lemon rind, and pour the mixture onto a lightly oiled slab.
4. Allow it to cool slightly, then fold sides to middle.
5. Cut in strips, using an oiled knife, and twist evenly (p. 107).
6. When the barley sugar is cold, store in airtight jars.

## Honeycomb Toffee

400 g granulated sugar
A pinch of cream of tartar
2 rounded tbsp. (30 ml) golden syrup
125 ml water
½ level tsp. (2.5 ml) bicarbonate of soda
2 tsp. (10 ml) water to dissolve bicarbonate

1. Grease a tin measuring 12 × 4 ins. (30.4 × 10 cm).
2. Dissolve the sugar, cream of tartar, golden syrup and water over a low heat in a heavy-based saucepan, stirring gently with the thermometer.
3. Bring to the boil and boil gently to 154°C (310°F)—hard crack stage. Remove from the heat.
4. Blend bicarbonate of soda with the 2 tsp. water and add.
5. Stir gently and pour at once into the tin. Mark into squares or fingers when half-set, using a buttered knife.

## Coconut Ice

450 g granulated sugar
140 ml milk
140 g desiccated coconut
Pink or green colouring

1. Oil or butter a tin measuring 8 × 6 ins. (20 × 13 cm).
2. Dissolve the sugar in the milk over a low heat.
3. Bring to the boil and boil gently for about 10 mins., or to 115°C (240°F)—soft ball stage.
4. Remove from heat, stir in the coconut and pour half the mixture quickly into the tin.
5. Colour second half and pour quickly over first; leave until half-set, mark into bars and cut up when cold.

## PRESERVES

### Raspberry Jam

| | |
|---|---|
| 900 g raspberries | 450 g sugar |

*Yield: 1¼–1½ kilos approx.*

1. Wash out 3 jam jars and leave in a warm place.
2. Put the fruit in a preserving pan and cook slowly till some juice is extracted; simmer gently until tender.
3. Add sugar, stir, and boil rapidly to setting point.
4. Pour the jam into the warmed jar to within 1 cm of top.
5. Place waxed discs over the jam and seal each pot with Cellophane, which should first be dipped in water; secure with elastic bands. Label with name of preserve and date.

### Three-fruit Marmalade

| | | |
|---|---|---|
| 2 grapefruit | to weigh a | 3 litres of water |
| 4 lemons | total of about | 2.2 kilos sugar |
| 2 sweet oranges | 1¼ kilos | A knob of butter |

*Yield: about 4 kilos*

1. Wash out 9 jam jars and leave in a warm place.

2. Scrub the fruit, cut in halves, squeeze out the juice and pips and slice the peel.
3. Put the sliced peel and fruit juice in a preserving pan with the water and the pips (tied in a muslin bag). Cook gently for 2 hrs., until the peel is soft.
4. Remove the bag of pips, after squeezing, and add the sugar; stir till dissolved, then bring rapidly to the boil and boil rapidly for 10–20 mins., at 104°C (approx. 220°F) until setting point is reached.
5. Allow to stand in pan for a few mins. to get rid of any bubbles. Add a knob of butter to remove scum.
6. Pot, cover and label as for jam.

## Lemon Curd

Grated rind and juice of 4 lemons
4 eggs, beaten
100 g butter
400 g sugar

*Yield: about 600 g*

1. Wash 3–4 small jars and leave in a warm place.
2. Put all the ingredients in the top of a double saucepan or in a basin standing in a pan of simmering water.
2. Stir till the sugar dissolves, and continue heating, stirring all the time, until the curd thickens.
3. Strain the curd into the jars and cover as for jam.

*Note*: For recipe for Curd and Jam Tartlets, see p. 207.

## Red Tomato Chutney

25 g mustard seed
3 level tsp. (15 ml) whole allspice
1 level tsp. (5 ml) cayenne
1,800 g red tomatoes, peeled
200 g sugar
25 g salt
375 ml white vinegar

*Yield: about 1 kilo*

1. Wash 2 jam jars and leave in a warm place.
2. Tie the mustard seed and allspice in muslin and add with the cayenne to the tomatoes. Simmer until reduced to a pulp—about $\frac{3}{4}$ hr.; add remaining ingredients.
3. Simmer until of a thick consistency, with no free liquid. Pot, and cover with vinegar-proof 'parchment'.

# BASIC RECIPES

## PASTRIES

*Note*: In recipes, '200 g pastry' means pastry made with 200 g flour, and other ingredients in proportion, unless bought pastry is specified.

| *Type* | *Uses* | *Oven Temp.* | *Baking Time, etc.* |
|---|---|---|---|
| **Shortcrust**<br>100 g plain flour<br>¼ level tsp (1.25 ml) salt<br>25 g lard<br>25 g margarine<br>Abt. 3 tbsp (45 ml) water | Flan cases (use either basic short-crust or the flan pastry variation) | 204°C (mark 6, 400°F) | 20 mins. in all, incl. 10 mins. with baking beans |
| | Jam Tarts and variations | ditto | 15–20 mins. |
| VARIATION — FLAN PASTRY<br>Replace water by sufficient beaten egg to bind in-gredients; for a sweet flan, in-clude 1 level tsp (5 ml) sugar | Savoury dishes, e.g. Egg and Bacon Flan | ditto to start, then 177°C (mark 4, 350°F) | 15 mins., then 30 mins. |
| **Flaky Pastry**<br>200 g strong plain flour<br>½ level tsp (2.5 ml) salt<br>150 g margarine and lard<br>About 90 ml water<br>1 tsp (5 ml) lemon juice | Sweet and savoury dishes | 232°C (mark 8, 450°F) | |
| | E.g. Jam Puffs | | 20 mins. |
| | Sausage Rolls | ditto | 25–30 mins. |
| | Meat Pies | ditto | 20 mins. at 232°C, then a further 40 mins. at 177°C (mark 4, 350°F) |
| **Rough Puff Pastry**<br>200 g strong plain flour<br>½ level tsp (2.5 ml) salt<br>150 g margarine and lard<br>1 tsp (5 ml) lemon juice | Sweet and sa-voury dishes | As for flaky pastry | As for flaky pastry |

PASTRIES (*contd.*)

| *Type* | *Uses* | *Oven Temp.* | *Baking Time, etc.* |
|---|---|---|---|
| **Suetcrust**<br>200 g self-raising flour<br>1 level tsp (5 ml) salt<br>100 g suet, chopped<br>About 125 ml water | Puddings, e.g. Steak and Kidney Blackberry and Apple<br>Jam Roly-Poly Dumplings | Steam<br>Steam or Boil | 2–2½ hrs.<br>1 hr. |
| **Choux Pastry**<br>40 g butter or margarine<br>125 ml water<br>65 g flour<br>2 eggs, lightly beaten | Éclairs, Choux Buns, Profiteroles | 218°C (mark 7, 425°F) | 30 mins. |
| **Cheese Pastry**<br>100 g plain flour<br>A pinch of salt<br>50 g margarine and lard<br>50 g Cheddar cheese, chopped<br>A little beaten egg | Cheese Flans, small Savouries | 204°C, (mark 6, 400°F) | 15–20 mins. |
| **Pâte Sucrée**<br>100 g plain flour<br>A pinch of salt<br>50 g butter<br>25 g caster sugar<br>½ a beaten egg | Sweet flan cases | 190°C (mark 5, 375°F) | 10–15 mins. |
| **Biscuit Crust Cases**<br>150 g wheatmeal or plain biscuits<br>1 level tbsp (15 ml) caster sugar<br>75 g butter, melted | Cheesecakes Flans made with a filling set with gelatine, or a thick creamy mixture | | Chill, leave to set |

## YEAST MIXTURES

| *Type* | *Uses* | *Oven Temp.* | *Baking Time, etc.* |
|---|---|---|---|
| **White Bread**<br>400 g strong plain flour<br>1 level tsp (5 ml) salt | Bread | 232°C (mark 8, 450°F) | 30–40 mins. (until cooked) |
| 2 level tsp (10 ml) fresh yeast *or* 1 level tsp (5 ml) dried yeast<br>250 ml water | Rolls | ditto | 20 mins. |
| **Brown Bread**<br>200 g each brown and strong white plain flour<br>5 g lard | Bread | As for White Bread | 30–40 mins. |
| 2 level tsp (10 ml) sugar<br>2 level tsp (10 ml) fresh yeast *or* 1 level tsp (5 ml) dried yeast<br>250 ml water plus 1 tsp (5 ml) | Rolls | ditto | 20 mins. |
| **Enriched Doughs**<br>200 g strong white plain flour<br>A pinch of salt<br>25 g lard<br>3 level tsp (15 ml) fresh yeast *or* | Breads<br>Teabreads | 190°C (mark 5, 375°F) | 30–40 mins. |
| ½ level tsp (2.5 ml) dried yeast and ½ level tsp (2.5 ml) sugar<br>1 level tbsp (15 ml) sugar<br>1 egg, beaten<br>5 tbsp (75 ml) warm water | Rolls | 218°C (mark 7, 425°F) | 20 mins. |

## SCONES

| *Type* | *Uses* | *Oven Temp.* | *Baking Time, etc.* |
|---|---|---|---|
| **Plain** | | | |
| 200 g self-raising flour *or* 200 g plain flour plus 4 level tsp (20 ml) baking powder; 25 g butter or margarine; 115–125 ml milk | | 232°C (mark 8, 450°F) | 10–12 mins. |
| **Fruit** | | | |
| Add 25 g sugar and 25 g dried fruit | | ditto | ditto |
| **Cheese** | | | |
| Add 75 g grated cheese | | ditto | ditto |

## CAKES

| *Type* | *Uses* | *Oven Temp.* | *Baking Time, etc.* |
|---|---|---|---|
| **Large Plain (rubbing-in method)** | | | |
| 200 g self-raising flour; ½ level tsp (2.5 ml) mixed spice; 100 g butter or margarine; 100 g sugar | Large cakes | 177°C (mark 4, 350°F) | 1–1¼ hrs. |
| 225 g mixed dried fruit; 1 standard egg; 75 ml milk and water mixed | Rock Cakes | ditto | 15–20 mins. |
| **Large Rich (creaming method)** | | | |
| 200 g plain flour; 200 g butter; 200 g soft brown sugar; 4 large eggs; 800 g mixed dried fruit; Spices to flavour | Christmas or Birthday Cakes | 149°C (marks 1–2, 300°F) | 3¾ hrs. |

CAKES (*contd.*)

| *Type* | *Uses* | *Oven Temp.* | *Baking Time, etc.* |
|---|---|---|---|
| **Victoria Sandwich** | | | |
| 100 g self-raising flour<br>100 g caster sugar<br>100 g margarine<br>2 standard eggs | Sandwich and layer cakes | 190°C (mark 5, 375°F) | 20–25 mins. |
| Filling and/or decoration | Small Cakes e.g. Fairy Cakes | ditto | 15–20 mins. |
| **Whisked Sponge** | | | |
| 2 standard eggs<br>50 g caster sugar<br>50 g self-raising flour<br>Filling if required | Sponge Cake<br>Sponge Flan<br>Swiss Roll | 190°C (mark 5, 375°F) | 20 mins. |
| **Genoese Sponge** | | | |
| 75 g butter<br>50 g plain flour<br>3 large eggs<br>75 g sugar | Large Cakes (increase amounts for slab cake to make Petits Fours, etc.) | 190°C (mark 5, 375°F) | 20–25 mins. |

## BISCUITS

| | | | |
|---|---|---|---|
| **Plain (rubbed-in)** | | | |
| 100 g plain flour<br>75 g margarine<br>75 g caster sugar<br>1 egg yolk | 'Elevenses' biscuits | 177°C (mark 4, 350°F) | 20–25 mins. |
| **Rich (creamed)** | | | |
| 100 g margarine<br>100 g caster sugar<br>1 standard egg<br>150 g plain flour | Shrewsbury Biscuits and variations | 177°C (mark 4, 350°F) | 15–20 mins. |

## SAUCES, GLAZES, SYRUP

| | | | |
|---|---|---|---|
| **White Pouring Sauce** | | | |
| 250 ml milk<br>15 g fat<br>15 g flour<br>Salt and pepper<br>Flavouring | Various sauces, e.g. Cheese, Parsley, Egg | | Cook until glossy |

SAUCES, GLAZES, SYRUP (*contd.*)

| *Type* | *Uses* | *Oven Temp.* | *Baking Time, etc.* |
|---|---|---|---|
| **White Coating Sauce**<br>250 ml milk<br>25 g flour<br>25 g butter or margarine<br>Salt and pepper<br>Flavouring if required | Used in such dishes as Fish Pie, Cheese and Vegetable Pie | | Cook until glossy |
| **White Binding Sauce (Panada)**<br>250 ml milk<br>50 g fat<br>50 g flour<br>Salt and pepper<br>Flavouring if required | To bind ingredients for Fish Cakes, Croquettes, Rissoles | | ditto |
| **Glaze for Flans**<br>125 ml fruit juice<br>$1\frac{1}{2}$ level tsp (7.5 ml) arrowroot | To pour over fruit filling | | Simmer for a few mins. |
| **Syrup for Fresh Fruit Salads**<br>125 ml water<br>2 tbsp (30 ml) lemon juice<br>50 g sugar | Dissolve sugar in liquids, steep prepared fruits in the syrup | | |

# FOODS IN SEASON

Whether you're planning a week's family meals or the menu for a special occasion, it's useful to check the foods likely to be available. It is true that nowadays, with the enormous range of canned, frozen and other preserved goods, most things can be bought in some form the year round. But if you relish the flavour of fresh foods at their peak of perfection, and if you want to keep catering costs within bounds, you'll find it still pays to buy vegetables, fish and so on in their seasons.

In the following lists we give first under each heading those items that can be obtained the year round; of course, they may not always all be found in every town and village, and the price may rise considerably at certain times, due to such factors as weather conditions or a switch-over to imported supplies. Any list can only be a general guide. If you are anxious to have a particular ingredient for a given date, consult your tradesman beforehand, and he may be able to order it for you.

## Fruit

*Available all the Year*: Apples, Bananas, Grapes, Grapefruit, Lemons, Melons (see note), Oranges, Pears, Pineapple.

| | | | |
|---|---|---|---|
| Apricots | May–Aug. | Mandarins | Nov.–March |
| Avocado pears | Oct.–Apr. | Nectarines | Aug.–Oct. |
| Blackberries | July–Oct. | Peaches | June–Oct. |
| Black currants | July–Sept. | Plums | July–Sept.; Jan.–Feb. (imported) |
| Cherries | June–Aug. | | |
| Chestnuts | Dec.–Feb. | Raspberries | June–Sept. |
| Cranberries | Nov.–Jan. | Red currants | June–Aug. |
| Damsons | Aug.–Oct. | Seville (Marmalade) Oranges | Jan.–Feb. |
| Figs | July–Aug. | | |
| Gooseberries | June–Sept. | Strawberries | April–July |
| Greengages | Aug.–Sept. | Rhubarb (treated as fruit) | Dec.–June |
| Loganberries | June–Aug. | | |

*Melons*: Honeydew melons are available more or less all the year; other types follow one another: Sugar melons, Apr.–Aug.; Charentais, Apr.–Oct.; Scarlet, June–July; Tiger, June–Sept.; Cantaloup, July–Sept.; Watermelon, July–Oct.; Ogen, Dec.–Sept.

**Vegetables, Salads**

*Available all the Year*: Aubergines, Beetroot, Cabbage (in various forms), Carrots, Mushrooms, Onions, Potatoes, Spinach, Turnips; Cucumber, Lettuce (round), Green and Red Peppers, Radishes, Tomatoes, Watercress.

| | | | |
|---|---|---|---|
| Artichokes, | | Cauliflower | March–Nov. |
| Globe | March–Nov. | Celeriac | Sept.–March |
| Jerusalem | Nov.–June | Celery | Aug.–Feb. |
| Asparagus | Apr.–July | Courgettes | May–Sept. |
| Beans, | | Leeks | Aug.–Apr. |
| Broad | June–Oct. | Lettuce | Summer |
| French | Feb.–March | (Cos, Webb) | months |
| Runner | June–Sept. | Parsnips | Sept.–Apr. |
| Broccoli | Oct.–Apr. | Peas | May–Oct. |
| Brussels | | New Potatoes | May–Sept. |
| Sprouts | Sept.–March | | |

**Fish, Shellfish**

*Available all the Year*: Cod, Haddock, Halibut, Herring, Mackerel, Plaice, Sole, Turbot; Crab, Lobster, Prawns, Shrimps.

| | | | |
|---|---|---|---|
| Salmon | Feb.–Aug. | Oysters | Sept.–Apr. |
| Trout | March–Aug. | Scallops | Nov.–March |

**Poultry**

*Available all the Year*: Chicken, Guinea Fowl, Pigeon; Duck and Turkey, though specially geared to the Christmas trade, are increasingly on sale throughout the year; Goose, Sept.–Feb.

**Game**

| | |
|---|---|
| Duck (Wild | Aug. 1st–March 1st |
| Grouse | Aug. 12th–Dec. 12th |
| Wood Pigeon | Aug. 1st–March 15th |
| Hare | Aug. 1st–Feb. 28th |
| Rabbit | Sept. 1st–Apr. 30th |

**Meat**

This cannot now be regarded as seasonal—with the merging of home-killed and imported supplies, most kinds of meat are on sale the year round. However, it's worth considering what is the best buy at different times.

*Lamb*: From New Zealand, new season's lamb arrives in December and extends through January to April, when the fresh supplies tail off and meat is released from cold store. In about May, English lamb appears and builds up to a flush of supplies from June to September or October, reinforced in August by Scotch lamb. Australian lamb fills the next gap and is usually cheaper than New Zealand, but has a short season, mainly November and December.

*Beef*: About 70 per cent. of our requirements are met by home-killed beef, available most of the year, though supplies are sometimes short from February or March to July. Imports arrive throughout the year and help to stabilise supplies and prices. They consist mainly of chilled beef from South America and frozen beef from Australia and New Zealand as well as South America, and also from some lesser-known sources such as Botswana.

*Pork*: We are self-sufficient in home-killed pork; supplies are fresh, not chilled or frozen. Although it is no longer true that pork is eaten only when there is an R in the month, the meat still tends to be more popular in winter.

*Veal*: Demand is fairly small, and home-killed and imported supplies are adequate. Veal is a good summer choice.

*Offal* (pleasantly known as 'variety meats' in the United States): Supplies follow the same basic pattern as for the main meats; it is worth remembering that oxtails, which are less in demand in summer, may then be bought fairly cheaply and put in the home freezer for later use.

# INDEX


Accelerated Freeze Drying, 34
Acid(s) and Preserving, 17–18, 32–33
  and Protein Coagulation, 20, 21
  and Spoilage, 28
  as Raising Agent, 8, 10
  Ascorbic, 48–49
  Phosphate, 10
Additives, 28, 34–35
Air as Raising Agent, 9, 10, 11
Albumen, 22
Alkalis, 8, 10, 28
Almond and Cheese Balls, 73
  Stars, 235
Ambrosia, 95
American Frosting, 215
Amino Acids, 31, 45
Apple and Cheese Salad, 146
  Pie, Spicy, 208
Apricot Gâteau, 217
Arrowroot, 16
Ascorbic Acid, 48–49
Asparagus, 94, 116
Avocado Pears, 116, 124

Bacon, 58, 59, 90
  and Cheese Quiche, 138
  and Onion Tartlets, 237
  Filling, 189
  Rolls, 21, 180
Bacteria, 26, 27–28, 30, 31, 32, 33
Baked Cheese Celery, 139
  Gammon, 155
  Stuffed Marrow, 186
Baking Blind, 41
  Powder, 8
Banana Tea Bread, 223
Barbecue(s), 66–67, 78
  Sauces, 160, 169
Barley Sugar, 107, 239
Barquettes, 235, 236
Battenberg Cake, 213
Bean(s) and Tomato Salad, 94
  Salted, 34
Beef Balls en Casserole, 156
  Cobbler, 149
  Goulash, 84
  Olives, 153
Belgian Pie, 188
Beurre Manié, 14, 15–16
Beverages: see Drinks
Bicarbonate of Soda, 8, 49
Biscuit(s), 224–225, 246
  Crust Case, 243
Blackcurrant Shake, 80
Blood, 21–22
Books, Recommended, 44, 78
Bottling, 32, 35–40
Bouillabaisse, 117
Bouquet Garni, 15
Brandy Butter, 210
Bread, 50, 58, 60, 114, 226–229, 233, 244
  Sauce, 180
  Stale, 89
Breakfast, 57–58
Breast of Lamb, Stuffed, 162
Broad Bean and Tomato Salad, 94
Budgeting, Food, 87–91
Buffet Parties, 68–69, 77
Butter Icing, 216

Cabbage, 90–91
Cake(s), 212–223, 245–246
  Decorating, 219, 221
Calcium, 46
Calories, 6, 51–52
Candies, 238–239
Canning, 32–33
Carbohydrates, 50, 51, 92
  and Diabetics, 53
  and Spoilage, 30
  See also Starch, Sugar
Carbon Dioxide, 7, 8
Casein, 20, 21
Casseroled Beef Balls, 156
  Kidneys, 157
Celery, Baked Cheese, 139
Cellulose, 7, 13, 50
Charlotte Russe, 195
Cheese, 21, 59, 68, 83, 136–147
  and Almond Balls, 73
  and Apple Salad, 146
  and Bacon Quiche, 138
  and Ham Pancakes, 142
  and Leek Pie, 139
  and Potato Cakes, 144
  and Salmon Quiche, 131
  and Tomato Bars, 145
  and Wine Party, 67–68, 78, 83
  Cake, 208
  Celery, Baked, 139
  Dip, 125
  Eggs, Curried, 137
  Fondue, 143

Cheese, Pastry, 243
Scones, 245
Soufflé, 136
Cheesy Tomatoes en Croûte, 122
Chicken Casserole, Creamed, 180
in a Basket, 117
Roast, 180
Salad, 84, 177
Sweet 'n Sour, 178
Chicory and Corn Salad, 93
Children's Lunch, 60
Parties, 71–72
Chilled Cucumber Soup, 118
Chilli con Carne, 151
Chocolate Biscuits, Hungarian, 224
Cups, 234
Leaves, etc., 65, 219
Sauce, 204–205
Choux Pastry, 9–10, 204, 243
Christmas Cake, 220–221
Eve Mull, 79
Pudding, 210
Chutney, Red Tomato, 241
Cider Lemon Cup, 79
Coagulation of Proteins, 7, 8, 9, 11, 19–24
Coating Fish, etc., 88
Cobbler, Beef, 149
Cocktail(s), Fish, 117, 119
Melon and Grape, 119
Party, 69
Savouries, 69, 236–237
Coconut Biscuits, 224
Ice, 239
Coffee, 85, 115
Party, 71
Shake, 80
Cold Drinks, 74–75
Cole Slaw, 192
Collagen, 20
Colonial Goose, 168
Connective Tissue, 20
Convenience Foods, 91–93
Coq au Vin, 179
Corn and Chicory Salad, 93
on the Cob, 116, 124
Cornflour, 16–17
Cottage Loaf, 227
Country Pasties, 152
Courgettes with Tomatoes, 187
Cream, 21, 104
Cheese Rhubarb Pie, 207
Horns, 218
of Tartar, 8
Creamed Cake and Biscuit Mixtures, 245–246
Chicken Casserole, 181
Creamy Walnut Gâteau, 216
Crème Caramel, 196
Crisps, Potato, 64
Croissants, 228
Crown Loaf, 227
Roast of Lamb, 161
Cucumber Garnish, 111
Soup, Chilled, 118
Curing; see Salting
Curried Cheese Eggs, 137
Egg Filling, 189
Eggs, Quick, 144
Curry, 166–167
Dip, 70
Custard, Egg, 24

Danish Pastries, 230–231
Decomposition, 25, 31
Decorated Fairy Cakes, 219
Decorating Cakes, 219, 221
Decoration, Food, 110–112
Table, 114–115
Dehydration, 33–34
Denaturisation, 19
Dessert, 60, 64, 85, 194–211
Dextrins, 50
Diabetic Diet, 53
Diet, 45–51
Diet, Diabetic, 53
Slimming, 51–52
Vegetarian, 52–53
Difficult Foods, Serving and Eating, 115–117
Dinner, 62–64, 113, 115
Party, 64, 69–70, 77
Rolls, 227
Dips, Savoury, 70, 125
Dishing up Food, 112–113
Doughnuts, 232
Dressings, Salad, 124, 191
Dried Herbs, 34
Yeast, 227
Drinks, 49, 58, 73–81, 85
Drying, 33–34
Duck, Roast, 182
with Cherries, 183
Dundee Cake, 222

Egg(s), 9, 10, 11, 22, 58, 59, 90
à la Mornay, 137
and Cheese, 136–147
and Prawn Kedgeree, 132
and Raising, 9, 10, 11
and Thickening, 22
Curried Cheese, 137
Custards, 24
Filling, Curried, 189
Glaze, 228
Ham and Rice Salad, 147
Mayonnaise, 146
Quick Curried, 144
Elastin, 20
Emulsifying, 11
Energy Foods, 45
Enriched Yeast Dough, 244
Entertaining, 66–85
Enzymes, 19, 20, 26, 31, 32
Exercises, 11–13, 24, 29–30, 34, 44, 61–62, 64–66, 94, 99
Expansion of Gases, 7–13

Fairy Cakes, 219

Family Menu for Four, 94
Fatless Sponge Cake, 9, 13
Fats, 49–50, 51, 92
  and Raising, 9, 10–11
  and Spoilage, 31
Fécules, 14, 17
Fermentation, 30, 31
Fish, 58, 59, 90, 126–135, 249
  Cakes, to Coat, 88
  Coagulation, 20
  Cocktails, 117, 119
  en Cocotte, 121
  Freezing, 43
  Frozen, 43
  Jalousie, 134
  Pie, Russian, 129
  Roll, Flaky, 130
Flaky Fish Roll, 130
  Pastries, 242
Flan, French Fruit, 202
  Glaze, 247
  Pastry, 242
Flour, 10, 14–16, 23
Fluorine, 46
Fondue, Cheese, 143
  Dinner Party, 70
Food Buying, 86–98
  in Season, 248–250
  on the Table, 109–117
  Preservation, 32–44
  Storage, 99–108
Forcemeat Balls, 168–169
Forcing Bag, Paper, 103
Freezer Storage, 107–108
Freezing, 33, 41–44
French Dressing, 191
  Fruit Flan, 202
  Onion Soup, 117, 123
Frosted Glasses, 74
  Orange Cream, 80
Fruit, 58, 248–249
  Bottling, Canning, 32, 35–40
  Flan, French, 202
  Freezing, 41–42
  Frozen, 42
  Juices, 58, 74
  Punch, Spicy, 78
  Salad, 85, 247
Fruit, Scones, 245
  Tea Bread, 229
Fruity Steamed Pudding, 211

Game, 90, 184–185, 249
  Pie, 159
Gammon, Baked, 155
  Rashers with Pineapple, 154
Garlic, to Use, 9
Garnish, Food, 54, 110–112
Gases, Expansion of, 7–13
Gâteaux, 212, 214, 216, 217
Gelatine, 19
Gelatinisation of Starch, 8, 9, 14
Genoese Sponge, 215, 246
Glasses, 76, 114
Glaze, Arrowroot, 16, 247
  Egg, 228
Globe Artichokes, 23, 116
Glucose, 13, 53
Glühwein, 80
Gluten, 7, 10, 11, 23–24
Gooseberry Sauce, 129
Goulash, Beef, 84
Granulose, 14
Grape(s) Gâteau, 212
  to Seed, 52
Grapefruit, Spicy Hot, 122
  to Prepare, 48–49
Gravy, Thin, 180
Green Salad, Tossed, 191
Guest Menu for Four, 94–95
Gums, 19

Haddock and Sweet Pepper Sauté, 93, 134
Ham and Cheese Pancakes, 142
  Bouchées, 174
  Egg and Rice Salad, 147
Hamburgers with Barbecue Sauce, 169
Heating and Food Preservation, 32–33
Herbs, Dried, 34
Herrings, Soused, 132
High Tea, 60
Honeycomb Toffee, 239
Horseradish Dip, 70
Hot Spicy Grapefruit, 122
Humidity and Spoilage, 28
Hungarian Chocolate Biscuits, 224

Ice Cubes, Decorated, 74
Iced Tea and Coffee, 85
Icing Cakes, 219, 221
Individual Tuna Pizza, 135
Instant Parties, 73
Insulin, 53
Iodine, 46
Irish Soda Bread, 233
Iron, 46

Jacket Potatoes, 91, 189
Jalousie, Fish, 134
Jam and Jelly Making, 17–18
  Raspberry, 240
  Tartlets, 207
Jamaican Crunch Pie, 209
Jellied Salad Mould, 193

Kebabs, 160
Kedgeree, Prawn and Egg, 132
Kidneys, Casseroled, 157
Kipper Pâté, 120

Lactic Acid, Lactose, 20
Lamb Breast, Stuffed, 162
  Crown Roast, 161
  Navarin, 163
Lancashire Hot-pot, 150
Larder Storage, 102–106
Lasagne, 171
Lattice Potatoes, 64

Latticed Meat Roll, 148
Leek and Cheese Pie, 139
Leftovers, 59, 86
Lemon Barbecue Sauce, 160
 Butterflies, 111
 Cider Cup, 79
 Curd, 241
 Fluff, 198
 Meringue Pie, 205
 Soufflé, 194
 Sponge, 200
 to Section, 48
Lipase, 26
Liver Casserole, 155
 Pâté, 120
 Stroganoff, 94, 170
Lobster Recipes, 117
Lunch, 58–62

Mackerel with Gooseberry Sauce, 128
Made-up Dishes, 84
Mandarin Barquettes, 235
 Cream Gâteau, 214
Marinading, 20
Marmalade, Three-fruit, 240
Marrow, Baked Stuffed, 186
Marshmallow Desserts, 196–197
Mayonnaise, Egg, 146
Meal Planning, 45–53, 54–81, 93–95
Meals, Quick, 93–95
 Special-occasion, 66–73
Meat, 58, 59, 62, 90, 148–175, 250
 Coagulation, 20
 Freezing, 42–43
 Frozen, 43
 Roll, Latticed, 148
 Roly-poly, 150
Meatballs Recipe, 94
Mediterranean Prawns, 117
Melon, 52, 116, 249
 and Grape Cocktail, 119
Menu Planning: see Meal Planning
Meringue(s), 185
 Mixtures, 24
 Pineapples, 200
Microbial Spoilage Agents, 25–26, 27–30, 32
Milk, 20, 26, 74, 80
 Shakes, 80
Mille-feuilles, 218
Mincemeat Tranche, 206
Minerals, 46
Mocha Mousse, 203
Moisture and Raising, 10, 11
 and Spoilage, 28
 and Thickening, 13, 14
Mornay Eggs, 137
Moulds and Spoilage, 25, 28, 31
Moules Marinière, 117
Moussaka, 165
Mousse, Mocha, 203
Mulls, 75, 79
Mushrooms, Stuffed, 187
Mussels, 117

Navarin of Lamb, 163
Nicotinic Acid, Nicotinamide, 48
Nitrates, Nitrites, 29
Nutrition, 45–51, 92–93

Obesity, 51–52
Offal, 90, 250
Oils in Flour Mixtures, 11
Omelette, Soufflé, 93
Onion and Bacon Tartlets, 237
 Soup, French, 117, 123
Orange Cream, Frosted, 80
 Sorbet, 199
 Tea Bread, 222
 to Section, 48–49
 Velvet, 198
Orange-Pepper Sauce, 164
Osso Bucco, 173
Oxidation, 26–27, 34
Oysters, 117

Packed Lunches, 61
Panada, 15, 247
Pancakes, Cheese and Ham, 142
Paper Forcing Bag, 103
Pappadums, 167
Paprika Dip, 70
Parties, 68–85, 242–243
Pasta, 89, 116, 117, 173
Pasties, 152–153
Pastries, 9, 242–243
 Danish, 230–231
Pastry Leaves, etc., 31, 35
Pâte Sucrée, 202, 243
Pâtés, 120
Pavlova Cake, 201
Pectin, 17–18
Petits Fours, 234–235
Phosphorus, 46
Pickles, 34
Pie Edgings, 29
Pigeon Casserole, 184
Pineapple(s) and Pepper Salad, 192
 Meringue, 200
 Whip, 94
Piping Cream, Icing, 104
Pizzas, 135, 140
Plaice, Stuffed Rolled, 126
Planned-overs, 86–87
Poor Knight, 89
Pork Chops in Orange-Pepper Sauce, 164
 Pie, 159
Potassium, 46
Potato and Cheese Cakes, 144
 Crisps, 64
 Flour, 17
 Jacket, 91, 189
 Lattice, 64
Poulet en Cocotte, 176
Poultry, 90, 176–185, 249
 Freezing, 43
 Frozen, 43
Prawn(s), 117
 and Egg Kedgeree, 132
 Cocktail, 117, 119

Preservation of Food, 32–44
Preserves, 17–18, 240–241
Profiteroles, 204
Progressive Dinner, 70–71
Protective Foods, 45
Protein(s), 10, 19, 45–46, 47, 52, 92
 and Spoilage, 31
 Coagulation, 7, 8, 9, 10, 11, 19–24
Proving Yeast Rolls, 233
Puddings, 60, 64, 85, 112, 194–211
Puff Pastries, 13
Pulses, 89
Punches, 75, 78

Quantities for Parties, 81–85
Quiches, 131, 138
Quick Curried Eggs, 144
 Meals, 93–95

Rabbit Casserole, 185
Raised Pies, 21, 158–159
Raising, Raising Agents, 7–13
Rancidity, 26, 31
Raspberry Jam, 240
Ratatouille, 191
Record Evening, 66
Red Tomato Chutney, 241
Refrigerator Storage, 99–102
Re-heating, 113
Rennin, 21
Rhubarb Cream Cheese Pie, 207
Riboflavin, 48
Rice and Salmon Moulds, 133
 Boiled, 170
 Egg and Ham Salad, 147
 Flour, 17
 Savoury, 170
Rissoles, to Coat, 88
Roast Chicken, 180
Roast Duck, 182
 Lamb Crown, 161
 Stuffed Breast of Lamb, 162
Rolls, 227, 233, 244
Rough Puff Pastry, 24, 242
Roux, 14–15
Rubbed-in Cakes and Biscuits, 245, 246
Rum Butter, 210
Russian Fish Pie, 129

Saccharin, 51, 53
Salad(s), 191–193, 249
 Broad Bean and Tomato, 94
 Cheese and Apple, 146
 Chicken, 84, 177
 Chicory and Corn, 93
 Dip Platter, 125
 Dressings, 124, 191
 Egg, Ham and Rice, 147
 Mould, Jellied, 193
 Pineapple and Pepper, 192
 Tossed Green, 191
 Winter, 192
Salmon and Cheese Quiche, 131
 and Rice Moulds, 133
 Shells, 130
Salt, Salting, 28, 34, 35
Sambols, 167
Sandwich Cake, 12–13, 24, 246
Sangria, 79
Santa Claus Decoration, 221
Sauce(s), 14–15, 113, 246–247
 Barbecue, 160, 169
 Bread, 180
 Chocolate, 204–205
 Gooseberry, 129
 Lemon Barbecue, 160
 Orange-Pepper, 164
 Tomato, 175
 White, 246–247
Sausages, 58
 en Croûte, 175
Sausage-meat Stuffing, 162
Savouries, Cocktail, 69, 82, 236–237
Savoury Barquettes, 236
 Rice, 170
Scones, 12, 245
Seasonable Foods, 248-250
Seasoning, 112
Service, Table, 115
Serving Food, 109–117
Setting Table, 113–115
Shellfish, 249
Sherry Party, 69
Shopping, 86–98
Shortbread Mould, 95
Shortcrust Pastry, 242
Shortening, 10
Slimming Diet, 51–52, 57
Smoked Foods, 34
Sodium, 46
 Bicarbonate, 8, 49
Sole Meunière, 127
Sorbet, Orange, 199
Soufflé(s), 24, 37
 Cheese, 136
 Lemon, 194
 Omelette, 93
Soup(s), 59, 62
 Chilled Cucumber, 118
 French Onion, 117, 123
Soused Herrings, 132
Spaghetti, 116
 alla Paesana, 84, 172
Special-occasion Meals, 66–73
Spicy Apple Pie, 208
 Fruit Punch, 78
 Hot Grapefruit, 122
Spoilage, 25–31
Sponge, Fatless, 9, 13, 246
 Genoese, 215, 246
 Lemon, 200
Starch, 7, 8, 9, 13–17, 23, 50
Steam as Raising Agent, 9–10
Steamed Fruity Pudding, 211

Storage, Food, 99–108
Store-cupboard, 91–95, 102–106
  Meals, 93–95
Strawberry Butterfly, 217
Stuffed Breast of Lamb, Roast, 162
  Jacket Potatoes, 189
  Marrow, 186
  Mushrooms, 187
  Rolled Plaice, 126
Suetcrust Pastry, 243
Sugar, 50, 51, 53
  and Preserving, 17–18, 29, 30, 35
  and Raising, 8, 10, 11
  and Thickening, 14
  Syrup, 36, 74, 247
Supper, 58–62
Sweet Course, 60, 64, 85, 112, 194–211
  'n Sour Chicken, 178
Syrup, Sugar, 36, 74, 247

Table Setting, 113–115
Tea, 85
  Breads, 222, 223, 229, 244
  Party, 71
Temperature and Preserving, 33
  and Raising, 7, 8, 10
  and Spoilage, 27–28
  and Thickening, 14
  Refrigerator, 99
Tête de Porc Vinaigrette, 90
Theatre Party, 72–73
Thiamin, 47
Thickening, 13–19
Thin Gravy, 180
Three-fruit Marmalade, 240
Time-table for Cooking, 56–57
Tin Loaf, 226
Toffee, Honeycomb, 239
Tomato(es), and Broad Bean Salad, 94
  and Cheese Bars, 145
  Chutney, Red, 241
  en Croûte, Cheesy, 122
  Juice, 94
  Pop-ins, 237
  Sauce, 175
  Tuna-filled, 190
  with Courgettes, 187
Tossed Green Salad, 191
Toxins, 32
Trifle, 85
Tuna au Gratin, 127
  Pizza, 135
Tuna-filled Tomatoes, 190
Turkey Julienne, 184
TV Evening, 66
Two-some Menu, 93–94

Veal and Ham Pies, Raised, 158
Vegan, Vegetarian Diet, 52–53
Vegetable(s), 59, 62–63, 90–92, 186–191, 249
Vegetable(s) Bottling and Canning, 32–33
  Freezing, 42
  Frozen, 42
Victoria Sandwich, 12–13, 24, 246
Vinaigrette Dressing, 124
Vinegar and Preservation, 35
Viscosity: see Thickening
Vitamins, 46–49, 92–93

Walnut Fudge, 238
  Gâteau, Creamy, 216
Water, 34, 49
Whipped Cream, to Pipe, 104
Whirligigs, 225
Whisked Sponge, 246
White Sauces, 246–247
  Wine Cup, 78
Wine, 75–78
  and Cheese Party, 67–68, 78
  Cup, 78
Winter Salad, 192

Yeast(s), 7, 8, 227
  and Spoilage, 25, 28, 30
  Mixtures, 24, 226–233, 244
Yorkshire Pudding, 10, 13

Zigzag Grapefruit, 49